ENVIRONMENTAL POLLUTION IN CHINA

WHAT EVERYONE NEEDS TO KNOW®

ENVIRONMENTAL POLLUTION IN CHINA

WHAT EVERYONE NEEDS TO KNOW®

DANIEL K. GARDNER

OXFORD
UNIVERSITY PRESS

OXFORD
UNIVERSITY PRESS

Oxford University Press is a department of the University of Oxford. It furthers the University's objective of excellence in research, scholarship, and education by publishing worldwide. Oxford is a registered trade mark of Oxford University Press in the UK and certain other countries.

"What Everyone Needs to Know" is a registered trademark of Oxford University Press.

Published in the United States of America by Oxford University Press
198 Madison Avenue, New York, NY 10016, United States of America.

Library of Congress Cataloging-in-Publication Data
Names: Gardner, Daniel K., 1950– author.
Title: Environmental pollution in China : what everyone needs to know /
Daniel K. Gardner.
Description: New York, NY : Oxford University Press, [2018] |
Includes bibliographical references and index.
Identifiers: LCCN 2017036679 (print) | ISBN 9780190696115 (hbk.) |
ISBN 9780190696122 (pbk.) | ISBN 9780190696139 (updf) |
ISBN 9780190696146 (epub)
Subjects: LCSH: Pollution—China. | Environmental policy—China.
Classification: LCC TD187.5.C6 G37 2018 | DDC 363.730951—dc23
LC record available at https://lccn.loc.gov/2017036679

1 3 5 7 9 8 6 4 2

Paperback printed by LSC Communications, United States of America
Hardback printed by Bridgeport National Bindery, Inc., United States of America

CONTENTS

ENVIRONMENTAL POLLUTION IN CHINA

WHAT EVERYONE NEEDS TO KNOW®

Part I

SETTING THE SCENE

Figure 1.1 Map of China

1

OVERVIEW

Why Should We Be Interested in China's Environmental Pollution?

Is it China's problem alone when its particulate matter makes its way downwind to Korea and Japan, blanketing them with hazardous smog? Is it China's problem alone when its particulate matter, carried by easterly winds, shows up as smog in the air over California or when mercury, carried by the same winds, is deposited in Oregon's Willamette River? How about when China's Songhua River crosses the border into Russia, carrying pollutants that affect the fish population there and the people's drinking water? As the saying goes, pollutants, whether in the air or the water, do not honor national boundaries, nor do they require visas to pay other countries a visit.

But wait: there's another side to the story. When big Western multinationals move their manufacturing base to China or contract with suppliers to manufacture, let's say, jeans or smartphones there—because costs there are cheaper and environmental laws more lax—don't they have some responsibility for China's pollution problems? And when people in the United States complain about the effect of Chinese pollutants on the air in California and Oregon, shouldn't they consider that 6% to 7% of China's air pollution results from goods produced for the US export market—and that part of the polluted air reaching American shores is simply a result of American consumers wanting cheaper clothes, toys, and electronics? These are perplexing questions, but no matter the answers, the questions themselves point to the need for mutual, international understanding of—and cooperation on—the pressing environmental problems China faces today.

Further, the policies China adopts to mitigate its environmental woes are sure to have global consequences. For instance, if China reduces its dependence on coal, as it has been doing for the past couple of years, how will that affect the economies of countries like Australia, the United States, and Vietnam? As coal demand in the United States continues to decline, American coal companies have been looking to export more of their coal to China. But if demand in China continues to soften, as appears likely, what will that do to the financial ambitions of large energy companies (think here Peabody Energy Corp. and Arch Coal Inc., which both filed for bankruptcy in 2016)? And how will softening demand affect the international price of coal?

Then there is food. If China, because of soil pollution and scarcity, turns heavily to international grain markets for its food supply, how will that influence international grain markets? And if prices rise internationally, might social and political stability, especially in poor countries, be affected?

Consider, too: as China relies more and more on imported foodstuffs, what does that mean for exporting countries—and the globe? How many acres of rainforest, for example, are Brazil and Argentina losing to soybean cultivation to service the Chinese market? How much will the loss of these rich carbon sinks in the Amazon contribute to global warming?

Acknowledging the environmental crisis that the country faces, the Beijing government is energetically promoting the development of clean energy and green technology. China's leaders are explicit about the goals. The first is to clean up the air, water, and soil that have been the hapless victims of China's modern industrialization. But the second is no less urgent: confident that clean energy and green technology will be the foundations of the 21st-century global economy, they are determined that China become the pioneer in that new economy. To understand China today, business and political leaders in the United States and elsewhere must understand these goals—and the range of measures China is taking today to achieve them.

I hope, and trust, that what follows will provide the reader with a more comprehensive answer to the question of why we should be interested in China's environmental pollution.

What Are the Particular Environmental Pollution Problems China Faces?

China suffers from a range of environmental pollution problems: air, water, soil, electronic waste, noise, and light. But air, water, and soil pollution and the scourge of electronic waste have been the most environmentally costly and have had the most dramatic effects on public health.

The various forms of pollution are intertwined, as pollutants are "transboundary," readily migrating from one medium to another. For example, mercury or sulfur in the air comes to be deposited in water and soil, fertilizer in the soil leeches into the rivers and the groundwater, cadmium and other chemicals that are discharged into the waterways make their way into the soil, and metals in electronic waste seep into the ground and the surrounding waterways.

Just How Bad Is China's Air?

It ranks among the most polluted air in the world. In a study released by Greenpeace East Asia in January 2016, 293 of 366 monitored cities in China failed to meet China's own national standards (35 micrograms per cubic meter [$\mu g/m^3$] of fine particulate matter [PM2.5]) in 2015, and none met the stricter World Health Organization (WHO) standards (10 $\mu g/m^3$).[1] The major sources of the country's foul air are no mystery: emissions from coal-fired power plants and vehicles.

The worst air in China is not in Beijing, as many might assume. Indeed, in 2015, 26 cities had higher pollution levels. According to the Ministry of Environmental Protection (MEP), Kashgar, in the western province of Xinjiang, had the worst, with an average level of 119.1 μg/m³, followed by Baoding in Hebei province at 107 μg/m³. (By comparison, in the same year, Bakersfield, California, the most polluted city in the United States, had an average reading of 18.) These levels, however, were improvements over the previous year, when Xingtai and Shijiazhuang, both in Hebei, averaged 155.2 and 148.5 μg/m³, respectively. Figure 1.2 shows air quality levels for 2014.

In the numbers game, Beijing's air may fare better than Kashgar's or Baoding's or Xingtai's, but it is nowhere near healthy. Its average PM2.5 reading of 80.4 μg/m³ in 2015 far exceeds both the WHO guideline and the country's own. But the average doesn't tell the whole story: because the city is

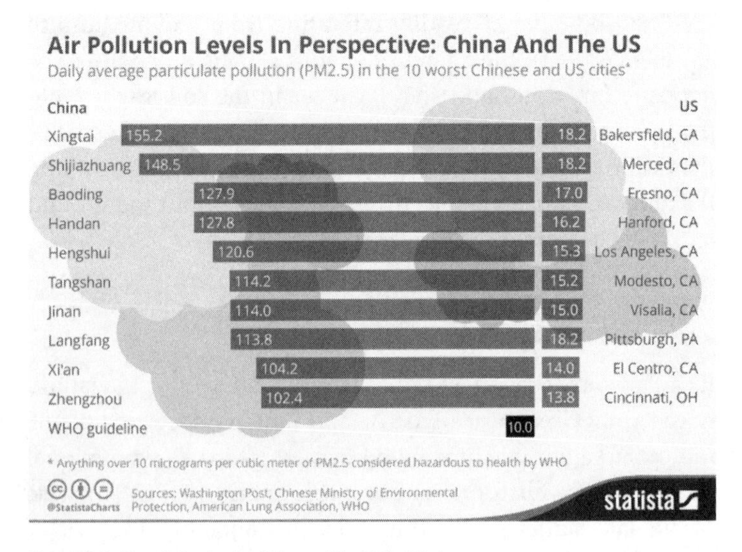

Figure 1.2 Air pollution levels: China and the United States

surrounded by mountains, a heavy smog can settle in for days, even weeks at a time. In the winter months, when the air is especially sooty with emissions from coal-fired heating plants, the air is so thick and soupy that the city's skyscrapers are rendered invisible. The air tastes acrid and metallic. At times like this, the PM2.5 level soars. For much of January 2013, the levels went "beyond index," meaning that the PM2.5 level exceeded 500 $\mu g/m^3$. Readings between 500 and 900 $\mu g/m^3$ were routine.

This polluted air takes a heavy toll on public health. Stinging eyes and coughs are the norm. More grave is the growing incidence of respiratory and heart diseases and lung cancer. Recent studies show that air pollution has become a leading cause of premature death in China—roughly 4,000 deaths per day.[2] The monetary cost, economists calculate, is more than 10% of China's annual gross domestic product (GDP).[3]

When Beijing's own mayor says that "Beijing is not a livable city" owing to the noxious smog,[4] and when respected Chinese scientists insist that if the country's smog persists conditions will be "similar to a nuclear winter,"[5] it would seem fair to say that China's air is in desperately bad shape. This is not the sort of public relations the country seeks—and may explain why foreign companies like Panasonic and Coca-Cola now offer a "hardship bonus" or "hazard pay" to lure workers to jobs in China.

How Extensive Is Water Pollution?

Many environmentalists argue that as bad as air pollution in China is, polluted water may be an even more serious problem. Statistics from the various Chinese state agencies and international organizations vary, but they all point to a startlingly high level of pollution in China's groundwater, rivers, lakes, and offshore water. What makes this pollution of the country's waterways especially problematic is that China has a scarcity of water resources in the first place. China holds 21% of the world's population, yet its share of global fresh water is just 7%. It can ill afford to contaminate the relatively little water it does have.

China's present annual per capita share of freshwater resources is as low as 25% of the global average. To put some specific numbers to this: the World Bank calculates China's freshwater resources for 2014 at 2,062 m^3 per capita (the United States, by comparison, had 8,846 m^3 per capita). In water-parched Beijing the figure these days is a mere 100 m^3 per person (just 1.69% of the world's average).[6] The United Nations considers any region with a level under 1,700 m^3 per person to be "water-stressed."

China classifies water quality into five grades: grades I, II, and III are described as "good," while grades IV and V are considered "poor," unsuitable for drinking, swimming, or, in fact, human contact of any sort. (Grade V+ is sometimes used to refer to water that is entirely unusable, including for industry and agriculture.) In 2014, of the 4,778 groundwater sites tested in 203 cities around the country, 60% were found to be grades IV and V/V+ (rising precipitously from 37% in 2000). As for the country's key rivers, 28% are deemed unfit for human contact (grades IV and V/V+).[7] And, in urban areas, 90% of the river water is badly contaminated.[8] (Twenty percent of the Yangtze River in the south and 50% of the Yellow River in the north are categorized as "poor.") Freshwater lakes fare still more poorly than the rivers, with 85% classified as grade IV or worse[9] (57.5% of the 40 major lakes in China were classified as either eutrophic or hypertrophic in 2005).[10] And more than 80% of the country's coastal seawater is heavily polluted.[11]

A pollution survey conducted by the Ministry of Environmental Protection found that 280 million people across the country lack access to safe drinking water.[12] Other studies put the figure at over 300 million. Whatever the precise number, it would seem that roughly one of every four people in China is without access to uncontaminated drinking water.

Inexplicably, according to Chinese regulations, grade V water, water regarded as unsuitable for industrial use and unfit for human contact, *is* considered suitable for agricultural purposes. Consequently, the polluted waterways we have described are the source of irrigation for much of the country's agriculture. Pollutants from the water thus can make their way into the food chain.

The sources of water pollution include waste and chemical discharge from industry, industrial accidents, human waste, pollutants suspended in the air and then deposited in the water (e.g., mercury and sulfur), and fertilizer and pesticide runoff from agriculture.

How Badly Is China's Soil Contaminated?

The country's soil has suffered a similar fate as the air and water. In a 2014 joint report, the Ministry of Land Resources and the Ministry of Environmental Protection found that 16.1% of China's soil is now contaminated; of the country's cultivated farmland, almost 20% is contaminated. Inorganic materials like cadmium, nickel, and arsenic are the major pollutants. The report asserts that "the main pollution source is human industrial and agricultural activities" and goes on to name, more specifically, industrial and factory waste, irrigation from polluted waterways, improper use of fertilizer, and the increased breeding of livestock as the key factors accounting for the massive degradation of farmland.[13] Acid rain should also be considered here as it falls on 11% of the land in southern China, especially in areas along the Yangtze River.

In late 2013, the Ministry of Land and Resources reported that over 8 million acres in China—equal to the size of Belgium—had become so toxic that farming on them should be prohibited.[14]

Some environmental activists believe that the government is grossly underreporting the severity of the problem. One, speaking of the 2014 report issued by the two ministries, told

Radio Free Asia, "These figures aren't accurate, because at least two thirds of China's agricultural land is polluted."[15]

Trying to feed 21% of the world's population on 7% of the world's arable land, China can hardly spare any loss of acreage to contamination. Already the country has one of the lowest arable land per capita rates in the world, at 0.197 acres per person (this metric has been on a steady decline since 1961). The world average is more than twice that; the US rate, by comparison, is 1.21 acres per person, six times that of China.

Chen Tongbin, a research fellow at the Chinese Academy of Social Sciences, told *Xinhua News* in 2014 that the joint report by the Ministry of Land Resources and the Ministry of Environmental Protection had set off "a loud alarm," and he noted that "Compared with air and water pollution, soil pollution is more difficult to control and remedy, taking a much longer time and needing more resources."[16]

Why Has Electronic Waste Been Such a Problem in China?

China is responsible for recycling about 70% of the world's electronic waste, or e-waste. E-waste refers to computers, televisions, mobile phones, printers, copiers, refrigerators, DVD players, batteries, and air-conditioning units—electronic devices of all variety—that have come to the end of their "useful life." The quantity of global e-waste has been swelling, especially as developing countries become enthusiastic consumers of electronic goods and as rapid technological innovation shortens the life span of the devices. Because e-waste contains valuable reusable materials (i.e., base metals, precious metals, and rare earth metals), much of it gets dismantled and recycled.

Until recently, up to 80% of what China recycled came from overseas, in particular from the United States, European Union countries, and Japan. However, today, as China's own middle class balloons, and with it the country's domestic consumption, about half of the e-waste China treats is domestically produced.

The city of Guiyu, in Guangzhou along the southern coast of China, has been the world's most popular destination for e-waste for a couple of decades now. Recyclers have found it cheaper to ship their e-waste there than to recycle at home, where they would have to comply with safe recycling practices. Employing roughly 80,000 to 130,000 workers, recyclers in Guiyu buy the e-waste—1.6 million tons per year—as it arrives on ships from abroad and via domestic transport. They then strip each device down to extract from it all the metals and parts of any value. It is estimated that the resale of metals and parts generates about $800 million for the town annually.

E-waste recycling, however, has wreaked havoc on the health of Guiyu's citizens and the environment. The plastic in the electronics is melted down to separate it from the metals, and the melting process releases into the air the chemical dioxin, a known human carcinogen, along with other toxins. Guiyu today has the highest level of cancer-causing dioxins in the world. The melting of lead solder off circuit boards has led to an epidemic of lead poisoning in Guiyu: 82% of the city's children have tested positive for this dangerous condition. In addition, 9 out of 10 city residents suffer from a skin, nervous, respiratory, or digestive ailment.

Dismantled e-waste has saturated Guiyu's soil with a variety of heavy metals in addition to lead (copper, zinc, tin, chromium, nickel, and cadmium), and they have contaminated the city's groundwater. Today Guiyu's groundwater is undrinkable, so drinking water must be trucked in from the outside.[17]

In late 2015 the government ordered Guiyu's more than 5,000 informal e-waste processing enterprises to shut down, requiring them to move their operations to a newly built industrial park.[18] The aim is to ensure more comprehensive oversight of the recycling process and stricter enforcement of recycling regulations by authorities. There is widespread concern, however, that such efforts to regulate the industry in

Guiyu will simply prompt unsanctioned recycling operations to move elsewhere.

E-waste recycling in China shows little sign of abating, especially as the country generates more and more of its own. But however profitable, it is contaminating the air, soil, and water in cities like Guiyu and damaging the health of the people who live there.

What Are the Challenges in Learning About China's Pollution and Environmental Issues?

Three challenges stand out.

First, the ministries, agencies, research institutes, and media reporting on the environment are by and large associated with the state and thus—we should assume—subject to occasional restraints in terms of what they make public. It is believed that sensitive environmental information and news sometimes goes undisclosed or is but selectively reported. Still, the leadership in Beijing—whether motivated by pressure from the public or the desire to amass public support in state campaigns to tackle air, water, and soil degradation—has become more transparent in recent years, increasingly willing to share information about problems such as the level of pollution in the air, the heavy metals in the soil, the cadmium in the rice, and the emission levels of industrial plants.

A second challenge in learning about China's environmental conditions is that, as a rapidly developing country, systematic monitoring of the environment has not been a top priority. This means that detailed, reliable environmental data for much of the country have been lacking. Only recently has the government ramped up its monitoring efforts. China has begun to track air quality, emissions levels, and energy use across much of the nation; it is also requiring local and provincial offices to submit pollution reports and energy intensity reports to the central government regularly. With more systematic monitoring and fuller reports from authorities on site, more accurate data should be available, making it easier to understand and assess environmental conditions.

Information from local officials, however, is not always dependable. Officials have been known to misreport data to satisfy the expectations and wishes of their superiors. In addition, since these data serve as the basis of their job evaluations, which in turn are the basis for future appointments, the temptation of officials to "massage" the numbers—even rather vigorously—can be strong indeed. Such falsification of data by local officials is a third challenge we face in learning about China's environmental problems. In recent laws and communiqués (see Chapter 11), however, Beijing has made clear its intention to hold officials accountable for accurate reporting. Time will tell.

2

HISTORICAL BACKGROUND

What Are Some of the Main Environmental Challenges China Has Faced Historically?

By the end of the first millennium BCE, the population in China was already 50 million; by 1000 CE it had doubled, and by the mid-19th century it had reached 400 million. Population growth of this magnitude necessarily put a strain on the country's natural resources. As the population expanded geographically, more and more forests were felled to make way for agricultural fields and to provide wood for heating and the construction of houses and ships. It is estimated that 75% of China was once forested; by the early 20th century that figure had shrunk to 5%. With deforestation has come loss of habitat for flora and fauna, soil erosion, disruption of water cycles, and other environmental problems.

In his book *The Retreat of the Elephants: An Environmental History of China*, Mark Elvin characterizes the China of the Zhou dynasty (1045 BC?–221 BC) as "a civilization based on deforestation" and goes on to say that "by the early first millennium B.C.E., if not considerably earlier, the focus of state economic concern was on farming."[1] Several verses in the Confucian classic the *Book of Poetry* (first millennium BCE) celebrate the efforts of the early Zhou people to clear the forested land for crop cultivation. One ode of thanksgiving reads,

> They clear away the grass, the trees;
> Their ploughs open up the ground.
> In a thousand pairs they tug at weeds and roots,
> Along the low grounds, along the ridges.
> There is the master and his eldest son,
> There the headman and the overseer.
> They mark out, they plough.
> Deep the food-baskets that are brought;
> Dainty are the wives,
> The men press close to them.
> And now with shares so sharp
> They set to work upon the southern acre.
> They sow the many sorts of grain,
> The seeds that hold moist life.
> How the blade shoots up,
> How sleek, the grown plant;
> Very sleek, the young grain![2]

In the writings of the great Confucian philosopher Mencius (fourth century BC) a few centuries later, celebration of the benefits of land clearance turns to despair over the despoliation of nature that results from it:

> There was a time when the trees were luxuriant on Ox Mountain. As it is on the outskirts of a great metropolis, the trees are constantly lopped by axes. Is it any wonder they are no longer fine? With the respite they get in the day and in the night, and the moistening by the rain and dew, there is certainly no lack of shoots coming out, but then the cattle and sheep come to graze upon the mountain. That is why it is as bald as it is. People, seeing only its baldness, tend to think it never

> had any trees. But can this possibly be the nature of a mountain? (*Mencius* 6A.6)

Human intervention, Mencius decries, had stripped Ox Mountain bare of its natural vegetative lushness.

Qu Geping, one of the "fathers" of environmental advocacy in the People's Republic, describes in *Population and the Environment in China* the 600 years from the Ming dynasty (1368–1644) to 1949 as a time of "escalated degradation" of the environment. The increasing population of those centuries, he argues, reclaimed forests at ever-increasing rates; peasant farmers would work the land aggressively for a few years, leaving it depleted of its nutrients, and then move on to clear new areas.[3]

China's long history of deforestation led to routine flooding and endemic soil erosion. Chinese chronicles are filled with accounts, from earliest times, of ravaging floods and the heroic efforts by rulers and their ministers to tame the water and protect the people from devastation. Yu, the great sage-king of China's legendary Xia dynasty (ca. 2000 BCE), was long revered by the tradition precisely because he is said to have brought the torrential flooding of the Yellow River under control by dredging channels for it. The ability to maintain effective control of the country's river systems remained one of the hallmarks of a "good" ruler throughout imperial China.

The geographic expansion of the population and the resulting widespread deforestation disrupted the habitats of native animal and plant species. It is stunning to realize that there was once a time when elephants roamed the region around Beijing, and that rhinoceroses, as recently as the 19th century, lived happily in many parts of southwestern China.

The gazetteer of Yushan county in China's southeast tells of the ill effects that the expanding human settlement had on local biodiversity:

> Old farmers say that at the beginning of the Qianlong reign [1736], when people were opening up the Huai and Yushan mountains, trees grew there in abundance, thickets of bamboo were dense, and herds of deer wandered by or rested at the side of the paths. Pheasants and hares were everywhere in the mountains, and could be caught without difficulty. Mandarin ducks and egrets frequently flew back and forth along the margins of Stone Drum Creek. Human beings and animals were used to one another, and paid each other no attention, though, on the other hand, wild boars, "field pigs," bears, black bears, and other, unknown wild beasts often did harm. Recently bamboos and trees have been ever more widely cleared, and human settlement grown denser. The wild beasts have not waited to be driven away, but have departed of their own accord.[4]

As the population swelled, per capita acreage declined and peasant families had to make do with less. The consequence, as Qu suggested above, is that families tended to work the land harder, overfarming it and stripping it of its nutrients. Land scarcity thus led to widespread soil depletion. In turn, competition for good land grew, especially in the 18th and 19th centuries, and frequently erupted into violence. Indeed, the greatest rebellion of the 19th century, the Taiping Rebellion, which claimed 20 million lives, had its roots in a struggle between ethnic groups over the scarce arable land in Guangxi province in the south of China.

Finally, some of the great monuments from China's past that produce so much wonder and awe today came at a hefty environmental price. Consider that the Great Wall, which extends for many thousands of miles, would have required an enormous amount of wood to heat the kilns for baking bricks, cooking food, and providing warmth for the laborers. Surrounding forested land would have been devastated. So, too, consider the spectacular Forbidden City, with its 1,000 buildings and 9,000 rooms. Floors of the main halls were paved with golden brick, baked with clay found in the area around the city of Suzhou; the pillars of these halls were made from whole logs transported to Beijing from as far away as the jungles of southwestern China.

How Has Tremendous Population Growth Since the Founding of the People's Republic in 1949 Affected the Environment?

Since the People's Republic of China (PRC) was founded in 1949, the population has more than doubled, growing from 541 million to roughly 1.38 billion today. Before 1949 the annual growth rate was 0.3%, but by 1960 it had risen to 3%. Scholars suggest a couple of reasons for this rise: (1) the establishment of the PRC in 1949 ended the unsettling civil wars and produced a new social stability and (2) the stronger health measures and better sanitation conditions introduced by the PRC government significantly lowered mortality rates.

This dramatic increase in population has had both direct and indirect consequences for the environment. To feed nearly 1.4 billion people, farming has become more intensive. Forests have been cleared to make way for more cropland, and much of the country's cropland has become overcultivated (i.e., shorter fallow periods and heavier use of fertilizers and pesticides). This heavy use of fertilizers and pesticides, in turn, has led to severe toxic runoff from the agricultural lands, which is a major contributor to the pollution of China's waterways. Much of the country's grasslands has been overgrazed, as larger numbers of livestock feed on them, particularly as the Chinese diet becomes more meat-oriented (see Chapter 4).

Together, deforestation, overcultivation, and overgrazing have produced a desertification crisis of enormous proportion, especially in the arid and drought-prone regions of northern China. The Gobi Desert is encroaching on the capital of Beijing, and a massive tree-planting campaign is under way to halt its expansion: the Great Green Wall of China is a program to plant a 2,800-mile-long belt of trees in the north of China. According to China's State Forestry Administration, 27% of China's territory, more than 1 million square miles (2.59 million square kilometers), is now desertified. Between 2005 and 2009 alone, more than 660,000 square miles (1.71 million square kilometers) became desert land. Desertification in China is not altogether new, but it is now a problem of huge consequence.[5]

Population growth has also led to increased water usage for agricultural, industrial, and domestic purposes, putting ever greater stress on China's relatively scarce water supply. And population growth has also brought with it a greater demand for energy, for heating, cooling, transportation, building construction, manufacturing of consumables, and the like. And since much of this energy over the past half century has come from fossil fuels, especially coal, the doubling of the population has to be considered, at least indirectly, an important factor in the rising toxicity of China's air, water, and soil (from sulfur and mercury deposition resulting from coal combustion) and in the country's world-leading contribution to carbon dioxide emissions.

What Is China's "Century of Humiliation" and What Does It Mean for the Environment?

The premodern Chinese were "exceptionalists"; they believed that their way of life was the envy of all other peoples. It was only natural, they thought, that their neighbors—the nomadic peoples to the north and west, the Japanese, the Koreans, and the Vietnamese—would want to become like them and to embrace their superior way of life. Even those who had visited them from the west—Marco Polo (13th century) and Matteo Ricci (16th–17th century), for instance—had expressed admiration for the prosperity and cultural richness of the Middle Kingdom.

But the 19th and early 20th centuries were challenging ones for the Chinese and gave them pause. The Manchu Qing dynasty that had ruled China since the mid-17th century had been weakened by huge corruption scandals and a succession of weak rulers. Western nations, Great Britain in particular, were pressing hard for expanded trade opportunities. When the Qing proved resistant to this pressure, the British went to war with China over the right to sell, of all things, opium. Easily defeating Chinese in the so-called Opium War of 1839–1842, the victors forced upon the Qing government the first in a series of "unequal treaties." The Daoguang emperor (r. 1820–1850) was required to cede Hong Kong to the British, open up the country's ports to foreign trade, grant foreigners living in Chinese cities the right of extraterritoriality (immunity from Chinese law), and pay the British Crown a huge indemnity. The remainder of the 19th century saw China agree to many more similar "unequal treaties" with other imperialist powers of the day.

Then, in August 1894, the Qing went to war with neighboring Japan over control of Korea. For the next six months, Japanese land and naval forces inflicted defeat after defeat on the larger Chinese forces. The Manchu government sued for peace, acknowledging the loss of Korea to Japan and the military dominance of Japan in the region—a hard pill for the Middle Kingdom, used to thinking of Japan as a subordinate and inferior, to swallow.

In 1911 the Qing dynasty fell, and the country descended into warlordism and civil war. By the 1930s, two parties were struggling for control of China: the Nationalist Party and the Chinese Communist Party. Before their contest could be resolved, Japanese forces invaded China, initiating the second Sino-Japanese War (1937–1945). The Japanese quickly captured Shanghai and then moved on to Nanjing, destroying the city in what would become known as the Nanjing Massacre. When the Japanese were defeated in 1945, China's civil war between the Nationalist forces and the Communist forces resumed with vigor, until 1949, when the Communists won a final victory and the Nationalists fled to Taiwan.

Chinese speak routinely of the period from the mid-19th to the mid-20th century as the "century of humiliation." It has become an integral part of the country's national narrative, a signifier for a time when China's greatness as the dominant cultural and political power of East Asia was momentarily eclipsed. Reference to the "century of humiliation" is a shorthand intended to convey the following message: in the country's long history, the period from the mid-19th to the mid-20th century was just a blip—but a blip whose memory must not be forgotten lest China again be reduced to a second- or third-class citizen of the world.[6]

How does this narrative of the century of humiliation play out environmentally? To be "modern" and "prosperous"—like the West—matters, and to be *seen* as "modern" and "prosperous" matters as well. Consider the pride the Chinese took in hosting the 2008 Beijing Olympics. It was, they claimed, their "coming-out party," an opportunity to broadcast to the world the phenomenal economic progress China had made since the time of Chairman Mao. From the grand Bird's Nest stadium, to the Water Cube (the swimming venue), to the colossal Terminal 3 at Beijing Capital International Airport, to the new high-speed rail system radiating out from Beijing, China spared no expense in showing off its capital. The city also constructed miles of new urban expressways and roads and added three new lines to the city's subway system. It tore down the *hutong*—the traditional courtyard alleyways—and replaced them with shiny high-rise offices, apartments, and condos. To be sure, Beijing is glisteningly modern, but the construction of towering buildings, the expansion of highways and roads, and the appropriation of once open land have had substantial environmental costs, both short and long term.

Some pundits argue that Chinese leaders are drawn to grandiose "megaprojects" because they offer opportunities for China to parade its 21st-century modernity and to demonstrate that its engineering and technological capabilities are the equal of any country in the world. The Three Gorges Dam on the Yangtze River near the municipality of Chongqing—an 18-year-long project completed in 2012—is the largest hydroelectric dam in the world (see Chapter 12). Its purpose is to produce much-needed energy for the country and to control flooding along the Yangtze. Another megaproject is the South-North Water Diversion Project, which is designed to move 45 billion cubic meters of fresh water annually, via three excavated canal systems, from the Yangtze in the south to northern China, where the water shortage is acute (see Chapter 6). It will not be completed until 2050, but already it has cost more than $80 billion.

Both of these are stunning engineering feats. But in the planning stages, scientific experts laid out what they regarded as serious problems and proposed less grandiose, more cost-effective alternatives. Some observers have concluded that these other proposals were dismissed at least in part because they did not offer the same opportunities for showcasing China's modernity and technological skill.

If being "modern" is good, the bicycle, which until the late 20th century ruled the roads of China, is under threat. Waves of black "Flying Pigeons," the ubiquitous Chinese-built bike, once flooded the streets of Chinese cities, often as far as the eye could see. Today the bicycle is not quite extinct, but close (though in heavily trafficked cities environmentalists and new bike-sharing enterprises are hoping to bring it back into fashion). The roads are so congested with automobiles that traveling just a few miles—at least in Beijing—can take up to a couple of hours. Yes, it is more comfortable in a car, where drivers can listen to music, turn on the heat or air conditioning, and escape the crowds. But bike travel can be much quicker, not to mention cheaper and healthier. Yet bikes carry some stigma; they are seen by many as "backward," a relic of a time when China was a "third world" nation, when people were poor, and when "modern" was something Chinese might see only in pictures of life in the West. Just as we in the West did after

World War II, China today is having a love affair with the car. Overnight the country has become the largest car market in the world, buying roughly 24 million units in 2016 (vs. 17.5 million in the United States). And car emissions have become a major source of the toxic air hanging over Chinese cities.

Why Did Mao Zedong Proclaim "Man Must Conquer Nature," and What Were the Consequences for the Environment?

In establishing the PRC in 1949, Mao Zedong was committed to ending China's humiliation at the hands of foreign powers. He was convinced—despite the warnings of economists about the dangers of overpopulation—that the road to global wealth and power lay in expanding the population and that China's lack of sophisticated technology could be effectively offset by a vast labor force. The five-character slogan of the day put it succinctly, "With many people, strength is great" (人多力量大 *ren duo liliang da*). And, from 1949 to 1976, the year Mao died, the country's population did indeed grow to "many," from 541 million to 933 million.

If, for Mao, modernizing required population growth, population growth meant reclaiming land, opening wastelands, felling forests, and filling in wetlands and even rivers and lakes with soil, all to increase the amount of arable acreage. Nature had to be made to yield all that it could, to serve the nation's cause. Mao cast the relationship between humans and nature in antagonistic terms, describing it as a battle wherein "man must conquer nature" (人定勝天 *ren ding sheng tian*).[7]

With 1958 and the launching of the campaign known as the Great Leap Forward, Mao's assault on nature intensified. Chinese peasants were mobilized into "people's communes" and instructed to produce "more, better, faster, cheaper." New techniques like "deep plowing" (five-foot-deep furrows) and "close planting" (12.5 million seedlings per 2.5 acres instead of 1.5 million) were introduced and fertilizers were applied countrywide. And since Mao believed that sparrows were consuming the country's grain seeds, he called for a campaign in 1959 to wipe them out; the people obliged by shooting sparrows from the sky and by banging on pots, pans, and drums to scare them from landing, forcing them to remain in flight until they fell to the ground exhausted or dead.

None of these steps proved effective; some, in fact, were positively harmful. Deep plowing and close planting may have sounded to Mao and others like reasonable steps, but neither had any scientific basis. Overfertilization and inappropriate fertilization degraded and contaminated the soil. The urgency to produce meant fields were not given sufficient fallow time. And it turns out that sparrows eat not only grain seed but insects: eliminating sparrows eliminated the most fearsome and effective natural predator of locusts, and locusts now came to infest large swaths of the Chinese countryside.

The Great Leap Forward aimed for a "leap" not just in crop production but also in industrial production. Mao urged the Chinese people on, saying that with their strength and determination, they could surpass the United States and England in iron and steel output. Hearkening to the call, people throughout the country set up "backyard furnaces," where they smelt "scrap" metal—pots, pans, knobs, bicycles, and the like, which they collected from their homes—to make steel. To fuel the furnaces, people cut down whole forests: an estimated 10% of China's forested area was lost during the Great Leap Forward. And, in the end, the "steel" produced in the backyard furnaces was so impure and of such low quality as to be useless.

The Great Leap Forward took a heavy toll on both the environment and the people. The campaign's misguided agricultural practices, the diversion of farm labor from crop production to steel production, the devastating locust infestations, and the government's failure to respond effectively resulted in one of the most horrific famines in history, one that took somewhere in the area of 40 million lives.[8]

Both nature and humanity were the victims of Mao's insistence that "man must conquer nature" if China were to reclaim its place in the world and to catch up with the West. Yet this antagonistic view toward nature has not entirely disappeared. In a 1997 speech commemorating the Three Gorges Project, then-president Jiang Zemin said:

> Since the twilight of history, the Chinese nation has been engaged in the great feat of conquering, developing and exploiting nature. The legends of the mythic bird Jingwei determined to fill the sea with small pebbles and the Foolish Old Man resolved to remove the mountains standing in his way and the tale of the Great Yu who harnessed the great floods are just some of the examples of the ancient Chinese people's indomitable spirit in successfully conquering nature.[9]

Jiang's speech reminds us that China had been engaged in a battle to control nature on and off for more than three millennia. The environmental consequences of Mao's war on nature may have been especially harsh, but the efforts to make nature submit to human control were hardly the first in the country's history.

What Do China's Major Schools of Thought—Confucianism, Daoism, Buddhism—Suggest About the Relationship Between Human Beings and the Natural World?

The schools of Confucianism and Daoism had their beginnings in China in the middle of the first millennium BCE and have remained tremendously influential ever since. Buddhism, unlike Confucianism and Daoism, is not indigenous to China, originating with the historical Buddha, Shakyamuni, in eastern India in the middle of the first millennium BCE and making its way to China via trade routes in the first century CE. By the fourth century, Buddhist teachings had become widespread and firmly rooted in Chinese soil, eclipsing Confucianism and Daoism in importance for the next half a millennium or so—when Confucianism would again become dominant. For much of Chinese history, these three schools have existed side by side and been known collectively as the *sanjiao* (三教), the "three teachings."

With different emphases, each of the three teachings speaks to the holistic nature of the universe, viewing heaven, Earth, and humankind as interrelated and constituting an organismic whole. Classical Confucianism claims that the realm of heaven or nature and the realm of humankind are inseparable (天人合一*tianren heyi*). Classical Daoism asserts that there is one true way, the way of nature, and that humans should behave in accord with it, harmonizing the human realm with the natural realm. And traditional Buddhism assumes that nothing has its own fixed or abiding identity; rather, it exists only in its interdependent relationship to all other things in the universe.

But while the three teachings could each express the ideal of a universe in which nature and humankind are in accord, none developed a sustained ecological discourse or agenda. And none called in practice for putting the interests of the natural world on equal footing with, or above, human interests. Even in the case of Daoism, the school most explicit in its praise of the natural order, nature was valued less in its own right than as an ideal of non-purposive, spontaneous, and un-self-conscious action (無為 *wuwei*) to be modeled by human beings.

I would even propose that Confucianism, the state ideology in imperial China, may have fostered a cultural mindset that regarded the physical world as something to be controlled and dominated. For although Confucian teachings argue for the inseparability of the human realm and the natural realm, they at the same time firmly believe that the natural world, in the end, exists largely to serve human needs and to provide for the material well-being of humanity. Confucius and his followers, like the great fourth-century philosopher Mencius, maintained that for most people sufficiency of food, clothing, and shelter is a precondition for Confucian moral self-cultivation. After all, the reasoning goes, people who are anxious about their mere survival and who are struggling to provide for elderly parents and young children "do not have the leisure to devote to ritual practice and righteousness" (*Mencius* 1A.7). Thus, it falls to the ruler to ensure his subjects' livelihood. Dong Zhongshu, a renowned Confucian of the second century BCE, lays out more specifically the worthy ruler's responsibilities in this regard: "He takes up the plough handle to till the soil, plucks mulberry leaves and nourishes the silkworms, reclaims the wilds, plants grain, and opens new lands to provide sufficient food and clothing."[10] In short, Confucian ideology has it that the good ruler is to take the lead in taming nature for the benefit of his subjects.[11]

Mao's "man must conquer nature" campaign, as we have seen, may have been particularly ruthless, but in its general call to rein nature in, to make it serve the needs of the Chinese people, it does not represent a major break in kind from traditional Chinese environmental practices or attitudes. As Judith Shapiro observes in her book *Mao's War Against Nature: Politics and the Environment in Revolutionary China*:

> The Mao-era effort to conquer nature can thus be understood as an extreme form of a philosophical and behavioral tendency that has roots in traditional Confucian culture. . . . State-sponsored resettlements and waterworks projects, extensive and excessive construction of dikes for land reclamation, political campaigns to change agricultural practices, and environmentally destructive land conversions in response to population shift can be found in imperial times.[12]

Nonetheless, in their belief that the universe is organismic, that heaven, Earth, and humankind are interdependent, each constituting an integral part of a larger whole, Confucianism,

Daoism, and Buddhism, the foundational "three teachings," may be capable of furnishing a China facing a postindustrial environmental crisis with the conceptual and linguistic resources to construct a meaningful native-based eco-centric philosophy. And, in recent years, various Confucian, Daoist, and Buddhist organizations committed to sustaining and protecting the environment have in fact emerged, aiming to elaborate doctrinally based eco-friendly programs capable of addressing China's 21st-century environmental challenges.

3

ECONOMIC DEVELOPMENT AND THE ENVIRONMENT

What Accounts for China's Economic Growth Since the Late 20th Century?

Mao Zedong died in 1976, and two years later Deng Xiaoping became China's paramount leader. Convinced that the Chinese economy was stagnating, Deng and others introduced a series of reforms meant to improve economic productivity and the living standards of the people. The reforms included decollectivizing agriculture, opening up China to foreign trade and investment, and allowing private enterprises to be established. Signaling that capitalism and personal wealth were no longer taboo, Deng is said to have proclaimed (though there is no documentary evidence), "To get rich is glorious"—a slogan that the Chinese people have embraced with enthusiasm.

The economic growth has been phenomenal. Prior to 1978, China's GDP was growing at roughly 3% annually; since 1978 it has enjoyed an annual rise of roughly 10%. In 2010 China overtook Japan as the world's second largest economy, just after the United States; the expectation is that it will surpass the United States as the world's largest by the mid-2020s.[1]

With agricultural decollectivization farmers were given partial ownership of the land and the right to sell surplus crops at market rates. In the years from 1978 to 1984 China's agricultural output skyrocketed by 47%. This increase did not simply enrich farmers; the surplus of food also allowed for the reallocation of labor from the farm to industry, especially to the town and village enterprises created by local governments.

China now set on a path of industrialization, rural and urban, state-owned and private. This industrialization was the engine driving the country's efforts to modernize and to challenge the global dominance of Western industrialized nations and Japan. Here we return to the subject of population: the huge and largely impoverished population made for a ready and cheap industrial labor force. Because textiles, furniture, toys, and electronics could be produced inexpensively by global standards, exports grew—and grew. China today is the largest exporter in the world and the second largest importer. In 2015, exports accounted for 22.4% of the country's GDP. (At their height in 2006, exports made up more than 35% of the country's GDP.)

Globalization has provided a big boost to China's economy. Accession into the World Trade Organization (WTO) in 2001, which liberalized China's terms of trade with other parts of the world, was a particular boon. Globalization and WTO membership provided the Chinese with more than export markets, though: multinational corporations (MNCs) from the West and from East Asia—GE, Johnson & Johnson, IBM, Philips, Toyota, Bosch, Audi, Microsoft, GM, and Apple, to name a few—have found it increasingly attractive to set up shop in China. Various factors have made China an appealing place for MNCs. Most significant perhaps are its cheap labor and lax environmental laws, which have made production there a relative bargain, and its growing consumerism, which has made the country an increasingly attractive market in its own right.

Globalization has also resulted in a tremendous amount of foreign direct investment (FDI) in Chinese enterprises: in 2014 alone FDI in China was around $120 billion, more than in any other country in the world (with the United States second at $86 billion).[2] Globalization has been a two-way street, especially in the past decade. China is also investing abroad, in places like Africa, the Mideast, South America, and, more recently, North America and Europe. In fact, for the first time ever, in 2014 China sent more FDI abroad than it received.

What Has It Meant for China to Be the "Workshop of the World"?

In the 20th century, the development of worldwide communications and transportation networks facilitated the globalization of trade. From 1978 to 2003 there was roughly a 40-fold increase in international trade; trade between Asia and the European Union, North America, South America, and Africa became routine.

China, in particular, benefited. Because of its (1) large labor force, (2) low wages, and (3) abundant supply of cheap energy (i.e., fossil fuels), the country had become a manufacturing powerhouse by the late 20th century, especially of inexpensive low-tech goods like textiles, toys, bicycles, paper supplies, and building materials. It was cheaper for countries around the world to import these products from China—even including transportation costs—than to produce them domestically. As mentioned earlier, it also became cheaper for MNCs (e.g., IBM, Bosch, Apple, GM, Toyota) to outsource the production of some of their goods, by setting up their own plants and factories in China or by contracting with Chinese suppliers, than to manufacture them at home.

Villages in China have even come to specialize in manufacturing a particular item: jeans, handkerchiefs, socks, and cigarette lighters, for example. In Yiwu, a village in China's southeastern Zhejiang province, the tree lights and trinkets, polystyrene snowflakes, and plastic Santas and reindeers that decorate houses all over the world during the Christmas season are made. Six hundred factories in Yiwu produce 60% of the entire world's Christmas decorations. Buyers from all over come to the wholesale market in the village to shop for Christmas ornaments, made by migrant laborers working

12-hour shifts for $300 to $400 a month, and ship them back to their home countries.[3]

In 2011, China surpassed the United States as the world's largest producer of manufactured goods. Data from the Natural Resources Defense Council show that in 2015 China was producing 40% of the world's washing machines, 50% of the textiles, 60% of the buttons, 70% of the shoes, 80% of the televisions, and 90% of the toys.[4] In recent years, China has added higher-value products to its list of manufactured goods: computer machinery, home appliances, aircraft, pharmaceuticals, and medical instruments, for instance.

With increased manufacturing comes increased energy consumption. Since 1980 the consumption of energy in China has more than quadrupled (between 2000 and 2010 alone, it rose 130%). And since coal provides the lion's share of China's energy needs, coal consumption has exploded, growing five-fold. China today consumes as much coal every year as the rest of the world combined. The "workshop of the world" has helped to bring prosperity to China and to lift hundreds of millions of Chinese people out of poverty, to be sure. But heavy emissions from coal-fired industries and power plants of sulfur dioxide, nitrogen oxides, particulate matter, mercury, and the greenhouse gas carbon dioxide have taken an unspeakable toll on the environment and the people's health.

A recent study found that the products manufactured for export accounted for more than 36% of the sulfur dioxide, 27% of the nitrogen oxides, and 22% of the carbon monoxide emitted by China.[5] We are thus left with the delicate and much-debated question: Whose pollution is this, China's or the importing countries'?

How Has Economic Growth Affected the Country's Environment?

In the first two decades of the reform period, China's efforts were focused on developing the economy at all costs. The environmental consequences of economic growth received little or no attention. The slogan "pollute first, clean up later" (先污染後治理 *xian wuran hou zhili*) encapsulated the government's priorities. And the economy has indeed prospered, and the material well-being of the people has vastly improved.

Today, China's priorities may be shifting, however: the country appears to be moving in the direction of the "clean up later" stage, as the people and the leadership alike recognize the devastating effects economic progress has had on China's physical environment. Beginning in 2014, Premier Li Keqiang signaled China's intention to shutter the "workshop of the world," saying that the country's economy must now move away from its dependence on the manufacture of cheap goods for export and pursue a new "low carbon and green growth" path focusing on the production of high-tech products and services for domestic consumption.

Economic growth has meant a heavy reliance on fossil fuels, most particularly coal, for the production of energy. At the turn of this century China was consuming 1.5 billion tons of coal annually; in 2013, the country consumed more than 4 billion tons. And because burning coal emits more pollutants and more carbon dioxide than any other source, China's economic development has been directly responsible for much of the smog that hangs in the country's air and nearly 30% of the greenhouse gases warming the globe. The toxins emitted into the country's air, in turn, have contributed to an increase in the country's morbidity and mortality rates. Teng Fei, a professor at Tsinghua University, estimates that the country's coal emissions were responsible for 670,000 premature deaths in 2012 alone.[6]

In addition, the coal industry—mining, processing, and power generation—is water-intensive, consuming approximately 20% of all of China's water resources. Thus, the ever-rising need for energy is a growing threat to the country's already limited water supply. It is estimated that since the 1990s more than 28,000 rivers in China have dried up, owing in large part to the withdrawal of water by industries located on riverbanks—as well as to climate change, population growth, and poor water management.[7]

The factories that have sprouted up along China's rivers and lakes account for much of the country's phenomenal economic development. However, because they dump their chemicals and wastewater directly into these waters, they account too for the contamination that makes much of the country's water—surface water and groundwater—undrinkable, even untouchable. The toxins introduced into the water supply and the soil by these factories and taken up by neighboring villagers in their drinking water and crops have resulted in an abnormally high incidence of cancer cases in the countryside. Some villages have been so severely stricken that they are referred to as "cancer villages," at least 500 of which are known to exist (see Chapter 8).

Finally, there are the inevitable industrial accidents that release metals and toxins into the air, the water, and the soil. One of the more notorious occurred in the northern province of Jilin in 2005 when a chemical factory exploded, sending 100 tons of toxic pollutants—benzene, aniline, nitrobenzene—into the Songhua River. Six people were killed by the blast and dozens were injured. Forming a 50-mile-long slick, the deadly spill then drifted downstream, reaching Harbin, a city of 10 million, and cutting off its water supply; from there it continued downstream, flowing into the Amur River and Russian territory.[8]

Turning the present question on its head, we can ask: What is the cost of environmental pollution to the country's economic growth? Economists tend to put the cost in terms of percentage of China's GDP. The figures range widely, from 3% to as much as 15%. But the figures are not based on a consistent set of metrics. Some focus on the costs of air pollution, some on air and water pollution, and some on air, water, and soil pollution; some calculate the costs according to the number of lost working days and productivity; some consider the cost of lost working days and the medical and hospitalization costs;

still others include the cost of lost working days, medical expenses, natural resource degradation, and environmental cleanup. The Chinese Academy of Social Sciences and World Bank put the annual total cost of environmental degradation in China at about 9% of the country's GDP.[9] The World Bank and the Institute for Health Metrics and Evaluation, in a study published in September 2016, calculated that in 2013 the cost to China of air pollution alone approached 10% of its GDP.[10]

What Has Economic Development Meant for the Growth of Cities?

With industrialization has come greater economic opportunity for China's less well-off rural population. The pace of urbanization has been remarkable, as farmers have fled the land for construction, manufacturing, and odd jobs in the cities. In the early 1950s urbanites were but 13% of the country's population and as recently as 1978, they represented only 17.9%. But by 2013, China had officially become "urban," with 53% of the people living in cities. In 2015, 56% of the population was urban.

In 1949 there were 132 cities in China. Today there are 655; 12 have populations of over 4 million (Figure 3.1). This "hyper-urbanization" is expected to continue apace, as the government is actively promoting the move from the countryside to cities. Reckoning that urbanization will reduce the number of rural poor and promote greater income equality, Premier Li and the Beijing leadership plan to move 100 million rural Chinese into cities by the end of 2020 (60% urbanization), and another 150 million by 2025 (70%), making for an additional 250 million new city dwellers. According to Li, China should be aiming for an 80% urbanization rate, the average rate for the world's developed economies.

While the move to urbanize may be good for the economy, it naturally has had consequences for the environment—and the environmental challenges will only grow as the flight to

Figure 3.1 The growth of cities in China

cities accelerates. First, urban expansion has come at the expense of arable land. From 2001 to 2013 the country lost more than 8 million acres of arable land to urban development. The farmland lost to urban growth has put the country's food security at risk. Urban expansion has also led to the reclamation of wetlands and lakes; in the past 20 years, the city of Wuhan has lost 70% of its lakes.[11] To the consternation of environmentalists and scientists, China in recent years has been bulldozing the tops of mountains and filling in the surrounding valleys to create level ground for urban development. Already, studies have documented the environmental effects of moving mountaintops on the environment: deforestation, soil erosion, landslides, air pollution, water pollution, and so on.[12]

As might be expected, the construction of wastewater treatment plants has not kept pace with the rapid growth in urban population, which means that cities are discharging much of their municipal wastewater directly into surrounding waterways. The larger numbers of people produce more sewage, which, like the wastewater, contributes to China's water pollution woes. An often-forgotten consequence of urban growth is the inevitable rise in solid waste. In 1976 Beijing generated 1.04 million tons of municipal solid waste; in 2007, the volume had grown to 6 million tons. Currently solid waste in the capital is increasing 8% annually, and 90% of it is sent to landfills, which already are filled beyond their designated capacities.[13]

Finally, there is the obvious air pollution, the result of urban industry, power plants, trucks and cars, mass transit, housing and utilities, and so forth.

The urbanization planned through 2025 brings with it opportunity. Cities *can* be thoughtfully designed, made to be greener and "smarter," and the present sprawl—and land encroachment—can be curtailed. Denser living could enable better and more efficient management of water, wastewater, and energy; the development of low-carbon public transit systems; and the reduction of private vehicles and their environmentally unfriendly emissions.

As the 21st Century Unfolds, Can Economic Prosperity and Environmental Protection Coexist?

This is the very challenge China's leadership has set for itself. Under Communist Party rule, China has become a global economic power and the lives of the Chinese people, materially, have improved dramatically. "Economic prosperity at all costs" has been the leadership's guiding principle—and the basis of its legitimacy—for the past few decades, but it turns out that those costs have been unacceptably high. Air pollution, water scarcity, food contamination, and a growing health crisis have made increasingly clear to the Chinese people all that has been sacrificed in the name of economic development. Environmental protests have become more frequent, as people insist that breathing clean air, drinking clear water, and eating foods free of toxins are basic human rights that need the government's protection.

As a consequence, there has been a seeming shift in the government's priorities. In the last couple of years, talk of the "economy at all costs" has given way to talk of building an "ecological civilization" (see the Epilogue). In 2012, then-President Hu Jintao remarked, "We must give high priority to making ecological progress . . . work hard to build a beautiful country, and achieve lasting and sustainable development of the Chinese nation."[14] The following year, the Central Committee of the Communist Party of China, under President Xi Jinping's leadership, picked up on the theme in a November communiqué:

> We must deepen ecological environment management reform by centering on building a beautiful China. We should accelerate system building to promote ecological progress, improve institutions and mechanisms for developing geographical space, conserving resources and protecting the ecological environment and promoting modernization featuring harmonious development between Man and Nature.[15]

Protection of the environment has taken on a new urgency for the Party. But the difficulty the leadership faces in promoting an "ecological civilization" is how to protect the environment *without* putting at risk the country's economic growth. When, for example, in the first quarter of 2014 the government shut down many of the high-polluting, energy-intensive steel, cement, and coal plants in Hebei, the province registered its lowest quarterly growth in 15 years.[16] And in 2015, when production was suspended at 57 energy-intensive plants in the city of Linyi in Shandong after the mayor was summoned to Beijing for failing to uphold environmental standards, 60,000 workers were reported to have lost their jobs.[17]

To this end, Premier Li Keqiang and others have been arguing since 2014 for the need to transform the very nature of the Chinese economy from one based on energy-intensive manufacturing of low-value goods to one centered on higher-tech products and services. In effect, this means a shift away from an export-heavy economy to an economy based on domestic consumption. And since urban dwellers have better incomes and on average consume two to three times as much as those who live in the country, the government, as we have learned, is intent on adding 250 million people to the urban rosters.

But while it is easy to see, as Li Keqiang does, how weaning the economy from dirty manufacturing and lessening the country's energy intensity might be beneficial for China's environment, it is less easy to see how vastly augmenting the number of urban dwellers—with the likely need for new building construction, the expansion of urban infrastructure, and the greater demand for automobiles, housing, heating and cooling, and utilities—can be environmentally beneficial. Only the coming years will tell whether Beijing's "hyper-urbanization" policy has taken adequate account of the potential environmental challenges it poses.

Still, there can be no doubting the leadership's intention. The many steps introduced by the government in recent years (see Chapter 11) make clear Beijing's wish to redress the three-decade imbalance in favor of economic growth. Li Keqiang's declaration of a "war on pollution" in March 2014 is but one indicator of Beijing's seriousness. Many observers of the Communist Party believe that much of its legitimacy today rests on the enormous economic progress the country has enjoyed under its leadership. The Party's legitimacy in the years to come may well depend on how effectively it continues to provide for the people economically even as it safeguards the environment and promotes the people's "quality of life."

4

CHINA'S NEW CONSUMERISM

What Are Some of the Consuming Traits of a More Well-to-Do China?

As China's GDP has grown, so has the wealth of its people. In January 2016 China was home to more billionaires than the United States (594 vs. 535). According to PEW Research, average income, perhaps a more meaningful marker, has quadrupled in the past three decades. China is becoming "middle class," with roughly 300 million people earning what economists describe as middle- or upper-middle incomes (compared to just 40 million as recently as 2001). A 2013 McKinsey report estimates that by 2022 a full 75% of urban households will qualify as having middle- and upper-middle incomes, with the majority earning in the upper-middle-income range ($15,000 to $34,000 annually). As the Chinese economy and personal incomes have skyrocketed, so too, unsurprisingly, has consumption.[1]

The eagerness to acquire and consume should be understood against the pre-1970s history of scarcity. With the liberalization of the marketplace under Deng Xiaoping, people became freer both to sell and to buy. The revolutionary ideology of equality quickly gave way to a culture of competitive consumption. In his 1997 article "Consumerism, Confucianism, Communism: Making Sense of China Today,"[2] Zhao Bin wrote,

"As a new and 'modern' way of life, consumerism appeared irresistible to the hitherto materially deprived," and described consumerism as "a para-belief system." Zhao explained that the bankruptcy of Marxism-Leninism-Maoism had left an ideological void, which "consumerism" now came to fill.

In the 1980s there were virtually no private (nongovernment) vehicles in China; those were days when Flying Pigeon bikes fanned out over broad avenues and country lanes alike, ruling the country's roads. Today, China has surpassed the United States as the largest automobile market in the world.

In 2000, China had just under 100 million mobile phone users; today there are more than 1.2 billion, four times the number in the United States.

In cities, the average floor space per inhabitant was 3.6 square meters (38.7 square feet) in 1978; today, even as the size of the urban population has surged, the average floor space per inhabitant is now 35 square meters (376 square feet), 10 times larger.

Between 1985 and 2002, China's people were buying up washing machines, refrigerators, air conditioners, and color televisions. A recent survey showed that the growth of these appliances has leveled off (with 91 washing machines, 89 refrigerators, and 120 televisions per 100 households).[3] These days the Chinese are turning their purchasing power to laptops, cellular phones, home computers, digital cameras, and other electronic goods.

The Chinese have also become the world's biggest consumers of luxury goods. McKinsey reports that by the end of 2015 the Chinese will be responsible for one-third of the money spent throughout the world on "high-end bags, shoes, watches, jewelry, and ready-to-wear clothing."[4] And it's not just the rich who are buying up these goods; a 2013 HKTDC survey found:

> The middle class is still as enthusiastic about international brand name products as ever. 81% of respondents

> have bought international brands in the past year, while 37% have bought luxury products costing more than their monthly personal income. Among the different types of international brand name products purchased in the past year, garments rank first based on mention rates (74%), followed by footwear (57%), electronic products (41%), and handbags/wallets/luggage (40%).[5]

In the 20th century, global luxury brands were hardly available in China, except in luxury hotels catering to tourists. Now, as we head deeper into the 21st century, Louis Vuitton, BMW, Rolex, Gucci, Armani, Prada, Dior, Cartier, Tiffany, and Chanel products can be found in stores and shopping malls everywhere throughout the country. Cartier alone has 30 standalone stores there.

The fondness for consumption in China is reflected in the huge popularity of the country's e-commerce market. Overnight, China has become the world's largest online retailer. In 2015, online sales there hit $630 billion; the United States, the world's second largest e-commerce market, had online sales of $340 billion.[6]

What Does a Wealthier China Do in Its Leisure Time?

Shopping, clearly, is one popular leisure-time activity. But as the country's income has grown, so too has the variety of leisure-time activities. Outdoor sports have become a passion, especially golf and skiing. In 2004 there were 176 golf courses in the country; even though in that year the government capped the number of courses that could be built, today there are roughly 1,000 courses. This is a sport for the well-heeled: a round of golf at a public course costs $150 or so, while membership in a private club costs about $150,000 (excluding monthly fees). No wonder golfing confers status in China; indeed, in President

Xi's anti-corruption campaign, golfing intermittently comes under attack for its profligacy.[7]

Then there is skiing—in a country that has relatively little snowfall. In 1996 there may have been 10,000 skiers in the entire country; today, according to the Chinese Ski Association, the number has swelled to 20 million. Like golf, the audience for the sport is the relatively rich, as a one-day lift ticket and gear rental costs over $100.

More leisure time has resulted in more frequent gatherings with family and friends. In the 2013 HKTDC survey mentioned above, 73% agreed with statement, "I now spend more of my free time with family/friends." The survey also revealed that friends and families are dining out more, going to movies, and taking many more weekend excursions into the countryside.

Theme parks have become a major leisure attraction in China. In 2013 they drew 166 million visitors; by 2020, the global architecture firm AECOM predicts, that number will reach more than 220 million. In *China Theme Park Pipeline Report 2013*, AECOM writes, "Based on increasing population in the middle and upper income groups, and booming tourism, we expect the theme park market to have doubled in size from 2010–2015, and nearly double again from 2015–2020. By 2020, theme park attendance in China is projected to exceed that of the US market today."[8] Roughly 60 new—and large—theme parks are scheduled for construction in China by 2020. International companies like Six Flags, Universal, and Disney are eager to get in on China's theme-park action. The Shanghai Disney resort, which opened in June 2016 at a cost of more than $5.5 billion, occupies a jaw-dropping 963 acres (1.5 square miles) of precious Shanghai land.

With more money and more leisure time at hand, the Chinese have become enthusiastic travelers, both domestic and international. Visiting family and friends, sightseeing, and shopping are the main purposes of leisure travel. By 2008, the Chinese had already taken to foreign travel, logging more than 48 million outbound trips in that year. In 2013, just 5 years later, that number had doubled to 98 million, with 100 million expected by the United Nations World Tourism Organization by the end of 2016. Not only do the Chinese constitute the largest group of world travelers, but they are now the top per-capita spenders when traveling abroad, having displaced the Germans and the Americans. Domestic travel is on a steep rise as well: in a population of 1.3 billion, 1.7 billion domestic trips were taken in 2008, increasing to 3 billion in 2012.

What Are Some of the Environmental Consequences Associated with the New Consumerism?

There are some obvious environmental consequences, even if they cannot all be precisely quantified.

Cellular phones, computers, televisions, microwaves, and other electronic gadgets and appliances all require energy, which today is largely generated by fossil fuels, especially coal. And when these goods die or are rendered "obsolete" by updated versions, they end up as waste in landfills. Landfills in Beijing are already full, which is why Beijing and other cities have moved forward, often against considerable opposition, with the construction of incineration plants. Chemicals leaching into the landfill ground contaminate the soil and also can make their way into the groundwater and nearby waterways. "E-waste cities" like Guiyu (see Chapter 1), which once treated mostly foreign waste arriving on ships, now treat waste generated in China.

Housing units, especially in cities, have grown more numerous and capacious. Their construction has frequently come at the expense of arable land, thus contributing to the growing threat to the country's food security. New housing has also contributed to urban sprawl and to the increase in the number of cars on China's roads and their polluting emissions. More cement, more steel, and more wood are all needed in the construction of new housing. And, of course, since the new housing units are larger, more energy—and more coal—is required, not simply to build them but also to heat, cool, and light them and to keep the appliances running. Finally, new housing, which tends to be fully plumbed, is a heavier drain on water resources than unplumbed traditional housing (20 or 30 gallons per day vs. 10 gallons).

China's new consumerism can also have direct environmental consequences for other countries. The Chinese fondness for carved ivory has made the country the largest ivory market in the world; as such, China must bear some responsibility for the ongoing decimation of the world's elephant population. Every year 30,000 African elephants are killed for their tusks; the population has shrunk to 400,000 or so, down from 1 million in the 1970s. (The government recently announced its intention to impose a complete ban on ivory trade by the end of 2017.) Similarly, demand among affluent Chinese for imperial-style furniture made of precious rosewood has led to the depletion of rosewood forests throughout Southeast Asia and Africa. Take Malagasy rosewood, a species native to Madagascar: today only 1% remains in Madagascar, and 98% has made its way, illegally, to China.[9]

The new leisure activities have environmental costs as well. Theme parks and golf courses eat up land that could be used for food production. A typical 18-hole course in China requires about 173 acres of land. The constant watering that the courses require—in a water-scarce country—makes them a particular environmental liability. And, of course, with the watering comes the constant application of fertilizers and pesticides. Since 2004 the government has intermittently imposed limits and bans on the construction of golf courses (though has not rigorously enforced them). Like golfing, the growing obsession with skiing constitutes a drain on China's limited water resources. Many of the ski resorts are located in the northeast, outside of Beijing, an arid region with often little snowfall. Thus, skiing is possible only because of manmade snow. At one resort for which we have figures, annual snow production requires an amount of water equal to the annual water use of 42,000 people.[10]

With domestic and international travel doubling since 2008, the number of miles logged in high-speed trains, planes, and cars has shot up, resulting in increased consumption of fossil fuels and thus boosting China's contribution of carbon dioxide, nitrous oxides, black soot, and PM2.5 to the atmosphere. In short, the leisure-travel trend of recent years is adding to both global climate change and China's more local air pollution crisis.

What Is the Status of the Automobile in China?

Before 1980 there was hardly a private car in China. Today, China represents the largest automotive market in the world (in 2016, 24 million units were sold in China vs. 17.5 million in the United States) and has more cars on its roads (approaching 200 million) than any country except the United States. People have eagerly given up their Flying Pigeons and pedal power for domestic- and foreign-made automobiles. The cost to the environment, especially in larger cities, has been huge. According to a 2017 Xinhua report, in Beijing, where smog routinely shuts down schools, grounds airplanes, and sends children and the elderly to emergency rooms with respiratory problems, car emissions account for some 31% of the PM2.5 in the air.[11] The only larger source of carbon dioxide and PM2.5 is emissions from coal-fired power and industrial plants.

As China's economy grew with Deng's program of liberalization, and as the Chinese people increasingly aspired to become "modern," modeling their lifestyle on that of already developed countries, the bicycle became unfashionable, a symbol of the country's "backwardness" and hardship. In the 1980s the government itself began promoting both the use and manufacture of cars. Designating automobiles a "pillar industry," the state poured subsidies into domestic car production and invited foreign auto firms like AMC, Volkswagen,

Honda, GM, Honda, and Toyota to come to China and forge joint ventures with domestic manufacturers. Thus, early on, foreign brands were more readily available than domestic ones, and they are still favored by Chinese consumers today (in 2016, 6 out of 10 cars sold in China were foreign-made).

Prior to Deng's reforms, cars were not much of a necessity. Citizens were assigned to a *danwei*, a unit that provided, in one general area, work, housing, schooling, health care, child care, and cultural activities. There was no need for commuting; the Flying Pigeon met the quite limited transportation needs of the day. But as Mao's collectivization experiment came to an end and the market economy expanded, people's workplaces became separated from their homes. And as cities grew, the distance between home and workplace frequently grew. Bicycles, because of their affordability, remained a popular mode of transportation, but public transportation, especially bus service, now appeared. By the late 1980s, taxi service also became available, at least in some of the bigger cities, though ridership tended to be limited to tourists and foreigners.

With urban populations growing, and with urban zones expanding, the government in the late 1980s and 1990s began building extensive subway systems in cities like Beijing, Shanghai, Guangzhou, and Nanjing. And as cities have continued to sprawl, the government has struggled to construct new lines to keep up with rider demand. As wide-ranging as some public transportation networks have become (see Chapter 11), many Chinese still live beyond the reach of public transit, and so turn to motorized bikes and automobiles.

It would be misleading to suggest, though, that automobile ownership in China has exploded out of necessity alone. For many, cars represent freedom and comfort, being able to go where you want when you want, sitting in a comfortable seat rather than standing on a bus or in a packed subway car with your face smashed against the window, listening to the music of your choice, with the temperature at just the right setting. As Zhu Chao, a website engineer in Beijing, put it in a *Washington Post* article: "I really like what the car brings to my life—convenience, freedom, flexibility, a quick rhythm. I can't imagine life without it."[12]

Car ownership also brings status: the car has become a centerpiece of China's competitive consumerism.[13] "People don't really think about whether they need a car, but feel they have to have one," car aficionado Zhao Cihang (owner of two BMWs, an Audi, and a Honda) told a reporter as he strolled through a Mini showroom in Beijing. Indeed, it's China that is keeping much of the global auto industry vital: "For GM, Hyundai, Nissan, Volkswagen, Audi, it's already the number one car market in the world. Take China out of their portfolio and their fortunes would reverse," says automobile analyst Michael Dunne.[14] In the past decade, escalating incomes have made the Chinese among the world's most eager consumers of luxury-brand automobiles, as the showrooms for BMW, Lexus, Infiniti, Cadillac, Land Rover, Lamborghini, Porsche, Rolls-Royce, Mercedes, and Audi along the country's city streets attest.

Since 2009, sports car clubs for the super-rich have sprung up all over China. Perhaps the best-known one is the Sports Car Club of Beijing, which had its start in the capital and now has branches all over the country. To become a member, one has to pay an annual fee of $1,600 and own a qualifying sports car. In the Beijing branch of the club, a $220,000 Porsche SE 911 is considered an "entry-level" model.[15]

The country's love affair with the car has made congestion a massive problem (Figure 4.1). With nearly 6 million cars on Beijing's roads and 3.5 million on Shanghai's, drivers in those cities, among others, spend more time idling—spewing out deadly exhaust—than they do driving. To get from one side of the city of Beijing to the other can easily take a couple of hours at rush hour. In a 2012 race across Beijing from west to east, a distance of 6.2 miles, a bicycle beat a Porsche by roughly 30 minutes.[16]

Figure 4.1 Traffic jam near a toll station in Beijing

But even as municipal governments have taken measures to limit automobile use (see Chapter 11), the country has vastly expanded its expressway network. The country's first expressway, the Shanghai–Jiading Expressway, opened in 1988 and was 17 kilometers (11 miles) long. By the end of 2014, the expressway system covered 111,950 kilometers (69,560 miles) and had overtaken the American system as the world's largest. This has meant paving over land that could be used for other purposes and creating tens of thousands of miles of impermeable surfaces, reducing the amount of rainfall and snowfall that can penetrate into the groundwater.

How Have Food-Consumption Patterns Changed?

Through the 1970s, prior to the economic reforms, the Chinese lived largely on a grain-based diet. That has changed. Meat consumption since then has risen four-fold to about 130

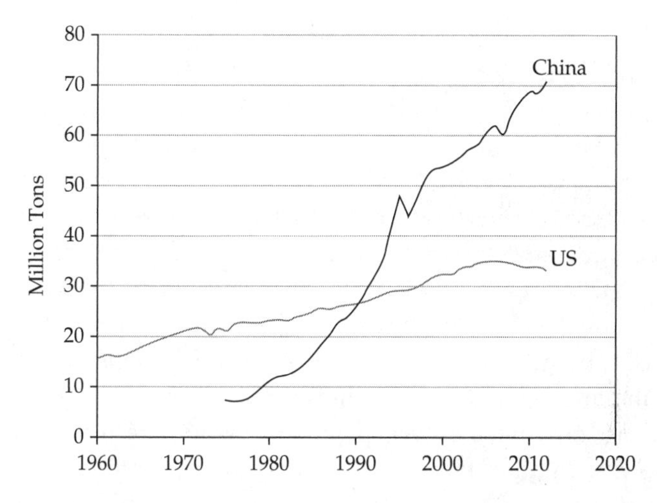

Figure 4.2 Meat Consumption in China and the United States, 1960–2012
Source: USDA

pounds per capita annually (82 pounds of pork, 29 pounds of poultry, and 20 pounds of beef). China now consumes about one-quarter of the world's meat, and twice as much as the United States (though per capita consumption in China is half that of the United States). City dwellers in China eat almost twice as much meat as those who live in the country; thus, as the pace of urbanization quickens in the next decade, we have to assume that China's meat intake will continue to escalate (Figure 4.2). Two main factors are driving this dietary shift to protein-rich foods: greater discretionary income and wider exposure to Western cuisine.

While more protein might be nutritionally beneficial for the Chinese people, the new diet poses a range of problems for the environment. Raising livestock requires land, especially for cattle. Deforestation is one way to provide it; another is to give up land that might otherwise be used for growing crops for human consumption. In addition to the land necessary to raise the animals, land for growing livestock feed is necessary. To produce 2.2 pounds of beef requires 17.6 pounds of feed;

pork requires 13.2 pounds of feed; and poultry requires 4.4 pounds. Because of land scarcity, China has had to turn to foreign markets for grain and soy to sustain their meat consumption. Sixty percent of the world's soybeans available for export are purchased by the Chinese. Much of this is coming from Brazil and Argentina, where grasslands and forested areas, including rainforests, are being cleared for soy farming to meet the demands of the Chinese market, thus reducing the world's precious carbon sinks (62 million acres in Brazil are now being used to produce soy).[17] Brazil is also giving more of its land over to the cultivation of corn as China's demand for corn balloons.

The growing livestock population is also resulting in a growing amount of fecal waste: a cow produces 45 to 75 pounds per day and a pig 10 to 13 pounds per day (a person produces one-quarter of a pound). This waste contains an enormous concentration of phosphorous and nitrogen, which is dumped, or runs off, into waterways, resulting in algal blooms, eutrophication, and then "dead zones."

Globally, livestock produces 14.5% of all anthropogenic greenhouse gas emissions. It accounts for 65% of the nitrous oxide and 37% of the methane released into the atmosphere. The implication is clear: China's growing appetite for meat is adding appreciably to global warming.

Some recent studies have calculated what they call the water footprint for various animals, which is the amount of "freshwater used to produce the product, measured over the various steps of the production chain" (i.e., feedcrop cultivation, livestock farming, food processing, retailing, consuming).[18] The following water-footprint figures suggest that meat consumption is taking no small toll on China's limited water resources:

One broiler chicken: 6,868 gallons/year
One pig: 137,369 gallons/year
One beef cow: 166,428 gallons/year
One dairy cow: 543,138 gallons/year.

The percentage of pork consumed in China is decreasing, while the percentages of poultry and beef consumption are increasing. Environmentally, this is an unfortunate development. An important 2014 study of livestock production in the United States concludes that beef is by far the least resource-efficient meat, requiring 28 times more land and 11 times more irrigation water per megacalorie than pork or chicken; it also produces 5 times more greenhouse gases. When compared with the production of staple crops, the figures are even more startling: beef requires 160 times more land and 8 times more irrigation water per megacalorie and produces 11 times more greenhouse gases.[19] One expert, having read the study, commented that "the biggest intervention people could make towards reducing their carbon footprints would be not to abandon cars, but to eat significantly less red meat."[20]

If we assume that these figures from the US study can be roughly extrapolated to conditions in China, the current dietary trend there toward red meat does not bode especially well for either China's environment or the global environment.[21]

Part II

THE POLLUTED ENVIRONMENT

5

WHAT'S HAPPENING TO CHINA'S AIR?

How Does China's Air Pollution Compare with Air Pollution Elsewhere?

It depends on who is doing the surveying (e.g., the WHO or World Bank), the metric used (e.g., PM10, PM2.5, or percentage of the country's population exposed to unhealthy air), and the period covered (one year or multiple years, and which particular year or years). By virtually any account, however, China is near or at the top of the list of the world's most polluted countries.

India, Pakistan, Afghanistan, Qatar, Iran, and Bangladesh, in terms of their particulate matter levels, tend to cluster with China at the top of these lists. In fact, Delhi, according to the WHO's 2016 report, is the most polluted city in the world, with an average annual PM2.5 reading of 153 (compared to Beijing's 56). Twelve other Indian cities appear on the WHO's list of the world's 20 most polluted cities. No Chinese city even makes the list.

But while India's cities may be smoggier than China's, the urbanized population of India represents a relatively small 33% of the country's people. In China, a full 56% of the population is now urbanized, so exposure to polluted air is considerably more widespread. And although Qatar and Iran are, to be sure, highly urbanized, the total number of affected people in these countries is quite small by comparison with China. We can perhaps best characterize the pollution contest this way: cities in India have some of the most polluted air in the world, but air pollution in China is more extensive and poses a health threat to more people.[1]

But India, a country that lags far behind China by all economic indices, is now—as China was for the past three decades—bent on revving up its economy and reducing the poverty that is rampant among its people. Looking to follow in China's economic footsteps, the government in New Delhi has exhibited restrained enthusiasm for taking environmental measures that might hinder the country's economic growth. India would do well to learn from the Chinese experience and give thorough consideration to the environmental consequences, long-term ones as well as short-term ones, as it looks to accelerate its economic development.[2]

What Are the Major Pollutants in the Air?

Carbon dioxide (CO_2), particulate matter (both PM10 and PM2.5 [see below]), carbon monoxide, sulfur dioxide, nitrogen dioxide, mercury, and ozone are the major pollutants in China's air. They come from a variety of sources, but most especially from coal combustion, vehicle emissions, and construction work. Coal combustion—in power and industrial plants and for home heating and cooking—produces significant amounts of CO_2, sulfur dioxides, nitrogen oxides, and particulate matter. Vehicles—cars and trucks, especially those that run on low-grade diesel fuel—are responsible for emissions of carbon monoxide, hydrocarbons, nitrogen oxides, and particulate matter. Construction, particularly on the massive scale taking place in China, kicks up a tremendous amount of debris and dust, which adds to the particulate matter suspended in the air.

The government periodically targets what it claims, perhaps in earnest, to be other sources of significant pollution as well. Since 2013 it has cracked down on open-air barbecuing, confiscating grills from street vendors and destroying them, and since 2015 it has requested that the people refrain from setting off fireworks, especially during the Lunar New Year. "Anti-pollution" campaigns like these inevitably invite ridicule by much of the public, which sees them as distractions by a government wishing to avoid addressing the real problem: industrial pollution. In January 2015, one official in the city of Dazhou even blamed the city's air pollution problem on the local practice of smoking bacon. (Respondents on the social media site Weibo were quick to point out that locals had been smoking bacon for centuries, long before the city's air turned to smog. One quipped, "Only a pig-headed person would think that air pollution was caused by smoking bacon.")

The pollutants from these three major sources—coal combustion, vehicles, and construction—largely make for the grimy air seen in images of cities like Beijing, Shanghai, Hangzhou, Lanzhou, Xi'an, Tianjin, Chongqing, Shijiazhuang, and Linfen that are broadcast around the world. These pollutants do not simply dirty the air, turning daytime into nighttime in these places; they also wreak havoc on public health (see Chapter 8). A 2015 Greenpeace study based on data from 2013 found that in the 31 provincial capitals, 1 out of every 7 deaths could be attributed to air pollution. This means that simply breathing the air in China poses the same risk of premature death as smoking cigarettes.[3]

What Exactly Is PM2.5?

PM2.5 refers to particulate solids or droplets—dust, dirt, smoke, organic chemicals, metals, and so on—that are less than 2.5 micrometers in diameter and are suspended in the air. PM2.5 has multiple pollution sources: manufacturing, coal burning, vehicle exhaust, waste incineration, biomass burning, sandstorms, construction dust, fertilizer application, chemical processes that occur in the atmosphere (e.g., sulfur dioxides, nitrous oxides, and ammonia can be transformed into the particulates sulfate, nitrates, and ammonium when exposed to light), and even barbecue grilling. Of these, coal combustion, vehicle exhaust, construction, and sandstorms are the biggest perpetrators.

PM2.5 is not, then, a single pollutant but a mixture of pollutants that come together in particle or droplet form. Most particulate matter results from chemical reactions between pollutants in the air (called secondary particulate matters). As a consequence, the precise composition of particulate matter varies from place to place and day to day. Scientists at the Research Center for Eco-environmental Sciences of the Chinese Academy of Science are now engaged in a long-term research study of PM2.5 "to investigate how it emerges, evolves, and can be reduced . . . Scientists will identify the types and sources of key pollutants, unravel the different formation mechanism of haze in different parts of China, and develop a suite of source-controlled based technologies for the monitoring, forecasting, and management of haze."[4]

PM2.5 poses the most serious and immediate health threat of all the pollutants in China's air today. When people breathe, these particles enter their respiratory system and can travel into their lungs and even their bloodstream. At a miniscule 2.5 micrometers in diameter—1/30 the width of a human hair—these tiny particles can make their way deep in people's lungs and lodge there. As we will see in Chapter 8, scientific studies in the past 20 years or so have shown that PM2.5 is closely linked to a range of health issues, including shortness of breath, asthma attacks, acute bronchitis, neurological disorders, decreased lung function, lung cancer, heart attacks, and premature death.

Particulate matter comes in a larger size as well, PM10. At 10 micrometers or less, these particles are coarser than PM2.5. They too can harm human health, but because of their larger size they are more easily combatted by the human body and cannot penetrate so readily into the lungs or bloodstream.

On account of the threat it poses to public health, PM2.5 has become the main measure of China's air quality. The scale measures from 0 to 500, which represents the micrograms of PM2.5 per cubic meter. Zero is the best, 500 the worst. Beijing has set what it calls "interim targets," temporary national standards, for PM2.5 levels: 70 $\mu g/m^3$ for a 24-hour period and 35 $\mu g/m^3$ for the year. These are considerably higher than what the WHO recommends: 25 $\mu g/m^3$ for a daily reading and 10 $\mu g/m^3$ for an annual reading. The "interim targets" are an acknowledgment that China has a way to go to meet the current WHO standards and would benefit from intermediate targets (as I write this, Beijing's reading is 406). By comparison, the US guidelines are 35 $\mu g/m^3$ for a 24-hour period and 12 $\mu g/m^3$, higher as well, though only slightly, than the WHO recommendations.

In January 2015 Greenpeace China released a study of air pollution in 190 cities. Every single one exceeded the WHO standard of 10 $\mu g/m^3$, and 179 exceeded China's own national standard of 35 $\mu g/m^3$.[5]

How Did PM2.5 Become a Household Term in China?

Mention PM2.5 to most Americans and they stare blankly, wondering whether it is the name of a rock band or perhaps a classified missile system. The Chinese people, on the other hand, are all familiar with the term: by the end of 2013 it was the third most popular meme on social media sites.

Here is the backstory. In 2008 the US Embassy in Beijing installed an air-monitoring device on its roof, tweeting out PM2.5 levels (@beijingair), with brief commentary, on the hour to inform its employees and US citizens of the severity of the pollution in the vicinity so they could plan their day's activities—and their children's activities—accordingly. Chinese authorities had yet to recognize PM2.5 as the standard measure for air quality; the less hazardous PM10 was the common measure, the one reported to the public. In 2009 the

Beijing Ministry of Foreign Affairs filed complaints with the embassy saying that tweeting information about China's air quality was a violation of Chinese law and demanding that the embassy stop the practice. The embassy persisted. The tweets were picked up by Chinese internet users ("netizens"), who retweeted the information much more widely on China's social media sites. Because these tweets focused on PM2.5 as well as PM10, they revealed the air in Beijing to be significantly more polluted and dangerous than what was reported by the Chinese government. People demanded that the government provide the same information as the US embassy. And in December 2011, influential real estate mogul and social media commentator Pan Shiyi carried out an informal poll among his millions of followers on Sina Weibo, asking whether they agreed that "the authorities should adopt the PM2.5 standard this year." Tens of thousands of people responded, with 95% of them expressing agreement. One month later, in January 2012, Beijing's own Environmental Protection Bureau began publishing air quality data that included PM2.5 levels.[6] Whether—and how much—Pan Shiyi and public opinion might have played a role in Beijing's decision to publish PM2.5 information, we cannot know.

The story continues: one year later, in January 2013, the now-notorious "airpocalypse" rocked China, hitting the capital especially hard. The smog was horrific; before deciding whether to go outdoors, send a child off to school, take a jog, or even open windows, people would consult the air quality index, especially PM2.5 levels. They actively turned to social media to share information—and vent—about the pollution and, especially, the stratospheric PM2.5 levels. Private citizens began developing air-quality apps, some showing both the levels recorded by their city governments and the levels recorded by the US Embassy and consulates. These days, almost every smartphone user in China has an air-quality app at the ready, and there are now air monitors recording PM2.5 levels in more than 360 Chinese cities.

What Was the Airpocalypse?

As we noted above, China measures its PM2.5 levels on a scale of 0 to 500 micrograms per cubic meter. You will remember, too, that 500 μg/m^3 is 20 times higher than the level considered safe to breathe by the WHO. During January 2013 in northern China, especially the area around Beijing, PM2.5 readings were regularly "off the charts" or "beyond index," meaning they exceeded the air-quality index limit of 500. There were many days when readings were in the 700 to 900 range. (One day it hit 993; by comparison, on the same day in New York City the reading was 19.) Over the course of the month, hundreds of flights in and out of Beijing were cancelled, industrial plants were shuttered, roads were closed, schools were shut down, cars were ordered off the road, and hospitals were overflowing with children suffering from respiratory problems.

To say that this smog caught China's attention, and indeed global attention, is an understatement. Every day, media in China and across the globe broadcast pictures of Beijing's soupy, sooty air, which darkened daytime skies and cloaked even the most massive skyscrapers in impenetrable haze. A report by Bloomberg that received widespread attention at the time showed that the daily average PM2.5 reading of the air over Beijing in January 2013 was 30 μg/m^3 higher than the average daily reading of the air in a typical smoking lounge in a US airport.[7] The difference is, of course, that going into a smoking lounge is entirely up to you; breathing the air in Beijing, if you live or work there, or happen to be visiting, is not.

While Beijing received most of the attention in January 2013, more than 30 cities and 600 million people over a 1-million-square-mile area were affected. The city of Shijiazhuang, the capital of Hebei, Beijing's neighboring province, for instance, recorded a reading of more than 1,000 μg/m^3.

Expatriates living in China dubbed this smog-blighted air the "airpocalypse," a term that has stuck and continues to be used when skies in China are especially smoky and registering high PM2.5 levels. Ever since, face masks have become daily apparel for those living and working in Beijing, and elsewhere in the country. The fashion industry has even designed lines of face masks for the style-conscious. Room air purifiers, costing $500 and up, have been hard for dealers to keep on the shelves. Social media sites like Weibo have been filled with advertisements for purifiers and netizens' questions and comments about how various brands of purifiers compare. Schools competing for students whose families worry about the health effects of the polluted air on their children have invested millions of dollars in constructing domes with hospital-grade filtration systems over their playing fields, the costs of which are reflected in the exorbitant tuition rates.[8]

International corporations have been finding it increasingly challenging to attract foreign recruits to work in Beijing and so offer "hazard pay" or "danger money" of up to 20% or 30%. The American Chamber of Commerce in China, in a March 2014 survey, asked, "Have you or your organization experienced any difficulties in recruiting or retaining senior executives to work because of air quality issues?" Forty-eight percent of the organization's 365 members said yes.

The airpocalypse is also having an effect on Beijing as a destination for tourists. In the one-year period following the airpocalypse, foreign tourism, with all of its economic benefits, was down 10% to 15% from the previous year.[9]

The airpocalypse of January 2013 was something of a defining moment, transforming daily life in cities like Beijing. Its effect has been lasting. The Chinese people are more aware than ever before of the pollution in their air. And no longer do the national weather media describe the air on days when the smog is heavy as simply *wu* (雾), "fog." They now call it what it is: *wumai* (雾霾) or *mai* (霾), "smog."

How Much Coal Does China Consume, and How Does China Compare to Other Countries?

Industrialization has driven China's economic development, and this industrialization, in turn, has been powered by coal. Coal today supplies about 64% of China's total energy consumption (the power sector uses the most, followed by the steel and cement industries), and the tonnage of coal has grown commensurately with the economy over the years. In 2013, the country used an estimated 4 billion tons of coal, almost three times more than it used as recently as 2000. The increase is staggering, as is the absolute amount: China now consumes yearly as much of the rest of the world combined (Figure 5.1).

It is coal combustion on this scale that accounts for much of the country's pollution: estimates have it that coal accounts for 50% of the PM2.5 in China's air and 90% of the sulfur dioxide. A study by Teng Fei at Tsinghua University revealed that in 2012 PM2.5 from coal combustion alone accounted for 670,000 premature Chinese deaths.[10]

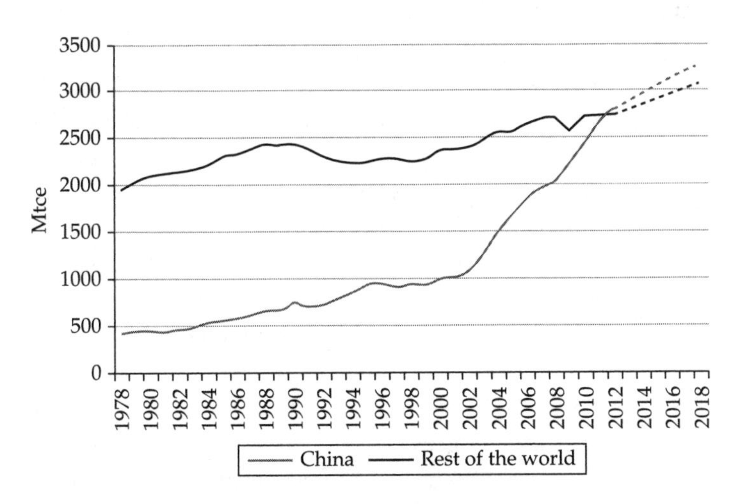

Figure 5.1 Coal demand in China and in the rest of the world

And then there is the carbon burden. China is the world's largest emitter of the greenhouse gas CO_2, releasing about 10.5 billion metric tons into the air in 2014. This represents nearly 30% of the world's emissions, and twice as much as the United States, the next largest emitter.

Recently, however, there has been some positive news. Data from 2014 and 2015 show that for the first time in the 21st century China's consumption of coal is falling: it decreased in 2014 by 2.9% and in 2015 by another 3.7%. A number of factors may help to explain the decline in coal use: a weakening global economy, the country's aggressive development and use of other energy sources, the government's more vigilant enforcement of environmental regulations, the shuttering of small and inefficient coal plants, and the removal of highly polluting vehicles from the roads. As promising as these recent figures are, it is hard to know whether they mark the beginning of a trend, though analysts like Nicholas Stern, Fergus Green, and Ye Qi suggest they do.[11]

What we can say with certainty is that the Chinese government is eager to reduce its reliance on coal. China's growing investment in alternative energy resources—wind, solar, hydroelectric, and nuclear—is one strong testament. Perhaps even stronger is the government's declaration to cap the country's total energy consumption by 2020 (at 5 billion tons). This is the first-ever talk of a national cap. At the same time, the government has stated its intention to reduce its carbon intensity 60% to 65% below 2005 levels by 2030; to increase the percentage of non-fossil fuels in the total energy mix from 11.2% in 2014 to 15% by 2020, and to 20% by 2030; and, finally, to peak carbon emissions by 2030 at the latest.

Still, given China's need for enormous amounts of energy to maintain economic growth, the ready availability of coal, and the time it takes to gear up the capacity of other energy resources, the widely held expectation is that coal will remain dominant for the foreseeable future, providing 60% of China's total energy mix through 2020 and 50% through 2030.

How Do Vehicles Contribute to China's Air Pollution?

Vehicle exhaust contributes to primary and secondary particulate matter, acid rain, and CO_2 emissions. After coal combustion, vehicle exhaust is the leading cause of PM2.5 pollutants in China. Since vehicles (including passenger cars, light- and heavy-duty vehicles, buses, and motorcycles) are more plentiful in urban areas, it is in urban areas that their emissions have the greatest effect on air quality. One recent study calculated that motor vehicles account for 15% to 35% of the local PM2.5 in Chinese cities. In Beijing the estimate is 31% of the PM2.5, in Shanghai 25%, in Shenzhen 31%, in Chengdu 20%, and in Hangzhou 33%.[12] These figures, however, should not be taken too literally; new studies, with varying figures, appear regularly. Distinguishing the sources of particulate matter (e.g., vehicles, incinerators, coal combustion, construction dust, road dust) is challenging, as it requires chemical analysis of the PM2.5, the methods for which are still improving.[13]

Whatever the precise figures, there is general acknowledgment that the PM 2.5 contribution made by vehicles is dangerously high—and growing. A 2015 United Nations Development Programme (UNDP) brief on China's air pollution concluded, "Vehicle emissions are now making a larger contribution to air pollution both in the form of direct particulate matter from incomplete combustion (soot, black carbon, etc.) and from NOx [nitrogen oxide] emissions, a precursor for PM2.5."[14]

Especially concerning, in my view, is that idling vehicles emit much higher levels of PM2.5. The *Beijing News* reported in July 2013 that a freely moving car on Beijing's West Second Ring Road produces 25 to 30 μg/m^3, while a car idling during peak congestion there produces more than three times as much (90–100 μg/m³). Traffic congestion, of course, is already a huge problem in Chinese cities. But consider what the congestion could be like in 2030, when it is estimated that there will be 500 million vehicles on Chinese roads, two to three times the current number (and more than double the number of total vehicles in the United States today). And then consider the possible effects on public health.

As the UNDP brief reminds us, the nitrogen oxide emitted by vehicles during combustion reacts in the air to form particulate matter. But it also reacts in the air to form acid rain—as does the relatively small amount of sulfur dioxide emitted by vehicles. And when acid rain falls, it forms mild solutions of nitric and sulfuric acid, harming waterways and the fish and aquatic life that inhabit them, and polluting the soil, making it difficult for trees and forests to survive. Finally, nitrogen oxide also reacts in the air to form tropospheric ozone, which can damage forests and crops and trigger a range of human health problems, particularly in the lungs and heart.

In 2014, of China's total carbon emissions—approximately 10 billion tons—roughly 730 million tons were attributable to the road transport sector. Not a small amount! In fact, the CO_2 that China produces from road transport alone is more than what Canada or the United Kingdom emits in total. If, as estimated, the number of vehicles on China's roads climbs to 500 million within the next decade and a half, the tonnage of CO_2 emissions could balloon to 1.3 billion or more. The potential for this sort of increase in vehicular CO_2 emissions is worrisome for a government intent on reining in air pollution and peaking carbon emissions by 2030.

The central government and municipal governments throughout the country have experimented with a number of measures to reduce the use of vehicles powered by fossil fuels (diesel fuel and gasoline) and their polluting emissions. The measures include the following:

- Building out subway and bus systems, especially in the larger cities, to encourage the use of public transit use
- Instituting Euro V fuel standards and planning for a phase-in of Euro VI
- Limiting the number of passenger cars by limiting the number of licenses issued
- Imposing alternate-day driving schemes on passenger cars based on license plate number
- Banning passenger cars from the road one day each week, based on license plate number
- Eliminating "yellow-label" cars—those not in compliance with higher emissions standards—from the roads
- Reducing or eliminating tolls and parking fees for hybrid and electric vehicles
- Offering significant rebates for the purchase of an e-vehicle (see Chapter 11)

In March 2015, the Chinese Ministry of Transport announced a plan to put 200,000 "new-energy" buses and 100,000 "new-energy" taxis on the country's roads by the end of this decade (in 2014, 15,000 "new-energy" buses were added to the roads).

How Are Smog and Climate Change Linked?

The blanket of sooty air that routinely hangs over much of China, especially the cities, is smog. The pollutants primarily responsible for this smog are PM2.5 and PM10. Once emitted into the air, particulate matters lingers relatively briefly (sometimes as a little as an hour and typically no more than a week or two) as rain, wind, and changing temperatures wash it away, disperse it, or transport it elsewhere.

Greenhouse gases emitted into the air, especially CO_2, but also methane and nitrous oxide, are what make for the warming temperatures associated with climate change. CO_2 is a colorless and odorless gas; it does not directly contribute to smog as particulate matter does, nor does it carry immediate risks to public health. The harm it poses comes from its greenhouse effect. Once released into the atmosphere, it accumulates and remains there for decades, even centuries, trapping the heat released by the planet's land and oceans and preventing it from passing out of the atmosphere into space. How this warming will ultimately affect humankind and Planet Earth is, of course, a matter of intense debate.

What links smog and climate change is that the particulate matter that spawns the smog and the CO_2 that warms the globe have a common source: fossil fuel combustion. That is, burning coal, oil, or natural gas emits a heavy burden of *both* particulate matter and CO_2. Thus, when the Chinese government, in waging a war on pollution, puts a limit on coal use; shutters coal-fired power and industrial plants; invests in alternative energy sources; eliminates old, polluting vehicles from the road; institutes higher fuel standards; encourages the purchase of new-energy vehicles; and promises to increase the percentage of non-fossil fuels in the total energy mix, it is at the same time reducing the country's harmful, planet-warming emissions.

By the same token, when in the lead-up to the 2015 Paris Agreement President Xi and Chinese climate representatives pledged on China's behalf to reach peak coal use by 2030, to cut CO_2 emissions per unit of GDP (carbon intensity) by 60% or more over 2005 levels by 2030, and to increase the non-fossil fuel share of the total primary energy consumption to 20%, they fully understood that these measures will at the same time "co-benefit" their goal to clean up the country's air. For them, taking on global climate change in large part addresses the nation's pollution crisis—and the growing health issues and costs associated with it.

By all accounts, the role China played in Paris in 2015 was far more conciliatory and constructive than the role it played in 2009 in Copenhagen. What had changed? Among other factors, in the intervening years China had become far more invested in facing its environmental challenges. Cooperating on climate change in Paris was, from Beijing's perspective, entirely consistent with its commitment to address environmental pollution at home. In short, tackling climate change was now viewed to be very much in the country's interest.

6

WATER CONTAMINATION AND WATER SCARCITY

What Is Contaminating China's Water Resources?

Viewed in the context of the skyrocketing industrialization, urbanization, and population growth of the past 30 years, the widespread contamination of the water supply that now plagues China would seem almost inevitable. Yet, because the country's water has been far less monitored than its air, and the data available to us are spotty and not very reliable, our present understanding of China's water situation is still quite limited. The good news is that in recent years investigation into China's water quality has become a high priority for the government—though critics maintain it has often been slow to release the information it collects.

China rates water quality using a five-point scale. Grades I through III are fit for fish habitat and drinking (with some degree of treatment). Grade IV is fit for industrial use and recreational activity in which there is no human contact with the water. Grade V is fit for agricultural and landscape use only. (Yes, this means—strangely—that water unfit for human touch and industrial use can nonetheless be used to grow crops that people eat.) A grade V+ is sometimes used to refer to water that is entirely unusable for either industry or agriculture.

To understand just how dire the condition of China's water supply is, consider the following:

- 60% of the country's groundwater is grade IV or V/V+ (unfit for drinking and human contact).
- 70% of the groundwater in the densely populated North China plain is grade IV or V/V+.
- 50% of the country's shallow groundwater is grade IV or V/V+.
- 50% of water from rivers, lakes, and waterways is grade IV or V/V+.
- 90% of river water in urban areas is polluted.
- More than 70% of 641 drinking wells tested by China's Ministry of Environmental Protection in 2009 were classified grade IV or V/V+.
- 300 million people (about 25% of the population) have no access to drinking water.
- The Danjiangkou Reservoir, which supplies Beijing with much of its drinking water, was found to have levels of lead 20 times higher than WHO standards in 2007–2010.

While air pollution in China has tended to receive more attention than water pollution—perhaps simply because sooty smog is much harder to ignore—the figures here help to explain why many are coming to view the contamination of the country's water supply as an equal, perhaps even graver, environmental threat.

Contamination of the country's water resources is owing mostly to industrial pollution, agricultural runoff, and human sewage. Industry and agriculture are the two largest water polluters nationwide, agricultural being the dominant polluter in the countryside, industry in the cities.

For decades, paper mills, chemical factories, steel plants, drug manufacturers, fertilizer and pesticide producers, textile plants, and tanneries have discharged waste and dumped chemicals directly into the country's waterways (Figure 6.1).

Figure 6.1 Chemical plant discharging waste directly into local river

Lax laws and even laxer enforcement—which we will consider in Chapter 11—have encouraged water degradation. With little risk of being found in violation of environmental regulations, industries have opted to pollute rather than to incur the costs of proper waste treatment and disposal.

An equally large share of water pollutants comes from the agricultural sector. Pesticides and fertilizers used for crop production are carried by rain, snowmelt, and irrigation into rivers, lakes, wetlands, coastal waters, and underground aquifers. (Phosphorous and nitrogen from fertilizer runoff, for example, make for the spectacular blue–green algal blooms in China's streams, lakes, and coastal areas.) In 1967 China's eutrophic lakes covered 52 square miles; in 2007 they had expanded to 3,360 square miles. In that year, 70% of Lake Tai, the country's third largest freshwater lake, was blanketed in a sheet of algal bloom nine inches thick.

Fecal waste from livestock production also makes its way into the country's water supply, either through direct excretion or through runoff carried by rain, melting snow, and irrigation.

In recent decades the livestock population in China has grown considerably (due to population growth and changes in diet). And before the turn of the 21st century, most livestock were produced by small farmers raising 2 to 20 animals annually, while today, factory farms (concentrated animal feeding operations) that produce thousands of hogs every year have become more usual. Human waste is also a significant pollutant, and not only in the countryside as one might imagine. In one study, 80% of 278 cities were found to lack sewage treatment facilities. With no sewage treatment plants, there are few places for the waste to go. It is estimated that roughly 90% of all household sewage in China is released into rivers and lakes without being treated.[1] As the urbanizing trend grows, domestic sewage discharge is increasing at a faster pace than industrial discharge.

One final source of water pollution should be noted: industrial accidents. This should not surprise us given the number of factories located along the country's rivers and lakes. Ten thousand petrochemical factories alone sit alongside the Yangtze River and 4,000 on the Yellow River. When accidents in factories on the water occur, as they inevitably do, water supplies in the surrounding region can be profoundly compromised:

In July 2010 two oil pipelines in the northern port city of Dalian exploded, sending 1,500 metric tons of crude oil into the bay off Dalian's coast, resulting in a 165-square-mile slick.

In December 2012, 39 tons of toxic anilines leaked from a ruptured drainage pipe belonging to the Tianji Coal Chemical Industry Group into the Zhuozhang River, severely contaminating the source of the drinking water for Changzhi, a city in Shanxi province. It then traveled farther downstream, through 28 more villages and cities, before reaching Handan in Hebei province.

In November 2013, an oil pipeline belonging to Sinopec, one of the country's largest oil companies, exploded in the eastern port city of Qingdao in Shandong province, killing at least 62 people; oil spilled into the rainwater drainage pipeline and contaminated the nearby seawater in Jiaozhou Bay.

In April 2014, a toxic oil leak in a Lanzhou Petrochemical pipeline released high levels (20 times the national safety standard) of the carcinogen benzene into the local water supply in Lanzhou, a city of 2.5 million in China's northwest. Residents were ordered not to drink the tap water; panic buying of bottled water ensued and the price per bottle shot up from $1 to $6.

What Are the General Consequences of Polluted Water?

The context here is crucial. China already has a scarcity of water: it has 21% of the world's population but just 6% to 7% of the world's freshwater resources. When rivers and lakes are contaminated with industrial pollutants and agricultural runoff, the country's water supply is significantly reduced, thereby worsening an already very bad situation.

Given the scarcity of water, many people have little choice but to drink water that is classified as unfit to drink or even touch. Various studies, including one in 2009 by the World Bank, concluded that 300 million people in China do not have access to safe drinking water. And this number assumes that the piped water in urban areas is regularly treated, which some observers doubt.[2]

Every year 190 million people in China—roughly 14.5% of the country's population—fall ill from drinking contaminated water. Diarrhea is by far the most prevalent of water-related diseases in China. According to a WHO report, in 2008 there were more than 487 million cases, resulting in almost 67,000 deaths. Children, because their intestinal systems are not as well developed, were hit hardest, accounting for 83% of all cases and 97% of the deaths.[3]

Even simple physical contact with contaminated water—when farming, swimming, bathing, and so forth—puts people at risk of infection from parasites, which in larval form can penetrate the skin. Children, because of their play habits and hygiene, are especially vulnerable to parasitic infection. It is estimated that today 865,000 Chinese people are infected with schistosomiasis, an intestinal disease caused by contact with fresh water infested with snails carrying the parasitic flatworms called schistosomes, and 30 million people living in tropical and subtropical zones are at risk of infection.[4] Scientists fear that as water temperatures rise with global warming, the transmission of schistosomiasis is likely to expand.

According to China's water-quality grading system, water that is unfit to drink is not necessarily unfit for agricultural use. Water that is too polluted for drinking or for use in industry can, as we have seen, be used to irrigate fields. Eating crops grown in these fields exposes people to some of the same health problems that drinking untreated water might—as well as other problems. Many farmers, according to media reports, are hesitant to eat the very food they have grown. As Hu Kanping of the Chinese Ecological Civilization and Research and Promotion Association said, "Farmers won't eat what they produce. They have fields for themselves and fields for the market."[5] In short, water contamination poses a real threat to the safety and security of China's food supply.

Today cancer is the leading cause of death in China. Lung cancer is the form that takes the most lives; next come the various digestive cancers—stomach, liver, and esophageal—which account for 1 million deaths every year. The high incidence of digestive cancers has given rise to hundreds of "cancer villages" along the rivers in China's countryside. Although hard scientific research analyzing the precise relationship between digestive cancer and contaminated water is still limited, one recent, quite rigorous study estimated that deterioration of water quality by a single grade leads to a 9.3% increase in the incidence of digestive cancer.[6]

Fish and marine mammals also suffer from contaminated water. Contamination, of course, is only one of the factors accounting for the reduction of freshwater wildlife in China's waterways (along with overfishing, loss of habitat, and river traffic), but it is a key factor. Indeed, it is often given as one explanation for the disappearance of the famous *baiji*, the Yangtze River dolphin, which was declared "functionally extinct" after a 45-day expedition in 2006 failed to detect any surviving specimen. At present, the Yangtze finless porpoise is "endangered" and on the verge of extinction, owing to much the same causes that made for the *baiji*'s demise.

Isn't Water Scarcity a Bigger Long-Term Problem Than Water Contamination?

More than two-thirds of China's 600-plus cities suffer from water shortages, but it is the per capita figures that really indicate just how grim China's water situation is. The annual global per capita availability of fresh water is roughly 6,000 m^3; China's is one-third of that, at 2,000 m^3. (The United States, by comparison, has 9,000 m^3 per capita per year.)

This is not the whole story, however, because there is a wide discrepancy in regional precipitation patterns: northern China receives 20% of the country's rainfall and snowmelt against southern China's 80%. The north, as a result, is far more arid. In Beijing, for instance, the annual per capita water availability is 100 to 150 m^3, not even 1/40th the world's average, and well below the UN's threshold of "absolute scarcity" (500 m^3) (Figure 6.2).

According to the government, agriculture and coal consume most of the country's available water. It is estimated that 65% to 70% of the water resources are used in the agricultural sector and 20% in the coal industry (to extract, wash, and combust coal), with little remaining for other uses. Cultivating one bowl of rice requires one bathtub full of water (70 gallons); processing one ton of coal requires somewhere between 800 and 3,000 gallons of water. Unfortunately, the agricultural and coal industries are largely concentrated in the north, where water

Figure 6.2 China's annual water resources per capita (m3) by province, 2003–10 average

Source: China Water Risk (based on National Bureau of Statistics)

and precipitation are extremely limited. (Two-thirds of the country's cropland and most of the country's coal industry are in the north.) The heaviest demand on China's water resources, thus, is precisely in the region of the country where they are least plentiful.

With precipitation and river runoff insufficient to meet the country's needs, especially in the north, China has drawn more and more on its groundwater. But experts worry that the groundwater is being withdrawn much too quickly, well beyond its recharging capacity. In many parts of the north, the water table has fallen to 328 to 984 feet (100–300 meters) below the ground, mostly within the past two decades.

Climate change is expected to make matters worse. If, as forecast, temperatures rise, evaporation is likely to increase, further stressing water resources. Climate experts also predict that, with the warming air, precipitation patterns will change; the south, they say, will get more moisture and today's dry north will get still less. Already, droughts in the Hai, Yellow, and Huai River areas have caused billions of dollars in losses. If the Himalayan glaciers in the west continue to melt and recede (having already shrunk by one-third over the past century), as all scientific studies suggest, the ice melt they provide to the east-flowing Yellow and Yangtze Rivers will decline by as much as 25% by 2050. This could be catastrophic for agriculture—and the people—along these rivers.

In the north and northwest, the shortage of precipitation, combined with overextraction of water, overlogging, and overgrazing, has already produced an ecological nightmare. Over 1 million square miles of China's land has become desert—that is, 27% of all of China's land. Four hundred million people have been affected by this massive desertification. Some of them have had little choice but to become ecological migrants, fleeing their homes in search of land that can sustain them. In 1978, in an attempt to fend off the desert's expansion, the Chinese people launched the world's largest tree-planting project ever. Since then they have planted 66 billion trees along the edges of the country's northern deserts. Like the Great Wall, this "great green wall" is intended to be a defensive structure, though this time the enemy is desertification, not nomadic invaders. When the project is completed, in 2050 or so, the wall of trees is expected to stretch more than 2,800 miles. Whether, ultimately, it will be any more successful than the Great Wall in keeping the enemy at bay is open to much debate.

Water scarcity on occasion can lead to conflict between villages, as it has, for example, along the Zhang River, a tributary of the Hai River that flows between Henan and Hebei provinces. In the 1950s, with the population growing, villagers in the region became increasingly intent on protecting the water needed for their agriculture. In the 1970s, villages along the Zhang even established militias to defend their water allocations. Occasional violence would erupt and, in 1976, one of the local militia chiefs was shot to death. By the 1990s, violence had escalated and the exchange of mortar fire between villages was not uncommon. On Chinese New Year in 1999, two of the villages took to bombing each other, injuring nearly 100 people and doing $1 million worth of damage to homes and water facilities in the area.[7]

A variety of measures to alleviate the country's water stress have been proposed. Those that have attracted the most interest include the following:

- Increasing the price of water, which now costs $0.46 per m^3 (vs. the global average of $2.03 per m^3)
- Implementing some sort of tiered pricing system for water
- Improving irrigation efficiency
- Charging farms based on the actual amount of irrigation water they use (volumetric pricing) rather than by acreage of land, as is still the case in many places
- Developing cost-effective desalination technology and plants
- Building a 100-mile-long canal from Tianjin to Beijing to carry potable, desalinated water from the Bohai Gulf
- Strengthening management of the country's water resources
- Increasing the country's food imports in order to conserve on agricultural water

How Have Groundwater Levels Become So Dangerously Low?

An increase in industrialization, urbanization, and population beginning in the mid- to late 20th century has resulted in the increasing depletion—and pollution—of China's surface waters. In recent years, a decrease in precipitation has further diminished its water resources. Consequently, China has turned more and more to its groundwater supply. Between 1949 and 2004 water use across the country increased, leading to an inevitable drop in groundwater levels.[8] China Water Risk estimates that today over 400 of the 655 cities in China rely on groundwater as their primary source of drinking water.[9] The north has been especially affected, as municipalities, industry, and agriculture there have all become dependent on groundwater for a significant share of their water needs—65%, 50%, and 33% respectively. As a result, in the north, groundwater levels have been dropping 3.3 feet (1 meter) every year.

Most aquifers are rechargeable (i.e., replenishable) through rainfall, although fossil aquifers are not. But China is drawing from the groundwater at too fast a rate for it to recharge adequately.

A related problem is the country's rapid development and urbanization. Land that was once permeable and allowed rainwater and water runoff to seep into the ground is now covered with impermeable surfaces like asphalt and concrete, meaning that the recharging rate has slowed substantially in the past couple of decades.

So now the groundwater itself is being depleted, a cause for deep concern. As recently as 2008, workers in Beijing could drill a couple of hundred feet and hit groundwater, but in 2010, they had to drill over 1,000 feet (305 meters) to reach it. The World Bank reports that some wells in Beijing must be drilled a half-mile (0.8 km) deep before hitting water. Villages throughout Hebei province, which surrounds Beijing, now have to dig 650 feet (198 meters) to find clean water, when just a few years ago it could be found at just over 65 feet (20 meters).

At 650 feet or 1,000 feet, accessing water is a challenge, and it is expensive. At these depths, tube wells are required. In a tube well, a metal tube or pipe is bored into the underground aquifer; equipped with a pump and filter, the tube then brings the groundwater to the surface. In 1965, there were about 150,000 of these wells throughout the country; by 2003 there were 4.7 million. This expansion represents a huge increase in the cost of accessing the water supply.

There are serious secondary consequences to groundwater depletion. One is subsidence, the sinking of land that results from the extraction of groundwater. Groundwater produces an upward pressure on the layers of soil above it; as the amount of pressure is reduced, through depletion, there is less support for that soil and so it begins to settle or sink, sometimes even collapsing in on itself. Subsidence can do real harm: it can damage buildings; rupture water, gas, and electric lines; buckle highways and rail systems; and increase the risk of flooding. More than 50 Chinese cities are experiencing subsidence. The city of Tianjin has been especially hard hit: in 2008, an area of 43,090 square miles (111,602 km^2) was found to have sunk 10.5 feet. Shanghai, the country's most populous city, has sunk more than 8 feet (2.4 meters). And one recent study concluded that Beijing is sinking by more than 4 inches (10.2 cm) annually.[10]

Another serious consequence is saltwater intrusion. This occurs when groundwater near the ocean is overextracted and the water table declines, allowing salt water to flow in and fill up the empty space in the aquifer. The intruding salt water can result in the contamination of the aquifer and soil salinization. Looking down the road, if China continues to overextract its groundwater, and if, as climate scientists predict, sea levels rise from global warming in the coming decades, the incidence of saltwater intrusion in China's aquifers—and the problems associated with it—could escalate steeply.

Why Are Some of the Rivers, Even Major Ones like the Yellow River, Drying Up?

Rivers all over China are drying up, even disappearing. History had never recorded a "no-flow" day for the mighty

Yellow River until 1972: for 15 days that year, the water ran so low that the river failed to reached its outlet in the Bohai Sea. From 1972 to the mid-1990s there were intermittent recurrences of this sort of dry-up. Then, in 1996, "Mother River," as the Chinese people have long called it, failed to make it to the sea for a full 133 days. The next year was worse: the river ceased flowing for 236 days.

The Haihe or Hai River flows through Beijing and Tianjin before emptying into the Bohai Sea. The volume of water in the Hai River has declined drastically in recent years as many of the smaller tributaries that feed it, and some of the major ones as well, have become dry river beds (about 2,500 miles [4,023 km] in total) for most of the year. In 2001, Xinhua news reported that the wetlands area along the Hai River had shrunk by 80% over the past 50 years, from 1,465 square miles (3,794 km^2) to 207 square miles (536 km^2).

In 2005 China's Ministry of Water Resources reported that of the 541 rivers it had surveyed, 60 had run dry in 2000. And in 2013, according to China's "First National Census of Water," of the 50,000 rivers with a flow area of 60 square miles (155 km^2) or more that were recorded in 1950, only 22,909 were found by surveyors; the other 27,000 could not be found.[11] Poor water-management programs and excessive withdrawal for irrigation are thought to be the likely causes (though some Chinese officials have argued that the 1950 figure of 50,000 was based on inaccurate estimates by cartographers using poor mapping techniques). Whatever the precise number, the trend is clear: China's waterways are drying up.

A number of factors, mostly already familiar to us, explain the trend. First is population growth. The jump from 541 million people at the founding of the People's Republic to 1.38 billion today has necessarily resulted in far greater extraction of natural resources like water. A significant share of river water is siphoned off for irrigation use, especially in the north, where water-intensive crops like wheat are grown and rainfall is slight. Industrialization, which has been the driver of the Chinese economy over the past 30 years, has brought a high demand for energy, especially coal, and, as we have seen, coal extraction, washing, and processing place a huge stress on water resources. China is attempting to turn from coal to other sources of energy in order to decarbonize, yet some of these sources—gas, nuclear, and hydropower—also require a great deal of water. Another factor explaining the "dry-up epidemic" is water diversion: water from rivers is increasingly being diverted to dams (built to control flooding and to generate hydroelectricity), reservoirs, and cities to supply the water needs of the increasingly urban Chinese population, roughly 700 million people.

Climatic changes factor in too. Scientists have calculated that from the 1950s to the 1990s years there was a 2.30°F (1.28°C) rise in air temperature in the Yellow River basin.[12] The warmer air has resulted in increased evaporation of the surface water and increased evapotranspiration by plants, which then require more watering. This century has also seen an increase in droughts, in both the north and the south. A March 2009 drought in China's southwest provinces reduced precipitation there by 90%; in 2011 a drought in the Yangtze River basin left more than 3 million people without sufficient water. In both cases, when the rains returned, they caused damaging flooding.

Finally, Chinese industry's inefficient use of water is a factor in the widespread river dry-up. It is estimated that Chinese industry uses somewhere between 4 and 10 times more water per unit of production than the average among developed countries.[13] Further, according to the World Bank, Chinese industry recycles only 40% of its water, compared to 75% to 85% in developed countries.[14]

What Is the South-North Water Diversion Project?

In a country where 80% of the relatively scarce water resources are in the south and just 20% in the north, where the population is split roughly evenly between the two regions (53% in the south, 47% in the north), and where 66% of the agriculture is in the north, the question of how the country's water resources might be more equitably distributed arises naturally. In the 1950s, Chairman Mao, during an inspection tour of the south, observed, "The south has plenty of water, but the north is dry. If we could borrow some, everything would be okay."

That is what the South-North Water Diversion Project, which broke ground in 2002, aims to do. The three channels (an eastern channel, a central channel, and a western channel) will move water from the wet south to the water-deprived north. Together the three channels will run more than 2,000 miles (3,219 km).Considered by many the biggest engineering project in history, it will move 45 billion m^3 of fresh water every year from the Yangtze River to the arid north.[15]

The eastern and central channels have been completed. As Figure 6.3 shows, the eastern channel originates in the lower Yangtze and threads its way north to the metropolis of Tianjin; the central channel begins at the Danjiangkou Reservoir and carries southern waters northward to Beijing (Edward Wong of the *New York Times* wrote that this was "like channeling the Mississippi River to meet the drinking needs of Boston"[16]). The western channel, connecting the headwaters of the Yangtze River to the headwaters of the Yellow River, is the shortest but technically the most difficult, as it will move water from the Yangtze across the eastern Himalayas; it is still in the planning stages and is not scheduled for completion until 2050. The cost of the transfer project thus far is $80 billion.

As desperate as the north may be for water, the South-North Water Diversion Project has raised many concerns. The eastern channel was constructed largely by linking up existing canals, rivers, and lakes, but much of the water in these waterways is polluted. Will the eastern channel simply be moving polluted water north? More than 400 wastewater treatment plants have been built along the channel (which come at a cost and require energy to run), but how effective will they be in treating the

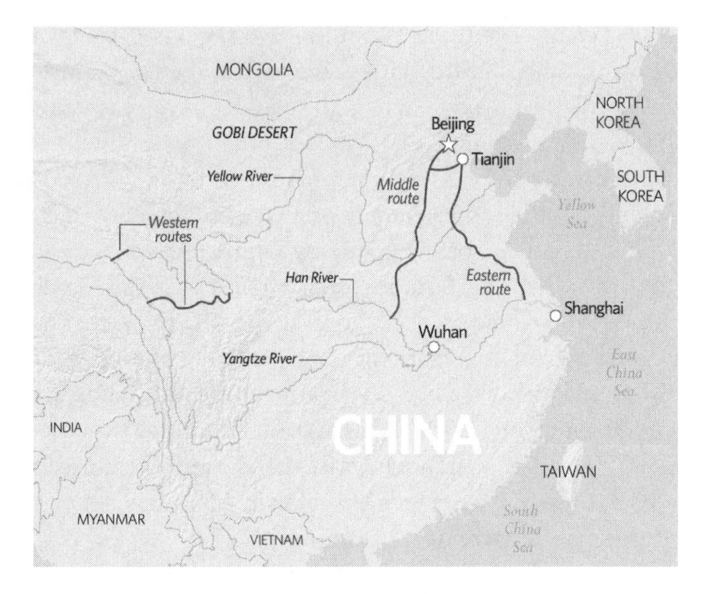

Figure 6.3 The eastern, central, and western routes of the South-North Water Diversion Project

water arriving in the north? For the moment, officials in the city of Tianjin say they still prefer to desalinate water—an expensive process—rather than drinking water pumped from the south through the eastern channel.

Cities and provinces along the channels have argued that they are being robbed of water in order to supply Beijing. For instance, officials in Hebei province say that in recent years the amount of available water in Hebei and its capital city of Shijiazhuang has declined by 50% as a result of the diversion project.

Estimates of the amount of runoff that will be diverted from the Yangtze vary. Most experts suggest roughly 5%, but some add that it could increase to as much as 20%, depending on the season and the weather. Whatever the amount, there is worry that the Yangtze and the cities and villages it serves will pay a price. In the last four decades, the amount of water entering the Yangtze from Tibetan glaciers has decreased 15%;

as the glaciers melt and recede over the course of this century this figure is expected to escalate. Thus, diverting even 5% of the Yangtze's annual runoff would be significant. Experts in Hubei's capital, Wuhan, a city of 8.3 million, contend that diverting water away from the Yangtze, the source of the city's entire water supply, especially during periods of lower runoff, puts Wuhan at grave risk. They wonder why supplying north China with water should be a higher priority to the state than maintaining a healthy water supply in their city. Meanwhile, Sichuan province has submitted an official complaint to the central government about the likely effects that the still-unbuilt western pipeline would have there: not only are water levels already dropping, but water pollution is a widespread problem.[17] The question that many critics of the project have is simply this: Will supplying the north lead to scarcity in the south?

There is also concern about the transmission of waterborne diseases from south to north. For instance, schistosomiasis, the chronic parasitic snail-borne disease mentioned above, has so far been limited largely to the lower reaches of the Yangtze River. However, some scientists believe that as water is diverted north from the Yangtze, the possibility of the disease spreading northward is very real.

Diverting water from the Yangtze poses risks to the health of the river itself. A decline in water level increases the likelihood that salt water will intrude into its estuaries. And a lower volume of water (and thus a slower flow) weakens the river's "environmental capacity" (its ability to clean itself of pollutants introduced into its waters). Today, roughly 40% of the country's wastewater is dumped into the Yangtze River, and diverting the water means there will be less water in the river to dilute the pollution.[18]

Finally, building the canals has required a massive relocation. More than 330,000 people have been forced to move from their homes to make way for the construction of the central channel and the expansion of the Danjiangkou Reservoir that feeds it.

7

SOIL POLLUTION AND AGRICULTURE

How Much of China's Land Is Contaminated?

China's land area is about 3.7 million square miles (world's third largest after Russia and Canada). Roughly 11.5% to 15%, depending on the source, is arable (approximately 334 million acres). This represents about 7% to 9% of the world's arable land—but, in turn, that 7% to 9% must feed more than 20% of the world's population. Between 2010 and 2015, per capita arable land in China was 0.2 acres (0.08 hectares); this compares to Germany at 0.37 acres (0.15 hectares) and the United States at 1.21 acres (0.49 hectares). Given these numbers, the country can ill afford to lose any of its arable land to contamination.

Yet, a seven-year government survey completed in 2013 (the results of which were initially classified by the government as a "state secret") found that 16% of the country's total land area is contaminated and 20% of all arable land—66 million acres—is contaminated. The Ministry of Land and Resources warned that 8.24 million acres were so severely befouled, so saturated with heavy metals, that they were unfit for farming and should be withdrawn from agricultural use.

When the results of this survey were finally publicly released in April 2014, environmental activist Zhang Changjian challenged the results of the survey, saying, "These figures aren't accurate, because at least two thirds of China's agricultural land is polluted," and went on to explain, "All of the major rivers are polluted, and a lot of agricultural land uses that water for irrigation, which means it must be polluted."[1] When we consider that 75% of the country's grain is produced on irrigated land, and when we remember just how contaminated the country's waterways—and irrigated water—are, Zhang's remarks may not be unreasonable.

What Are the Sources of Soil Pollution?

Agriculture, industry, and polluted air are the main sources of China's soil pollution. As the need to feed more people has grown over the centuries, so has the pressure to increase agricultural yields. That pressure has intensified in recent years as desertification, contamination, and conversion of land to urban and industrial use have taken a large bite out of the country's available arable land. Eager to maximize the productivity of their holdings, farmers, with the state's encouragement (at least until recently), make liberal use of fertilizers and pesticides. But the problem is that today's synthetic fertilizers and pesticides introduce into the soil chemicals that can degrade its composition and render it less fertile. And when overapplied, the excess fertilizers and pesticides that are not absorbed by the soil make their way into the groundwater and nearby rivers and lakes.

Food exposed to pesticides like DDT, endosulfan, endrin, heptachlor, and lindane, which bind to the soil, can be toxic to humans. Most of these have been banned in China, but reports say they are still commonly used. Pesticides that do not bind to the soil present another problem: they move easily into runoff and contaminate water supplies.

Industry is the biggest polluter of soil. With the rapid industrialization of the past three to four decades, plants and factories have grown up along the rivers throughout rural China. Their waste, often completely untreated, flows into the rivers, and from the rivers into irrigation canals. This waste carries a burden of heavy metals, including cadmium, nickel, arsenic, chromium, copper, lead, zinc, and mercury—which then make their way, either through leaching or irrigation, into the nearby fields. More than 82% of the land that the 2013 government survey determined was polluted was contaminated by heavy metals.

The threat to human health comes when people eat crops grown in soil that has absorbed these metals. Cadmium, a heavy metal emitted from non-ferrous metal mines and smelting plants, leads the list of contaminants in China's soil. Ingested, it causes renal failure, liver diseases, osteoporosis, and various cancers. A recent study in the heavily industrialized province of Hunan found the cadmium level in some locations to be 200 times higher than the national standard. Meanwhile, in a 2013 investigation, the Guangzhou provincial government took samples of rice being sold in Guangzhou and found 44% of them to have excessive levels of cadmium. The public was quick to express its displeasure. One social media user angrily asked, "Now before every meal must we all first wonder: Does this rice have too much cadmium? Are the vegetables laced with pesticide?"[2] Even the *China Daily* chimed in; according to a 2013 editorial, "soil contaminated with heavy metals is eroding the foundation of the country's food safety and becoming a looming public health hazard."[3] Chinese officials now estimate that every year the country produces more than 12 million tons of grain contaminated with heavy metals.

Industrial accidents, which inevitably occur, can also send agrochemical, petrochemical, and other chemical spills into nearby waterways. If this water is not prevented from entering the irrigation systems, it eventually makes its way into the neighboring land on which local crops are growing.

Agriculture and industry do the most damage to the country's soil, but a third source of the country's soil pollution is air pollution. Mercury emitted into the air during fossil fuel combustion—from power plants, industry, and automobiles—gets deposited by wind and rain on the land and in the water, contaminating crops ("mercury rice" is almost as big an epidemic in China as cadmium rice) and freshwater wildlife. And carbon dioxide, normally associated with atmospheric warming, is now thought also to affect the nutritional values of major food crops like wheat, rice, maize, and soybeans. An international study done in 2014 concluded that as the level of carbon dioxide in the air increases, the content of certain nutrients, especially zinc and iron, in major field crops decreases.[4] The biological mechanism causing the decrease is not well understood, but any reduction of zinc and iron in wheat and rice is worrying for a country where these are dietary staples—and where zinc and iron deficiencies are already of public health concern.[5]

How Much Fertilizer Is Used in Chinese Agriculture?

Population growth since the time of Mao Zedong has put pressure on agricultural yield. Consequently, fertilizer use has skyrocketed. Average fertilizer application in 1961 was 11.9 pounds per 2.47 acres (5.4 kg/hectare); a half-century later, in 2010, it was 1,115.5 per 2.47 acres (506 kg/hectare), an astounding 9,274% increase.[6] Today, the internationally accepted limit of nitrogen fertilizer is 225 kg/hectare, so China's average application is more than twice the international standard.

The more fertilizer use, the greater the degradation to the soil and waterways. But overfertilization is not just damaging; it is also inefficient. A number of recent studies have shown that in China the increase in the application rate over the years has not produced a commensurate increase in crop yield. One study found that "from 1977 to 2005, total annual grain production in China increased 283 to 484 million tons (a 71% increase). . . . However, synthetic N [nitrogen] fertilizer application increased from 7.06 to 26.21 million tons (a 271% increase) over the same period."[7] Another concluded that over the past five decades the "human population in China doubled . . . the total grain production more than tripled, and fertilizer use increased 10-fold."[8] Figures vary, but the scenario is the same: farmers are not getting payback on their fertilizer use.

Agricultural experts argue that China could reduce its use of nitrogen fertilizer by as much as 30% to 60% without any reduction in the crop yield. But getting farmers to reduce their use will not be easy: the attitude, engrained over decades, is that if some fertilizer is good for the crops, more must be better. A 2009 scientific report remarks:

> Although this trend [i.e., applying rates far higher than crop demand] has been recognized by the scientific community since the late 1990s, on-farm practices are difficult to reverse after 10 to 15 years of effort. Persuading farmers to limit fertilizer inputs is difficult because many of them still hold to now traditional opinions that higher crop yield will be obtained with more fertilizer. Application rates of N therefore often include an extra "insurance" component to prevent yield loss rather than matching inputs to crop demand.[9]

The Chinese government shares some responsibility for the country's fertilizer overuse. Anxious about food security and about its ability to feed a population of a billion-plus, for decades it has subsidized the fertilizer industry and kept the price of fertilizer at artificially low rates. The aim has been to promote adoption of fertilizer use by hundreds of millions of farmers throughout the country, encouraging them to get as much from the land as possible. And, while clearly that aim has been achieved, a profound consequence of government efforts has been widespread nutrient pollution.

Even now the subsidies continue, in large part because fertilizer is an important export industry. Indeed, over the 10 years from 2004 to 2014, subsidies of the industry increased by 670%;

in 2010 alone, they amounted to $18 billion, roughly as much as the government spends annually on education.[10] However, beginning in 2009, the government relinquished control of prices, partly with the hope that market prices would lead to more judicious use of fertilizers by farmers. Experts have suggested additional measures the government might consider taking to curb fertilizer use, such as (1) strengthening the regulations governing the management practices of fertilizer products, as Canada, Japan, and the European Union have, and (2) establishing "a sound multidimensional information delivery system that provides scientific services to farmers and guides fertilization practices."[11]

What Is the State of Organic Farming in China?

Organic farming arose in China in the 1990s, mostly to meet international demand. Green tea from Lin'an, destined for the Netherlands, was the first product to receive organic certification. Processed vegetables, soybeans, honey, grains, green teas, and herbal medicines have made up the bulk of organic exports since. Whole Foods, for instance, imported 50% of its organic soybeans from China in 2009.

But in the past decade the domestic demand for organic food has boomed. China is now the fourth largest consumer of organic products in the world, after the United States, Germany, and France. The reasons for the popularity are not hard to find. Food safety has become a prominent concern. In a fall 2015 PEW poll in China, 71% of the respondents said that food safety was a very big problem or a moderately big problem.[12] This comes in the wake of numerous food scandals. Most notoriously, perhaps, in 2008 hundreds of thousands of infants were sickened after drinking melamine-laced milk and powdered infant formula made by the Sanlu Group. Six infants died and more than 50,000 were hospitalized. The company had added the industrial chemical melamine to boost the appearance of protein content in milk and infant formula that it had watered down. Other scandals include the following:

- Workshops mixed pork with chemicals such as paraffin wax and sold it as beef.
- Dealers bought up diseased pork, processed it in illegal workshops, and sold it at market.
- Shanghai Husi Food Company distributed expired meat to international companies like McDonald's, KFC, and Starbucks.
- Gangs smuggled in frozen meat up to 40 years old (so-called zombie meat) from foreign countries and sold it to restaurants in China.
- Small factories collected waste oil, or "gutter oil," from sewer drains, restaurant fryers, and grease traps; cleaned and packed it; and then resold it as cooking oil.

The list, unfortunately, could go on.[13]

Public confidence in the food supply thus is low. It was not much improved when the news broke in 2011 that high-ranking officials at Communist Party headquarters in Zhongnanhai in Beijing were getting food directly from organic farms run by the government and that many provincial and municipal governments had their own dedicated organic food suppliers. At the same time, public awareness of the detrimental environmental effects of pesticide and fertilizer use has been on the rise. So, too, has recognition that crops grown in the country's contaminated water and soil may well be toxic. As a result, the domestic market for organically grown food has been expanding and in the past five years has overtaken the export market. Today, between 5 million and 7.5 million acres (2–3 million hectares) of the country's farmland is now organically certified, the second largest area of certified organic land in the world (this represents 0.75–2.5% of China's arable acreage, depending on the source).

Of course, China's economic development is also a factor in the expanding market. As the middle class has grown, so too has the number of people able to afford the high costs of organic foods, which sell at up to 500% more than conventionally produced foods. (A recent study concluded that "white-collar" families make up 40% of the organic food market.) Driving the market as well, especially in big cities, are the expatriate communities and higher-end hotels and restaurants.

Food labeled "organic" must go through a certification process, but trust in this process is apparently quite weak. In a September 2015 article, *The South China Morning Post* quoted one professor at China Agricultural University in Beijing as saying, "Trust is a big problem. . . . Organic producers want to make money. The certification centers for organic produce also have to make a profit. Some problems exist in the products' authentication process."[14] The article went on to claim that this lack of trust has spawned more than 500 community-supported agriculture (CSA) farms, in which CSA members buy produce directly from the farm and can thus feel more assured of its quality.

Is China's Ability to Feed Its People at Risk?

In 1995, the environmental analyst Lester Brown, in his book *Who Will Feed China?*, predicted that massive urbanization and population growth would require China to turn to the international grain market to support its people and speculated on what the global consequences might be.

China's response to Brown, issued by the state council in "White Paper—The Grain Issue in China" (1996), was quick and unambiguous: China will feed China. The state council said:

> The basic principle for solving the problem of grain supply and demand in China is to rely on the domestic resources and basically achieve self-sufficiency in grain. China endeavors to increase its grain production so that its self-sufficiency rate of grain under normal conditions

> will be above 95% and the net import rate five percent, or even less, of the total consumption.[15]

Ever since, grain self-sufficiency has been something of a state mantra. As recently as 2011, Han Changfu, the Minister of Agriculture, announced, "To ensure national grain security, it is important that China adheres to the principle of self-sufficiency. The livelihood of the Chinese people cannot end up in the hands of others. Depending on international trade to ensure food security is unreliable."[16]

China is not simply responding to the gauntlet thrown down by Brown. Vivid memories of starvation linger among the Chinese people, including those in the Chinese leadership. The 1950s and 1960s were hard years, and the famine associated with the Great Leap Forward is engrained in the national consciousness. The government is determined that mass starvation must never again visit itself on the land and its people.

China's pursuit of "grain independence" also reflects its reluctance to become food dependent on other countries at a time when the international order is in considerable flux and today's friend may become tomorrow's adversary. This, no doubt, is one of the takeaways of the harsh break between China and the Soviet Union in the late 1950s and early 1960s.

Today China's leaders still hold to the 95% grain self-sufficiency target, but meeting this target could prove difficult as China's population hits 1.4 billion and is expected to grow to anywhere from 1.45 billion to 1.6 billion by 2030. We have already touched on many of the challenges China's land faces. The amount of arable land has been shrinking since the late 20th century due to a number of trends associated with economic development, such as the following:

- Conversion of arable land for urban use (e.g., houses and apartments, office buildings, airports, shopping centers, leisure space [golf courses, parks, and the like])

- Proliferation of industries and factories in both cities and rural areas, especially with the development of township and village enterprises beginning in the mid-1980s
- Widespread contamination of the soil from industries and agriculture
- Acid deposition from polluted air (between 650 and 1000 tons of mercury enter China's soil every year)
- Dietary shifts and the growth of the livestock industry, which cuts into available crop land
- Erosion and desertification

For a decade the state council has said that to be 95% grain independent the country must have no less than 297 million acres (120 million hectares) of arable land—what the state calls the "red line." In 2015 the government claimed that in late 2013 there were 336 million acres (135 million hectares) of arable land, well above the red line.[17] However, some authorities suspect this figure is too high, given the quantity of farmland that has been converted to urban use in recent years or contaminated with heavy metals and other pollutants.[18]

Whatever the figure, it is clear that foreign imports of grains like soybeans, sorghum, maize, corn, and barley have been on the rise. Reliable figures for domestic grain production versus foreign imports are difficult to obtain, but most observers agree that China's grain self-sufficiency rate today is probably closer to 90%, and is likely to decline further.[19]

This would mean a still greater reliance on grain imports, which raises two urgent questions: (1) Which countries, if any, have the surplus agricultural capacity to supply the food needs for a country the size of China? (2) If China does become more dependent on imports, how might international commodity markets be affected? At an extreme, consider the Arab Spring uprising of 2011: many observers have argued that the uprising was fueled in part by the skyrocketing costs of bread. The drought in China, they contend, contributed to the crisis, as China turned to the international grain market to provision itself, thereby driving up the costs of wheat worldwide. Concerns about the global impact of China's growing reliance on international markets notwithstanding, the World Bank has encouraged China to consider abandoning its objective of self-sufficiency in order to preserve the country's increasingly scarce land and water resources.[20]

Recently, as part of its overall strategy to secure food resources for its huge population, China has been buying large tracts of foreign farmland in Africa, the Ukraine, Brazil, Chile, Australia, and the United States.[21] It has also been buying foreign agricultural companies, whose expertise and patent-protected products have the potential to boost the country's agricultural output. For example, ChemChina recently paid $47 billion to buy Syngenta, a Swiss seeds and pesticide group. A source close to the deal told Reuters, "Only around 10% of Chinese farmland is efficient. This is more than just a company buying another. This is a government attempting to address a real problem."[22]

Even if China has the ability to feed its population, however, these 1.4 billion people do not have equal access to food. It is estimated that more than 130 million Chinese, mostly in the countryside, now suffer from malnutrition—even as one-quarter of China's urban dwellers suffer from obesity.[23]

8

POLLUTION AND PUBLIC HEALTH

What Are the Major Health Consequences of Air, Water, and Soil Pollution?

When the smog settles in, coughing, wheezing, watering of the eyes, and shortness of breath are common, but these are relatively benign effects of air pollution. More serious respiratory problems associated with exposure to polluted air include asthma, bronchitis, pneumonia, and chronic obstructive pulmonary disease. It is now known, too, that long-term exposure to fine particulate matter (PM2.5) in polluted air results in an increased risk of lung cancer and cardiovascular disease.

Staying indoors is no guarantee of protection against pollutants. According to the *Wall Street Journal*, a report released in December 2015 based on a study of 160 office buildings in Beijing found that indoor air quality in 90% of the city's offices is no better than the outdoor air quality.[1] (The same study found that 75% of the PM2.5 in the outside air makes its way indoors.) Room air filters (costing $500 or more) have become the appliance of choice for affluent urban dwellers. On social media sites, netizens frequently discuss topics like whether it is better to open windows or keep them shut, at what times of day to allow outside air in, which air filters are most effective, and where to buy inexpensive PM2.5 monitors.

The air inside rural homes can be particularly toxic, as many villagers use low-quality, high-polluting, solid charcoal briquettes for heating and cooking. Despite a government subsidy program, beginning in 2004, to outfit rural homes with ventilating chimneys, many homes still lack them, so residents inhale the smoke from the burning coal, and the pollutants are deposited on the food.

Moreover, the coal used by the villagers in some regions of the country has a high content of fluorine, which is then released into the air or deposited on the food. Data from rural Shaanxi, for example, show that fluorine levels inside homes are up to 97 times the legal standard, leading to a high incidence of dental and skeletal fluorosis, which results in damaged and broken teeth and bones. In some regions the coal contains high levels of arsenic, which is released into the air when the coal is burned. Arsenic poisoning is linked to cancer and neurological disease as well as to digestive and urinary problems. Again in Shaanxi, a 2001–2003 study concluded that the coal burned there had five times the allowable level of arsenic, and in southern Guizhou province, 38,000 cases of arsenic poisoning related to coal have been confirmed.[2]

Exposure to China's contaminated water presents a different range of health risks: typhoid, malaria, diarrhea, lead and mercury poisoning, intestinal parasites, and digestive cancers. Cases of typhoid, diarrhea, and intestinal parasites (e.g., schistosomiasis) are especially widespread in the warm region of south China. While the incidence of malaria has declined dramatically, from 24 million cases in the late 1970s to just tens of thousands today, it remains endemic in southern and central China, particularly in Yunnan and Hainan provinces. Digestive cancers—esophageal, liver, stomach, and bladder—have become the leading cause of death in rural China. Without ready access to piped water, villagers draw their drinking, cooking, and irrigation water directly from local streams, rivers, and lakes. Scientists believe that the metals, agrochemicals, pharmaceuticals, human and animal waste, and other pollutants in these water sources are largely responsible for the cancer blight spreading in China's countryside.

Eating food grown in soil contaminated with heavy metals (e.g., cadmium, arsenic, mercury, and lead), petrochemicals, pesticides and fertilizers, and animal and human waste can likewise lead to digestive cancers—as well as to renal disease, osteoporosis, neurological damage, and a variety of other cancers.

Exposure to and contact with contaminated soil can lead to an assortment of human health problems. In one recent, widely publicized case, CCTV (China Central Television) reported that nearly 500 students at an elementary school in Changzhou (in Jiangsu province) had come down with illnesses ranging from bronchitis and eczema to lymphoma and leukemia; investigators suggested that the illnesses were linked to high concentrations of toxins found in the soil around the school, which had recently moved to a site near where three chemical plants used to operate.[3]

What Are "Cancer Villages"?

In February 2013 China's Ministry of Environmental Protection issued a document stating, "In recent years, toxic and hazardous chemical pollution has caused many environmental disasters, cutting off drinking water supplies, and even leading to severe health and social problems such as the emergence of cancer villages."[4] This was the first admission ever by the Chinese government that "cancer villages" existed, although journalists and environmentalists had been writing and speaking about the phenomenon since 2001.

A cancer village is a village where the incidence of cancer is abnormally high. There are now thought to be roughly 500 of them throughout China (Figure 8.1). Most are located in the eastern part of the country, along the major rivers—the Yellow, the Huai, and the Yangtze—and their tributaries, and there are a number in the south as well, in the Pearl River delta

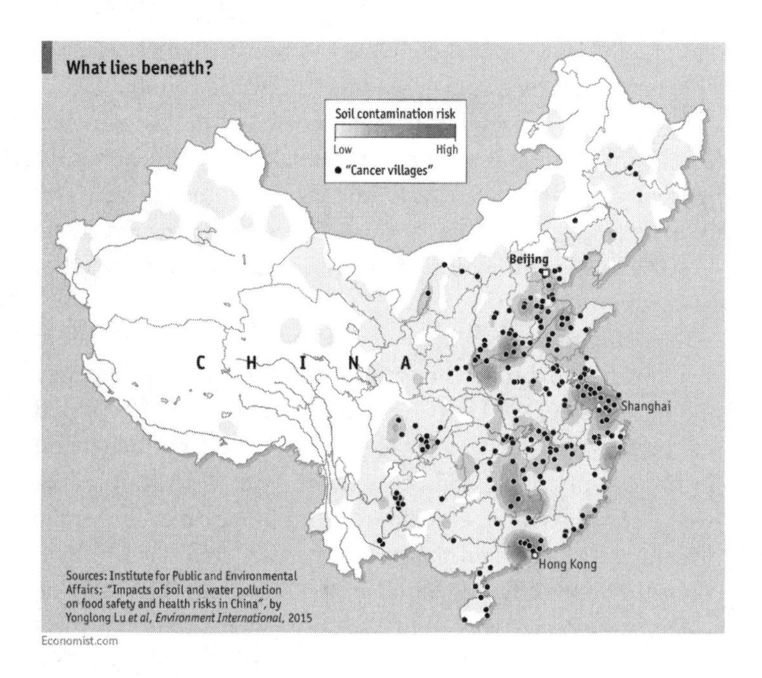

Figure 8.1 Cancer villages

area. It is along these waterways that tens of thousands of tanneries, paper mills, chemical plants, textile factories, food manufacturers, and other industries have cropped up since the 1980s, releasing into the surrounding air, soil, and water a wide variety of pollutants that the villagers believe to be the cause of their cancer. Wastewater discharge into nearby water systems is the most common source of cancer, as villagers often draw their drinking and cooking water directly from these sources. That same wastewater can also seep into adjacent fields where crops are grown and livestock graze. Foodstuffs contaminated by the polluted water are thus another source of the cancer.

For almost two decades now villagers have been lodging complaints with government officials against factories they hold responsible for the spread of the disease. But officials have not been especially responsive, partly because these factories contribute to the local economy and partly because it is difficult to draw a causal connection between one particular factory (there may be many of them in the general vicinity spewing various chemicals into the stream or river) and the rash of cancer cases in the village. As Wu Yixu, a toxins campaigner for Greenpeace, noted, "You need to establish the fact that it's a certain chemical that's causing certain cancers, and this chemical is being discharged from this very factory."[5]

Stricken villages suffer from more than the cancer alone. The toxins in the water and soil make their produce unfit for sale, thereby leaving the inhabitants without a livelihood. Poor and diseased, these villages desperately require aid. In recent years, nongovernmental organizations have been active in focusing the public's and state's attention on their plight (see Chapter 10). But it is unclear whether, in the end, the government will, or can, institute an effective, targeted remediation program for the hundreds of cancer villages.

What *is* clear is that the state thus far has been considerably more attentive to the problems associated with urban pollution. Cleaning up the cities has been the first line of attack in Beijing's "war on pollution." But even should the government aggressively take its war on pollution to the villages, the question is this: Will those factories and industries that are shuttered simply move their operations farther inland and set up shop elsewhere? That is, will the cancer-inducing pollution simply be outsourced to poorer "pollution havens" to the west?

Is Food Safety an Issue in China?

Food safety has become a serious concern. As we have seen, 71% of the respondents in the 2015 PEW survey said food safety was either a "very big problem" (32%) or a "moderately big problem" (39%). In 2008, just five years earlier, only 12% of the respondents had seen it as "very big problem." High-profile scandals—melamine-laced infant formula in 2008, gutter oil in 2011, and the 40-year-old frozen meat in 2015—account for some of the mistrust on the part of the Chinese public.

But such sensational "additive" scandals aside, the public has become increasingly aware that food processing involves a series of steps, and that foodstuffs can become contaminated in any of the steps along the way. Improper application of agrochemicals, fertilizers, and pesticides can result in unsafe compounds in food products. Water used to grow the food can be contaminated with untreated sewage that enters the waterways from local villages, contributing to the transmission of foodborne diseases. Industrial pollutants—heavy metals and chemicals (e.g., cadmium, lead, iron, chromium)—in the water systems and soil can taint the food supply and pose a considerable hazard to human health. The water used in processing and preparing the food can transmit harmful microorganisms and chemical pollutants. It is such worries over the quality of food that help explain the growing popularity of organic farming and the preference, among those who can afford it, for purchasing foodstuffs that have been produced outside of the country.

The government has introduced important measures to safeguard the country's food supply, most notably the 2009 Food Safety Law. But implementation of food-quality standards is challenging and progress has been slow—owing both to the lack of coordination among the national, provincial, and local government authorities and the enormous size of the country's food industry. A *Lancet* study calculated that there are more than 450,000 food-production and food-processing companies in China, and that 350,000 are small operations with fewer than 10 employees.[6]

What Are Some Recent, Notable Health-Related Findings?

In 2014, 60% of China's groundwater was found to be unsafe for drinking (or even touching).

On a scale of 0 to 500, with 300 to 500 representing hazardous air and above 500 representing "beyond index," many cities in China, including Beijing, Shanghai, Harbin, Taiyuan, and Shijiazhuang, have recorded levels as high as 1,000, 40 times higher than the standard (25) deemed safe to breathe by the WHO.

In 2012 the Institute for Health Metrics and Evaluation released the influential *Global Burden of Disease Study 2010*, which found that in 2010 alone 1.2 million people in China died prematurely from exposure to "ambient particulate matter pollution" and 1.1 million people died prematurely from exposure to "household air pollution from solid fuels." A later assessment by Berkeley Earth concluded that 1.6 million people in China died annually (4,400 each day) from health problems related to outdoor air pollution. Still another study, done this time by the Max Planck Institute and published in *Nature* in 2015, put the number of annual premature deaths from ambient air pollution in China at 1.4 million.[7] According to research by Teng Fei, a professor at Tsinghua University, the particulate matter emitted by coal combustion *alone* was responsible for 670,000 premature deaths in 2012.[8]

In the past 30 years, the death rate from lung cancer in China has increased 465%. Most of the increase, according to medical studies, is due to exposure to air pollution. A 2015 Greenpeace–Beijing University study of the mainland's 31 municipalities and provincial capitals found that in 2013 people were as likely to die from breathing the air as from smoking cigarettes. Of every 100,000 deaths, 90 were attributable to PM2.5.[9] In 2013, the WHO's International Agency for Research on Cancer announced that because there is "sufficient evidence that exposure to outdoor air pollution causes lung cancer," it is now classifying both outdoor air pollution and PM2.5 as "carcinogenic to humans."

In 2013, an international team of researchers published an influential study showing that because north China over the years 1981–2000 was more dependent on coal than the south (for heating during the winter), particulate matter levels there were significantly higher; and as a consequence, the life expectancy of people living in the north was a stunning 5.5 fewer years than their counterparts in the south.[10]

A Duke University study in 2016 found that rats exposed to Beijing's polluted air had a much higher risk for obesity and diabetes than rats not exposed to the air. After only 19 days, the exposed rats had 50% higher LDL cholesterol, 46% higher triglycerides, and 97% higher total cholesterol; their insulin resistance level, a precursor to type 2 diabetes, was also higher. After 8 weeks of exposure, male rats were 18% heavier and female rats 10% heavier than their counterparts breathing clean air. "If translated and verified in humans, these findings will support the urgent need to reduce air pollution, given the growing burden of obesity in today's highly polluted world," said Junfeng Zhang, the lead author of the study.[11]

In the city of Guiyu in Guangdong province, the e-waste capital of China, the melting of lead solder off circuit boards has resulted in an epidemic of lead poisoning. Over 80% of the children there have tested positive for the harmful disease.

In May 2013, officials in Guangzhou, one of China's largest and most prosperous cities, informed the public that 44% of rice samples sold throughout the city contained dangerous levels of the metal cadmium.

He Dongxian, an associate professor at China Agricultural University, said her studies show that when thick smog settles over Beijing, so much sunlight is blocked that plant photosynthesis is slowed and crop growth is stunted. She concluded that, on a larger scale, photosynthesis-impeding smog could reduce the nation's food supply, warning that if the air pollution continues or intensifies, China's agriculture would face conditions "somewhat similar to a nuclear winter."[12]

What Measures Do China's Residents Take to Protect Themselves from the Health Effects of Pollution?

The first thing many residents in China do when they awaken is to consult one of the many air-quality index apps available on mobile devices. For some, the air-quality reading helps determine what they do that day. Will they leave the house? Will they let their kids play outside? Will they bike to work or take another mode of transportation? Will they jog? Will they swim outdoors or indoors? Will they wear a facemask?

Increasingly, residents own room air filters and run them when pollution levels are high. High-end residential and commercial builders have installed whole-building filtration systems to attract potential buyers. Likewise, high-end car manufacturers tout the benefits of innovative air-filtration systems in reducing the particulate matter in the cabin of the car. The chairman of Geely, Volvo's parent company, stated in an interview on Chinese television, "Volvo's interior air quality system provides you with an air quality inside the car as good as that of Northern Europe while the outside is as bad as that of Beijing."[13] Affluent parents are sending their children to schools that have built $5 million inflatable domes that enclose the playgrounds and filter the air.

Boiling drinking water is a standard practice throughout China, whether in the cities or the countryside. Boiling vaporizes the microorganisms in polluted water but does not affect the toxic metal content. Because water drawn directly from streams, rivers, and lakes tends to have an especially high content of chemicals and heavy metals, those who drink it are especially vulnerable to toxic buildup in the body. Water drawn from the tap (72% of the country's drinking water) has typically gone through a process that filters out most of the microbial matter but is less effective in removing the heavy metals. People can install water-filtering systems in their homes (usually attached directly to the tap); they can install water-storage tanks and subscribe to a water-delivery service; or they can purchase bottled water at the local convenience store or the supermarket. All of this is costly and does not completely eliminate the risk: people have been told by the government that 50% of Beijing's bottled water is counterfeit, simply drawn from the tap.

In a country where water scarcity is already at a critical point, the prospect of a more affluent China turning in greater numbers to bottled water is unwelcome. Production of bottled water is energy- and water-intensive: three extra bottles of water and a quarter-bottle of oil are required to produce one bottle of drinking water. Already China has surpassed the United States as the world's leading consumer of bottled water (15% of the bottled water worldwide). In 1997, China consumed 2.8 million cubic meters of bottled water; in 2013, that number was 39.5 million. And in the last five years, sales of bottled water have doubled.

Water safety concerns, thus, are inexorably leading to a crisis of water security. China Water Risk, a nongovernmental organization based in Hong Kong, has done some outstanding work highlighting the problems surrounding the consumption and production of bottled water in China.[14]

As we have seen, the Chinese people are increasingly concerned about the safety of their food and have been turning to organically raised crops and meat. China is now the fourth largest consumer of organic products in the world. Urban farming has also become popular: city dwellers have begun converting their balconies and rooftops into gardens for growing their own green beans, tomatoes, cabbage, eggplants, herbs, and so on. Observers note that in the big cities, imported-food stores have proliferated; while as recently as 5 to 10 years ago they catered largely to foreigners, today they are filled with Chinese patrons. These recent changes are all attributable to worries over food safety.

In recent years, there has been a steady retreat of urbanites moving from large cities to smaller towns and villages—where the sky is bluer and the water clearer—in places like Yunnan province in southwestern China. Surveys indicate that the rich especially are eager to move. Emigrating abroad is increasingly popular: a 2014 survey by Hurun Reports found that 64% of Chinese millionaires have already emigrated to other countries or are eager to do so. Two of the most frequent reasons cited for leaving or wishing to leave were pollution and food safety (though I suspect that protecting their wealth is at least as strong a factor).[15]

Does Pollution Affect Different Populations Differently?

The study of how different populations in China are affected by environmental pollution is in its early stages and needs further study. Preliminary research, however, indicates the following.

Rural dwellers have far less access to filtered tap water than urban dwellers, and their surface water has a much higher content of heavy metals and chemicals. Experts believe that enforcement of water standards has been much less rigorous in rural areas than in urban areas, because (1) rural populations have been less environmentally demanding and (2) rural officials have been slower to impose regulations that might hurt the local economy. This helps explain the "cancer village" phenomenon and the high incidence of diarrheal diseases and waterborne parasites in villages. It also explains why digestive cancers are more frequent in the countryside and why lung cancer, from exposure to air pollution, is more common in the cities.

There is a marked disparity between rural and urban areas in the availability of medical professionals and hospital care. In cities there are three physicians for every 1,000 people, but in rural areas there is just one.[16] In cities there are 6.24 inpatient beds for every 1,000 people, but in rural areas there are just 2.80.[17]

The *hukou* registration system, instituted in the 1950s to limit migration from countryside to city, is another source of environmental inequality. In the *hukou* system, each individual in China is given either a rural residency card or an urban residency card. In the past 30 years, rural residents have moved to the cities in large numbers because of job opportunities, especially in construction work and factories. However, while they may work and reside in cities, they are not entitled to the same employment, educational, health, and social welfare benefits provided to those who have an urban *hukou*. They live as "migrant workers," a decided subclass of the urban population in China. Even though they are a subclass, the migrants number over 250 million, almost, but not quite, the entire population of the United States. Studies have shown that they tend to live on the urban fringes, in cheaper places where heavily polluting industries and power plants are more likely to be located; thus, the migrants are more susceptible to the harmful effects of air and water pollution.[18]

Similarly, well-off Chinese generally suffer less from the ill effects of pollution than the poor. They can more readily afford health care—doctor visits, hospital stays, and medications. They can equip their homes and workplaces with air-filtration devices. They can live in neighborhoods farther away from coal-fired power plants, incinerators, and landfills. And their jobs are typically white collar, in offices, rather than outdoors on construction sites or farms or indoors in bleak factories. They are more likely to heat their stoves and homes with electricity rather than with solid coal briquettes or wood. And they can afford to send their children to schools where the quality of the air and water is safeguarded.

The old and the young are especially susceptible to some of the hazards of environmental pollution. For instance, preliminary studies indicate that people over 50 are considerably more likely than any other group to die prematurely from respiratory and cardiovascular diseases associated with air pollution. Older women living in areas with excessive levels of PM2.5 may be more likely to experience cognitive decline and to develop dementia.[19]

Children, because they spend more time outdoors and because their immune systems are still undeveloped, are especially vulnerable to asthma and acute respiratory disease. Evidence also indicates that air pollution compromises the neurocognitive development of children.[20] Finally, while diarrhea is a common disease throughout China, the morbidity and mortality rates for children under five years old are particularly high, as they are in most low-income and middle-income countries.[21]

9

CHINA'S POLLUTION AND THE WORLD

How Has Globalization Contributed to China's Pollution?

As discussed in Chapter 3, globalization has fueled much of the economic growth China has enjoyed since 1980. With its large labor force, low wages, and large supply of cheap energy, the country became the "workshop of the world" in the late 20th century, manufacturing inexpensive low-value-added products, including textiles, toys, bicycles, paper supplies, electronic gadgets, and building materials for global consumption. Entry into the WTO in 2001 significantly expanded China's role in global trade. Today, China is the leading exporter in the world; in 2015, exports accounted for 22.4% of its GDP.

But skyrocketing manufacturing has been accompanied by skyrocketing pollution. The coal that powers all the factories and plants has thickened the nation's air with dirty pollutants and greenhouse gases, and factories in the pulp, paper, petrochemical, and, most especially, textile industries have discharged toxic waste into the country's waterways. To be sure, the economy has prospered, but China's air and water have been the victims.

At the same time, MNCs such as IBM, Apple, Toyota, Ford, Bosch, and GE have found it attractive to outsource some of their production to China, either by building plants there or by contracting with Chinese suppliers. Multinational apparel retailers (Armani, Calvin Klein, and Zara, to name but a few) have been especially aggressive in developing supply chains in China. There are now said to be more than 50,000 textile mills in the country.[1] Lower labor costs and lax environmental regulations have made it more profitable for MNCs to establish operations in China—even taking into account transportation costs—than to expand their operations at home. And, of course, when MNCs outsource their production to China they are also outsourcing their pollution. Whether it is the toxins and particulates their plants and factories—and those of their suppliers—release into the air, or the chemical waste and dyes the plants and factories discharge into the waterways, MNCs are contributing appreciably to the degradation of China's environment.

The shipping necessitated by global trade has an environmental cost as well. China is now home to 7 of the 10 busiest ports in the world, mostly along the east coast in highly populated cities; with the cargo carried to and from these ports comes air pollution from the diesel fuel operating the vessels. Barbara Finamore, Asia Director for the National Resources Defense Council, estimates that "one container ship cruising along the coast of China emits as much diesel pollution as 500,000 new Chinese trucks in a single day."[2] China has announced plans to control emissions from container ships calling at its ports beginning in January 2017, but pollution from shipping activities is certain to continue, if at a reduced rate—all part of the price China pays for active participation in a globalized economy.

Global trade does have beneficial effects as well, according to some. First, it enables the transfer of both knowledge and technologies that can mitigate environmental pollution. Second, when companies with the heft of Apple and Nike insist that their suppliers in China follow—or exceed—the country's environmental standards, they elevate the environmental expectations of other MNCs operating in China, and, indeed, of China's own companies, and help to generate a higher environmental awareness among the Chinese people.[3] One example of this sort, perhaps, is an announcement by Apple in October 2015 that the company "is launching a new initiative to drive its manufacturing partners to become more energy efficient and to use clean energy for their manufacturing operations. Apple will partner with suppliers in China to install more than 2 gigawatts of new clean energy in the coming years."[4]

How Are Neighboring Countries Affected by China's Pollution?

The study of transboundary pollution in East Asia is just beginning, but it is clear that pollutants from China routinely make their way to the neighboring countries of South Korea, Japan, and Vietnam. When China's smog is blown downwind across the Yellow and East China Seas to Korea and Japan, the two countries see and feel the effects. Local media in South Korea have taken to calling the invasive smog from China "air raids." While sources disagree over just how much of Korea's smog is attributable to China, Greenpeace, in a study it completed with Harvard University researchers, suggested a figure of somewhere between 30% and 50%.[5] In Japan, recent research concluded that China is responsible for 40% of Tokyo's annual PM2.5 levels and 60% of Kyushu's.[6] While these numbers should be regarded as tentative, it is evident that China's air is contributing to the pollution over Korea and Japan.

Part of the mix that makes for China's smog is mercury, which is released into the air when coal is combusted. A 2013 study in Japan claimed that China's dirty air moving eastward is responsible for the high level of mercury deposition now found on Mount Fuji.[7] There is worry too that, with rain, the mercury carried in the air from China is falling into the western Pacific Ocean (East China Sea and Yellow Sea), harming the ocean water and marine life. Indeed, a recent study showed that "mercury levels in yellowfin tuna caught in the Pacific Ocean have been rising at a 3.8% annual rate since 1998" and suggested that coal burning in China is to blame.[8]

Sulfur dioxide and nitrogen oxide are also byproducts of fossil fuel combustion, mostly coal combustion. These pollutants, once emitted into the air, can be transported by wind for as much as 1,000 miles; eventually they dissolve into water droplets and fall to Earth as acid rain, damaging forests, soil, water, and fish.

Since the early 1990s studies have linked the acid rain that falls on Korea and Japan to coal plants in China, with estimates of China's contribution to Japan's acid rainfall ranging from 30% to 50%.[9]

In addition to mercury and acid rain, the waters in the western Pacific Ocean bordering Korea and Japan, as well as China, are prone to nitrate spikes, resulting in excessive water pollution, algal blooms, and "dead zones" with low oxygen levels. The spikes arise when nitrogen oxide from fossil fuel burning and ammonia from agricultural runoff enter the seas. While all three countries bear some responsibility, the lion's share is placed on the growing population density and industrial activity along China's eastern seaboard.

There is also the issue of how much China contributes to "mismanaged plastic waste" in the world's oceans. A 2015 report in the journal *Science* found that in 2010 China's coastal population generated more plastic waste than any other coastal population in the world (8.82 million metric tons, or 27.7% of the world's total) and that between 1.32 and 3.53 million metric tons of it ended up as marine debris.[10] A 2014 survey by Japan's Ministry of the Environment, released in June 2015, reported that approximately 80% of the washed-ashore debris in Ishigaki City (in Okinawa) originated in China; of the debris washed ashore on the Sea of Japan side of the country, 20% to 30% came from China.[11]

It is not only countries to the east that are affected by environmental conditions in China: to the southeast, Vietnam also feels their effects. Scientists at the Vietnam Institute of Meteorology, Hydrology, and Climate Change have found that in seven northern provinces bordering China there is considerable cross-border pollution; 52% of the sulfur dioxide, 48% of the nitrogen dioxide, and 30% of the carbon monoxide migrate to these provinces from China.[12] The pollutants are carried largely by the monsoon winds that blow in from the northeast from October through December.

Rivers with headwaters in China that flow through countries in Southeast Asia—the Red, the Black, the Mekong, and the Salween—have "high levels" of heavy metals, organic nutrients, and industrial chemicals, endangering the biodiversity and ecology of these waterways and, crucially, the livelihood of the Southeast Asian people who depend on them.

Additionally, industrial accidents along China's waterways have had occasional consequences for neighboring countries. Perhaps most notoriously, when a chemical plant exploded in Jilin province in 2005 and 100 tons of benzene, aniline, and nitrobenzene spilled into the Songhua River, the Songhua moved the toxins downstream into the Amur River in Russian territory, threatening the water safety of the Russian city of Khabarovsk, with its more than 600,000 residents.

What Are the Implications of China's Transboundary Pollution for Relations with Neighboring Countries?

Relations among countries in the region are already somewhat stressed: a dispute between China and Japan over who owns the Senkaku/Diaoyutai Islands in the East China Sea is ongoing; a quarrel between China and South Korea over maritime borders in the Yellow Sea remains unresolved; Japan's opposition to China's unilateral 2013 declaration of an air defense identification zone continues; and China's continuing efforts to build islands on reefs in the South China Sea, complete with port facilities, airstrips, and military outposts, have angered Vietnam, Malaysia, Taiwan, Brunei, and the Philippines, who have competing territorial claims in the South China Sea, and riled neighboring powers Japan and South Korea. The stream of toxic air and water migrating from China, polluting the air, water, and soil of its neighbors—and the finger pointing that at times comes with it—risks straining relations in the region still further.

A hopeful observer, however, might see China's migrating pollution as a problem capable of fostering better, more constructive diplomatic relations between the three countries. After all, it is a problem that is less political than others, and one that all parties are eager to address. Sitting down at a table to talk about how to cooperate over improving air and water quality might gradually lead to a relaxation of tensions over other more political, more contentious issues. This was a hope expressed by Xie Zhenhua, vice chairman of China's powerful National Development and Reform Commission, in a 2014 meeting with officials from Japan: "Through our cooperation in the environment and energy conservation, I believe we will be able to add positive elements to political relations between the two countries."[13]

It appears from press reports that bilateral and trilateral meetings are, in fact, taking place. In 2014, environmental ministers from China, Japan, and Korea met in South Korea, focusing in particular on the severe PM2.5 plaguing the region. At the conclusion of the two-day meeting they issued a joint statement announcing an agreement on behalf of their three countries to work cooperatively in reducing air pollution and protecting water quality. Importantly, they also agreed to share technologies for cleaning the air.[14] Later in the year, the Japanese press reported that the Japanese Ministry of Environment announced its support of "a China–Japan cooperative urban project" in which 9 Japanese municipalities would provide technical support and guidance to 10 municipalities in China for reducing the emission of pollutants from factories and vehicles.[15] In June 2015 environmental ministers from the three countries met again, in Shanghai, and signed a five-year (2015–2019) action plan in which, according to the Chinese government, "the three countries will conduct research and cooperation on issues such as sandstorms, smog, and maritime pollution."[16]

Does China's Pollution Affect the United States?

Yes, there is a range of consequences, environmental and economic.

Research in this century has shown that pollutants in China's air—sulfates, ozone, mercury, black carbon, and desert dust—can ride the prevailing westerly winds and make their way across the Pacific Ocean to the west coast of the United States in as little as four days. Studies have estimated that of the particulate matter hanging in the air over California, between one-quarter and one-third is from Asia, mostly China; that nearly one-fifth of the mercury deposited in Oregon's Willamette River originates in Asia, again mostly from China; and that 10% to 30% of all mercury deposition in the United States comes from Asia, yet again largely from China.[17]

Additionally, China's air pollution may be affecting weather in the Pacific Ocean and North America. Scientists at NASA's Jet Propulsion Laboratory have begun speculating that the smog particles in China's air mix with the jet stream and are carried to the United States, where they form "cloud nuclei," which, in turn, make for bigger and heavier clouds—and thus bigger and heavier rainstorms and snowstorms.[18]

China's environmental crisis, of course, has consequences for the US economy as well the environment. If, for example, China is serious in weaning itself from dependence on fossil fuel energy, those coal companies in the United States that have pinned their hopes of future growth on the Chinese market (because the US market has shrunk in favor of natural gas) will be disappointed. In 2016, Arch Coal and Peabody Energy filed for bankruptcy, largely as a consequence of the weakening Chinese market. If China's coal consumption continues to decline, other US coal-related companies are sure to feel the effects.

There is a flip side: China's increasing concern with environmental protection also presents opportunities for US businesses. To offer just an example or two: in 2014 IBM was hired by the Beijing environmental protection bureau to develop models and technologies to allow for accurate pollution predictions 10 days in advance. The purpose of this "Green Horizon" initiative is to enable Beijing officials to anticipate "pollution events" better and to determine which strategies might be most effective in dealing with them (e.g., restricting vehicular traffic, suspending outdoor construction, shutting down factories, closing airports and schools). Since then, a number of other Chinese cities have contracted with IBM for similar services, including Zhangjiakou, the co-host with Beijing of the 2022 Winter Olympics. Meanwhile, the environmental protection bureaus in Fujian and Sichuan provinces have turned to Microsoft Corporation to develop tools to predict air quality for their regions. On a lesser scale, Alen Corporation, a small Texas-based company that makes air purifiers, has built a strong Chinese presence in recent years by building and marketing models aimed at the Chinese consumer's worry over PM2.5.

In short, as China transitions from its 30-year-old economic strategy of "pollute first, clean up later" to a strategy of promoting both economic growth and environmental protection, business opportunities are changing. To succeed in China in the 21st century, American businesses will have to be alert to the country's shifting economic and environmental priorities.

US businesses with offices and plants in China are facing another sort of environmental challenge these days, one that is rather more immediate: air pollution there is making it difficult for these businesses to recruit, and retain, workers. The evidence is largely anecdotal but nonetheless compelling. In 2014 National Public Radio was told by three relocation companies in Beijing that more expatriates are now leaving the city than coming—and that the driving reason for the outflow was air quality. In a 2014 survey conducted by the American Chamber of Commerce in China, 48% of 365 companies said they had had trouble recruiting or retaining senior executives to work in China because of air-quality issues; in 2010 that figure was only 19%.[19] One result is that some companies, like Coca-Cola, offer an "environmental hardship allowance" or "hazard pay" (roughly 15% on top of base salary) to compensate their employees in China for simply breathing the country's air.

But, in my view, perhaps the most serious consequence of China's pollution for the US economy is one that is easy to overlook, in part because it is indirect: the pollution crisis has spurred innovation in China. In both the 12th and 13th Five-Year Plans (2011–2015 and 2016–2020) China has placed a high premium on the development of green technology, spelling out its intention to invest heavily in research and development of green technology and in the build-up of green industries (see Chapter 11). The motivation is two-fold: (1) to clean up the country's pervasive pollution and (2) to recast its outdated economy, moving it away from the manufacture of heavily polluting and low-value goods. China's bet is that clean energy and green technology will be the foundation of tomorrow's global economy, and its hope is to become the leader of that economy.

Here, I am reminded of a speech that former US energy secretary Steven Chu gave a number of years ago now, making the point that investing in greener and cleaner technology is not just good energy and environmental policy, but good economic policy as well, and warning the country's leaders that the United States must not stand still and cede the development of green technology and its related industries to the Chinese.[20] Have US political leaders and the business community taken sufficient notice? Where and how do clean energy and green technology fit into the country's overall economic strategy in the 21st century? Is the United States at risk of ceding its economic leadership role in the world?

Does the United States Play a Role in China's Environmental Pollution?

Yes. A team of researchers, in an influential and oft-cited study published in 2013, calculated that 36% of the anthropogenic sulfur dioxide, 27% of the nitrogen oxide, 22% of the carbon monoxide, and 17% of the black carbon that China released into the air came from factories manufacturing goods for export. And of this export-related pollution, 21% was attributable to products that would be exported to the United States. In other words, American consumption of products made in China contributed significantly, roughly 6% to 7%, to the pollution plaguing the country's air. It is an ironic twist that some of that very pollution is picked up by westerly winds over China and carried to the west coast of the United States. Indeed, according to the team of researchers looking at the export trade, China's export-related pollution accounted for as much as 12% to 24% of the sulfate, 2% to 5% of the ozone, 4% to 6% of the carbon monoxide, and 11% of the black carbon particulate over the West Coast of the United States on any given day.[21]

More directly, in the last 20 years, American corporations—Apple, Nike, Starbucks, Pepsi, Coca-Cola, Ford, and others—have been setting up shop or establishing supply chains in China. Labor there is cheaper, environmental laws are laxer, and China and its neighbors represent an attractive and growing market. China and its people have prospered economically from the presence, and investments, of these corporations. Still, their plants and mills—and those of their suppliers—contribute to the pollution in the country's air and water, and the ships that transport their products to the rest of the world pollute the country's port cities and add to China's share of global carbon emissions.

Manufacture of goods for export also contributes to China's greenhouse gas emissions. Having overtaken the United States as the world's leading emitter of carbon dioxide, China today is responsible for up to 30% of the global total. A significant chunk of its emissions (between 16% and 33%) comes from the production of exports,[22] and 5% to 14% (estimates vary widely) comes from the manufacture of goods for export to the United States alone. In 2014 *Forbes* ran an article titled, "Here's One Thing the U.S. Does Export to China: Carbon Dioxide."[23]

The pollution emissions from China's export trade with the United States have led to an interesting debate. Economists, environmentalists, and others are asking: Whose pollution is it? Is it China's (the country of production), or does it belong to the United States (the country of consumption)? As one economist put it:

> Here's the problem: if a Chinese steel mill sells steel to Toyota in Japan, which uses it to make cars sold to Americans, which country is responsible for the steel mill's emissions? America seems like the logical answer; the Chinese emissions happened in order to make something that was bought and used in the United States. Those emissions, however, belong to China in all standard statistics, and in most discussion of climate targets and responsibilities for emission reduction.[24]

Arguments that China bears the responsibility for the pollution—all closely related—include the following:

- Guided by a policy of "pollute first and clean up later" (*xian wuran hou zhili*) for the past 30 years, China has knowingly sacrificed the environment and public health in pursuit of economic growth.
- China is a "sovereign country" that, in the interest of undercutting global competition, has failed to enforce its own laws against violators, be they Chinese companies, MNCs, or "shadow" factories that are part of the extensive MNC supply chains.

- The government has not invested the necessary resources—financial or human—in environmental protection efforts. Because of insufficient funding and staffing, neither the Ministry of Environmental Protection in Beijing nor the local environmental protection bureaus can do their jobs effectively.
- China's trade policies and lax pollution laws have encouraged American companies to move their production to China. Can China, then, turn around and complain that the United States is outsourcing its pollution emissions?

Arguments that the United States, the consuming country, should bear some responsibility for the pollution include the following:

- US consumers want the cheap goods made in China, but China pays for the damage the production of those goods does to the air, water, and soil.
- Don't consumers and consuming countries have a moral responsibility to consider the environmental consequences of the products they consume?
- US companies have leverage with the Chinese factories and plants in their supply chain to enforce compliance ("if you don't, we'll take our business elsewhere") but have not actively exercised it.
- The United States has reduced its greenhouse gas emissions in the past decade in part by exporting them to China. Has the United States really reduced its total contribution to global warming?

This debate over the China-to-United States export trade is a reflection of a general controversy over pollution emissions that has arisen in the recent analytical literature. The standard approach has been to allocate emissions to the country that has produced them, a reasonably straightforward process. But many environmental experts argue that as "emissions embodied in exports" grow, constituting an ever-larger share of global emissions, a more detailed, more accurate "consumption-based" accounting system is in order.[25]

Why Is China Importing Coal?

China's proven coal reserves are second in the world (170 billion tons), surpassed only by those in the United States (237 billion tons). It is an abundant and inexpensive resource and has long been a major export. China's coal exports peaked in 2003 at 94 million tons; imports that year amounted to 11 million tons. Yet, only six years later, in 2009, the balance had changed: China had become a net importer of coal for the first time, bringing in 126 million tons from abroad. And, by 2011, it had become the world's largest coal importer. What accounts for this 21st-century shift from net exporter to net importer—in a country with its own vast domestic resources? There are a number of factors to consider.

Most obviously, industrialization has skyrocketed in the 21st century, especially with China's entry into the WTO. Powering that industrialization has been coal, supplying up to 70% of the country's total energy mix. Taking into account that its economy has been growing nearly 10% annually until 2014 and that its energy consumption nearly tripled between 2001 and 2011, China is drawing on its reserves more conservatively and budgeting for the long term.

Another consideration is the inefficiency and high cost of transporting coal in China from where it is mined to where it is needed. The majority of the country's coal resources are found in the western and northern provinces of Shanxi, Shaanxi, and Inner Mongolia, but the coal is consumed in the urban and industrial centers in eastern China and along the southeastern coast. As coal consumption has increased since 2001, the strain on the transportation infrastructure has also risen. Railways and roads have simply not been able to keep pace with the growing coal-mining industry, so shipping coal in from nearby countries like Indonesia and Australia has been an attractive option, more efficient and economical than dealing with the domestic transportation bottlenecks.

The location of coal reserves in the west and the north poses another serious environmental challenge, because these are the regions of China that are most arid and the most water-stressed. Mining coal, as we have seen, is a water-intensive process; the more extraction and washing that is done, the less water there is for agriculture and drinking. By importing coal from other countries, the state can shut down small, inefficient, and highly polluting coal mines in the west and north and thereby offer some relief from the water stress there. Other environmental benefits accrue as well, including reduced water and soil pollution, lower levels of particulate matter, and less severe acid rain.

The country's largest foreign suppliers of coal by far are Indonesia and Australia, which make up almost 60% of the import market. Most of the coal from Indonesia is steam coal, used for power generation, while the coal from Australia is coking coal, a coal with fewer impurities, used in iron and steel production. China's neighboring countries, Vietnam and Mongolia, are the next largest suppliers. The United States is also a supplier, but it is small by comparison, providing only 3% of the total (5 million tons)—though American companies, of course, would like to see that share increase.

But, as China moves away from its dependence on coal and builds up its wind, solar, hydroelectric, and nuclear energy resources, coal imports will decline, and coal-exporting countries will feel the effects of reduced demand and reduced prices on their economies. Already, in 2015, China's coal imports were down a whopping 30% year-over-year; both Indonesia and Australia, two heavy coal-producing, coal-exporting countries, saw their exports to China drop a corresponding 30%. Neither country is expressing optimism about a turnaround any time soon.

Why Is China Building Coal-Fired Power Plants Abroad?

At a time when China is cutting back on its coal-producing capacity, shuttering hundreds of coal mines and suspending approval of new ones for a few years, a review of public documents by the *New York Times* revealed that Chinese state engineering firms have built, or have reached agreements to build, 14 coal-fired power plants along the Vietnamese coast. Loans from the state's China Export–Import Bank are subsidizing the ventures. The article went on to claim that since 2010 Chinese state enterprises have built, begun to build, or reported plans to build 92 coal-fired power plants in 27 countries, mostly in the developing regions of Asia, Africa, and South America.[26]

What explains this building spree? With domestic demand for coal falling, as a result of a slowing economy coupled with a determination to lessen dependence on the dirty fossil fuel for energy, the building of coal-fired power plants is tailing off in China. As a consequence, many state-owned engineering firms are out of work and are being encouraged by the government to pursue power-generation projects in foreign countries.[27] Because of their financial distress, these firms are offering, in the words of one energy consultant, "bargain basement prices," which developing countries eager for cheap sources of energy find hard to resist. So, while China is intent on reducing emissions of pollutants and greenhouse gases at home, it is facilitating the emissions of pollutants and greenhouse gases in countries around the world. Today, Chinese banks and companies are involved in 79 coal-fired power projects outside of China, with a total capacity of 52 megawatts.[28]

Part III

RESPONDING TO ENVIRONMENTAL POLLUTION

10

POLLUTION AND THE PUBLIC RESPONSE

What Are the Public's Sources of Environmental Information?

Environmental information is more widely available than ever, from an increasingly wide range of sources.

News Media

The state-operated television network, CCTV, and state-directed news outlets, like *Xinhua*, the *People's Daily*, *China Daily*, *China Youth Daily*, and the *Global Times*, routinely run stories about China's environment. Television stations throughout the country have programming dedicated to the environment (e.g., China Educational TV's *Environmental Focus* and Jiangsu TV's *Green Report*).

The *Southern Weekly* (南方周末 *Nanfang Zhoumo*), published by the Nanfang Media group, has had a strong history of watchdog journalism, reporting on everything environmental: industrial pollution, urban sewage, soil pollution, agricultural runoff, contaminated water supplies, Apple's suppliers operating in violation of the law, and so on. However, censorship of the paper since 2013 has compromised its coverage.[1] Caixin (财新), a Beijing-based media group founded in 2010 and led by the much-respected Hu Shuli, publishes periodicals, online content, mobile apps, and television programs focused on financial and business news and reports widely on stories at the nexus of the economy and the environment.[2]

Official Information

While the state does not disclose environmental information as fully and transparently as the 2008 "Measures on Open Environmental Information" (see Chapter 11) might require—and some environmentalists might like—the Ministry of Environmental Protection does publish an annual "Report on the State of the Environment." The ministry and other government agencies also publish periodic reports on issues they deem timely. For example, in 2014, the ministry's website reported the results of a seven-year land survey completed in 2013, which showed that 16% of China's total land area, and 20% of the arable land, is contaminated with heavy metals. In 2013 China's "First National Census of Water" revealed that, during the previous 20 years, of the 50,000 rivers with a flow area of 60 square miles, 28,000 could no longer be found. In the same year, the Guangzhou Food and Drug Administration announced that 44% of the rice samples it had taken from around the city were contaminated with dangerously high levels of cadmium.[3]

Importantly, the Chinese government compiles a yearly database, the China Statistical Yearbooks Database, which brings together statistics and information from hundreds of important statistical yearbooks published by mainland presses. The database covers a wide variety of environmental, economic, and social topics. It is fair to assume that while it comprises a great deal of up-to-date and useful environmental information, it is not a resource that the general public customarily consults.

Social Media

With over 7 million internet users, China's microblogs like Sina Weibo, Tencent Weibo, and Renren and text-messaging services like WeChat are popular platforms for sharing information and for conducting wide-ranging discussions relating to the environment.[4]

Mobile Apps

China is home to 1.3 billion mobile phones. Apps like China Air Quality Index (AQI) monitor the air quality in cities around the country, reporting the levels of ozone, sulfur dioxide, nitrogen dioxide, carbon monoxide, and particulate matter (2.5 and 10) in real time. An app produced by the Institute of Public and Environmental Affairs has maps that display the names and locations of industries in violation of the country's air-pollution and water-pollution standards (see below).

Nongovernmental Organizations

Environmental nongovernmental organizations (NGOs) like Friends of Nature and Global Village of Beijing first emerged in China in the 1990s. The goals of most of these NGOs were similar: to inform the public about environmental issues. And while that continues to be a central interest, NGOs have become more active in promoting agendas. Take the mission statement of the Global Village of Beijing, for example:

> Founded in 1996, GVB's mission is to promote a sustainable development model in China by raising awareness and creating an environmentally conscious culture. GVB's focus areas include theories and practices of green consumption, green community development, ecological remedy and conservation, and youth environmental education and exchange.

For more on NGOs, see below.

What Role Have Social Media Outlets Played in Engaging the Public in Environmental Issues?

Social media outlets have been instrumental in promoting environmental awareness among the Chinese public. They have served, often simultaneously, to spread environmental information widely, to invite public participation in protection of the environment, and to organize environmentally related protests.

It was through the US Embassy twitter feed, @Beijingair, for instance, that Beijing's PM2.5 levels were first brought to the public's attention. In 2008 the embassy installed an air-quality monitor on its rooftop and tweeted readings hourly. Chinese citizens who consulted the embassy's tweets found a considerable discrepancy in the air quality reported there and the air quality reported by the Chinese government. They were quick to understand why: the embassy's readings included data for PM2.5 and the Chinese readings did not. A call on Sina Weibo for the Beijing government to measure PM2.5, and to report it publicly, grew.

The government resisted. In fact, in 2009 officials in the Chinese Ministry of Foreign Affairs met with officials in the US State Department to protest the embassy's tweeting of the PM2.5 readings, claiming that the discrepancy was causing "undesirable 'social consequences' among the Chinese public." Still, awareness was escalating. What happened next, in 2011, is fascinating for the initiative it showed. An NGO, Green Beagle, purchased its own PM2.5 monitoring device and loaned it out to concerned people throughout the city. These volunteers would take measurements and send the data back to Green Beagle, which would then post them online. NGOs in other cities, like Green Hunan and Friends of Nature Wuhan, followed suit.[5] A more accurate perception of air quality in China was gradually taking root. So, too perhaps, was the view that citizens had the right to know how air pollution might be affecting their lives.

At this point, Chinese celebrities with millions of followers on Weibo, people like real-estate mogul Pan Shiyi, children's author Zheng Yuanjie, and entrepreneur Xue Manzi, began posting PM2.5 readings on their Twitter feeds as well as information about the health effects of PM2.5. Their followers then reposted the tweets.

Pressure continued to build, and on January 6, 2012, the Beijing government announced it would begin monitoring PM2.5 levels in the city and reporting them publicly. Today, most Chinese cities are monitoring their PM2.5 levels and publishing them hourly online. And today PM2.5 is a household term; in fact, it was #3 on the list of most popular memes in the country in 2013.

Microblogging has made it possible for activists to rally public participation to their causes and to bring more national attention to them. In 2013, for instance, Chinese environmental activist Deng Fei posted this question to his 4 million followers: "How is the river in your hometown?" He added this request: "While you're home for the holidays, take a photo of the river and stream in your hometown and upload it to Weibo for us to see." The message was retweeted by other popular Weibo users, and within a few days thousands of people had responded with pictures of rivers and streams, making Deng Fei's tweet one of Sina Weibo's "trending topics."

Charles Custer, an astute China observer, commented at the time:

> What's interesting about this is not so much that some Chinese rivers are full of trash—this should not come as a great shock to anyone—but that it is a clever way of making a local issue into a national one. Sina Weibo has been fertile ground for this . . . While one river being full of trash is a local problem, *everyone's* rivers being full of trash might point to a larger problem (italics are his).[6]

A few months later, a *Financial Times* report commented that Deng Fei's call for photos—and the massive response—had "prompted a series of press articles and shamed several local governments into cleaning up their waterways."[7]

In another case, on January 4, 2015, a netizen in the southwest municipality of Chongqing took a picture of Yangtze River water "thick with excrement" flowing under the Egongyan Bridge and uploaded it to Sina Weibo. Untreated septic waste was being dumped upstream into the river from a 16-foot-wide outfall. The picture went viral, as did the public outrage. Posts lambasted local officials for their inaction. A day later, the *China Daily* reported that "local authorities have removed the pollution source and vowed to punish the company responsible."[8]

Wang Chunsheng, who won the "best citizen journalist" award at the 2014 China Environmental Press Awards, began blogging (@VegetableVillageSword) in 2011 to spread the word about soil pollution in his hometown in Shandong province. The blog invited local residents to question how local crops were being grown—that is, were toxic pesticides and fertilizers being used, was the soil in which the crops were grown contaminated, was the irrigation water free of toxins, and so on.[9]

Social media outlets have also been an especially powerful tool in bringing people together, on short notice, to take to the streets in the name of environmental causes. One of the country's earliest environmental protests (May–June 2007) provides as clear an illustration as any of the potential of social media to mobilize people quickly. Upon being informed that a chemical plant producing paraxylene (PX), a benzene-based chemical used in plastic bottles and polyester, would be built outside the city of Xiamen in the southeastern province of Fujian, a (still unknown) netizen began circulating a message from his cell phone saying that building the plant would be like "setting off an atomic bomb in all of Xiamen," and pleading, "For our children and grandchildren act! Participate among 10,000 people, June 1 at 8am, opposite the municipal government building! Hand tie yellow ribbons! SMS all your Xiamen friends." It is estimated that the message was sent and re-sent more than 1 million times. At the appointed time, 10,000 to 20,000 citizens gathered at the municipal government building and began their "stroll" (散步 *sanbu*) through the city. Participants sent text messages and photos from their cell phones to bloggers in other parts of the country, who posted real-time reports, so that news of the PX protest in Xiamen spread everywhere. A year of mediation ensued, and the government's decision to build the plant in Xiamen was rescinded (though the plant would eventually be built elsewhere).[10]

In 2012, Chang Cheng, a prominent environmentalist, wrote: "'Xiamen PX' marked the dawning of a new savvy among the wider public," adding that "the rise of social media in the last decade has given China's citizens the tools with which to organize."[11] Later that year, an editor for Greenpeace in Beijing, referring to a string of recent environmental protests, echoed Chang's sentiments:

> These demonstrations represent a new grassroots force made possible by social media tools such as Weibo (China's Twitter), the messenger service QQ and online forums. These protests can be characterized by how swiftly they are organized and the way they happen outside more formal structures such as unions, NGOs or political parties.[12]

Deng Fei, the activist who asked followers to post photos of their hometown streams and rivers on Weibo, put it still more simply: "Chinese people were like shattered glass before we had Weibo. There was no way to unite."[13]

How Widespread Is Public Environmental Awareness?

There is no way to gauge the degree of environmental awareness with any precision. But, if social media attention, the proliferation of environmental NGOs, and the results of various polls are any indication, environmental awareness in China is gaining considerable momentum.

When asked by a Gallup pollster in 2011 whether "protection of the environment should be given priority, even at the risk of curbing economic growth," 57% of the respondents agreed. Asked whether "economic growth should be given priority, even if the environment suffers to some extent," only 21% agreed.[14] Similarly, a 2014 Jiaotong University survey of urban Chinese found that 60% favored environmental protection over economic growth; 72% of respondents said they had reduced their outdoor activities.[15] And when the PEW survey in 2015 asked Chinese people what their top concerns were, air pollution and water pollution ranked second highest, just after official corruption, and ahead of wealth inequality, crime, health care, unemployment, and other concerns. In 2014, the research agency Motivaction interviewed 48,000 people in 20 countries about their values and behaviors and found that while 64% of Chinese people identify themselves as environmentalists, only 30% of Europeans and Americans do.[16] Finally, a 2016 survey commissioned by the China Renewable Energy Industries Association found that in the 10 cities it covered, more than 90% of the subjects were willing to pay higher bills for green electricity produced from renewable sources like wind, solar, and biomass.[17] So while there are no precise measures of environmental awareness in China, it is clear that people generally have become more concerned about the country's environmental conditions.

Another indication: on February 28, 2015, the documentary *Under the Dome*, produced and narrated by investigative reporter Chai Jing, was posted online on the *People's Daily* website. For 104 minutes she walks to and fro, TED Talks style, in front of a large screen, weaving graphs, statistics, vivid photographs, interviews, and personal stories into an arresting narrative of China's pollution crisis. The audience hears that:

- Coal and cars are the main sources of pollution.
- At least 500,000 Chinese people die prematurely from cardiovascular and cardiorespiratory disease every year.
- The country has abundant environmental regulations, but enforcement is weak to nonexistent.
- The Ministry of Environmental Protection is sorely understaffed and underresourced.
- Local officials throughout the country often turn a blind eye to polluting industries.
- The powerful oil and gas industries—mostly state-owned—resist raising fuel standards as the higher costs of production, they fear, will fall on them.[18]

To say the documentary went viral is an understatement. Before the government called for its deletion from all social media on March 6, it had attracted some 200 million to 300 million viewers. Such a massive audience speaks to the deepening interest of the Chinese public in learning about the state of the country's environment; at the same time, it no doubt did much to engender still greater awareness.

While environmental awareness in China is certainly growing, we can assume that it is not by any means uniform across all sectors of the population. For instance, it is thought that urbanites, the middle class, and the more highly educated are generally more knowledgeable about environmental issues than rural dwellers, the poor, and the uneducated. Here, we await sound statistical research.

Also, environmental awareness is selective and tends to be most acute over domestic and local issues such as drinking water, sanitation, indoor pollution, air pollution, and water pollution. Studies find that more national issues, like deforestation, desertification, and acid rain, invite less interest. An article summarizing available Chinese-language surveys of Chinese attitudes toward the environment concludes that "The vast majority of Chinese are concerned about their domestic home environment and perhaps their neighborhood but not the surrounding area, often even their immediate surroundings. In short, the Chinese people say that they care about problems that affect them directly in space and time."[19]

As the Public Learns More, How Have They Responded?

Self-Protection

They have taken steps to protect themselves and their families from the harmful consequences of pollution. Consider the face mask. As people have come to learn that what is in the air is not simply "fog" (as the government and state media once insisted) but instead is smog filled with particulates that can wreak havoc on the human respiratory system, face masks have become a common sight in China. In a survey of 3,000 internet users in 2015, 83% of the respondents said they owned face masks. Face masks of all variety, quality, and costs—from paper masks to cotton masks to canister-style respirators—can be purchased at online retailers and in stores everywhere. Even high-end fashion designers have jumped into the game: Masha May created a face mask covered in Swarovski crystals for Paris Fashion Week in 2014; Nina Griffee showed a line of masks for pairing with evening gowns during the 2014 Hong Kong Fashion week; and Yin Peng has designed running gear with chic mouth covers.

But since indoor air may be no better than the air outdoors, middle-class urbanites have been buying up room air filters for their apartments (at $500 and higher) and filtration systems for their homes. One million air purifiers were sold in China in 2010; by 2015, the figure had quadrupled to over 4 million.

The *Lancet* recently reported that room air filters capable of filtering out 95% of PM2.5 have been developed; still more recently, the *South China Morning Post* reported on a new air filter made of soya bean protein that is 99.94% effective.[20] (For those interested in a robotic air purifier that seeks out and sucks up air pollutants, the Atmobot A630 is now available for just over $1,000.) When choosing schools for their children, many Chinese are tempted by those equipped with air-filtration bubbles over the playground area—though their exorbitant tuition costs put them out of the reach of most.

Inexpensive and portable PM2.5 meters that monitor indoor and outdoor air (the Laser Egg may be the best known) are widely available. They alert people to turn on their air-filtration systems when the indoor air is bad or to shut the windows when the outdoor air is bad. These devices, and mobile AQI apps, also help people to schedule their day—to decide, for example, whether the air quality is "safe" for outdoor exercise, to take an outing with a child, or even just to run a simple errand. And when they do head out, with these gizmos in hand they can decide which restaurant, this one or the one across the street, is a healthier space to take a break for food. When the food is served, they might pull out a pair of *Baidu kuaisou* (to be sure, still a novelty item), smart chopsticks that detect with a sensor whether the food was cooked in contaminated gutter oil.

Eating in their homes, they can steer clear of contaminated food by buying organically grown products or by becoming members of an ever-greater number of community-supported agriculture farms. And (carefully selected) bottled water provides some confidence that the water they drink and cook with is uncontaminated.

During spells of "airpocalyptic" air, the Chinese people have begun turning to international travel for relief. In December 2016, as PM2.5 readings rose to hazardous levels, an estimated 150,000 "smog refugees" headed abroad to relatively nearby places like Australia, Indonesia, Japan, and the Maldives to escape the assault, according to Ctrip, the China's largest online travel agent.

The ultimate protective measure some take is to emigrate, either to less polluted regions in the country or to countries abroad. In 2012–2013, nine million Chinese sought residency elsewhere. Many factors account for this number, but environmental quality is certainly one of them.

To underscore the obvious here: these measures are not equally available to all people. Those of means can "buy" protection against some of the threats to human health posed by pollution. But the less well-off, and the rural Chinese especially, cannot hope to clean their indoor air with expensive filtration systems, purchase organic food, escape to foreign countries, or use bottled water rather than drinking water from the tap or a local waterway.

Calls for Transparency

The Chinese people have called on the government to be more transparent and to disclose more fully to its citizens environmentally related information and data. As we have seen, in 2011 it was social media pressure for more reliable PM2.5 readings in Beijing that resulted in Beijing's decision in 2012 to monitor and publicly report hourly figures, not only for the capital but for cities throughout the country. (Today, there are more than 1,500 AQI monitoring stations in China.)

As early as 2008, the Ministry of Environmental Protection made promises to disclose environmental information to its citizens in the "Measures on Open Environmental information." Chapter I, Article 3 states, "the environmental protection department of local people's governments at the county level and above shall be responsible for organizing, coordinating and supervising open environmental information work within their respective administrative areas." Article 5 of the same chapter adds, "Citizens, legal persons and other organizations may request environmental protection departments to obtain government environmental information." Studies since 2010 have shown that the government, nonetheless, routinely fails to comply with the transparency requirements, often invoking the "state secret" article in the "Measures" (Chapter II, Article 12): "Environmental protection departments may not disclose government environmental information that involves state secrets, trade secrets, or individual privacy." The problem, of course, is that no definition of what constitutes a "state secret" is outlined in the document.[21]

Thus, in January 2013, when lawyer Dong Zhengwei requested the results of a multiyear nationwide soil-pollution survey completed by the national government in 2010, he was denied on the grounds that they were a "state secret." Dong responded defiantly: citing the "Measures," he called the refusal a "clear denial of the public's right to know and right to monitor." Standing his ground, Dong appealed. As pressure from the public and from the media mounted the government relented and released the sobering information in April 2014.

NGOs like the Beijing-based Institute of Public and Environmental Affairs have worked to promote greater transparency. Beginning in 2009, a year after the "Measures" were put into effect, the institute, in collaboration with the Beijing office of the National Resources Defense Council, an American NGO, has tracked how well 113 cities have complied with the pollution-disclosure requirements, publishing the findings annually in the Pollution Information Transparency Index. Compliance thus far has been rather low, but figures have improved each year since 2009.[22]

Public Participation

Increasingly aware of the harmful effects that environmental pollution can have on human health, the public has become more insistent about having its voice heard in the environmental impact assessments of local projects. The public was first granted the right to participate in environmental impact assessments in 2003, in Article 11 under the "Environmental Impact Assessment Law of the People's Republic of China":

> In the case of a plan that may cause adverse effects on the environment or may have a direct bearing on the rights and interests of the public in respect of the environment, the authority that draws up the plan shall, before submitting the draft of the plan for examination and approval, hold demonstration meetings or hearings, or solicit in other forms the comments and suggestions from the relevant units, specialists and the public on the draft report on environmental effects, except where secrets need to be guarded as required by State regulations.[23]

Studies, however, have shown that consultation with the public, as required by this law, occurred infrequently, at best.[24]

Observers agree that the spread of environmental protests in the past few years reflects not only the public's anxiety over the threat that pollution poses to their health, but also the growing anger they feel over their marginalization in the environmental impact assessment process. Having no effective, legitimate venue for voicing their views, they take their views to the street instead (on protests, see below). As Ma Tianjie, now managing editor of *ChinaDialogue*, said in 2012 after the protests in Shifang (Sichuan) over plans to build a copper alloy plant, "In Shifang and other recent environmental protests we're not simply seeing demands that a project close down or move away, but calls for openness, transparency and participation."[25]

Dark Humor

The public has resorted to dark humor in responding to the pollution (Figure 10.1). As one example, in late 2012 celebrity millionaire and publicity hound Chen Guangbiao started selling, for 80 cents apiece, fresh air in soda cans, in atmospheric

Figure 10.1 Even the stone monkeys at the Beijing Zoo were seen wearing face masks on this smoggy day in December 2016

flavors like "pristine Tibet," "revolutionary Yan'an," and "post-industrial Taiwan." According to Chen (who has been known to exaggerate) more than 10 million cans were sold in January 2013 alone, when the infamous "airpocalypse" enveloped Beijing.

Two years later, returning from a business trip to Provence, France, Beijing artist Liang Kegang brought with him a small glass jar of clean Provence air. He put the jar up for auction before a group of 100 artists and collectors, where it sold for $860, garnering the jar of air—and Liang—national and global attention.

On social media, needless to say, humor lampooning the pollution is frequent. When, for instance, the story of cadmium-laden rice broke in 2013, one netizen posted on Weibo: "By the time we finish eating rice from around the country, we'll probably have the entire periodic table in our systems."

Pollution humor even makes its way into marketing. Jing-A Brewery in Beijing recently began selling an Airpocalypse IPA, an unfiltered beer that the owners describe as particularly "hazy," and which they discount more deeply as the

PM2.5 levels in the city rise. A Facebook post from December 2015 read:

> You asked for it, and we're gonna give it to you! Considering this week is the first ever Red Alert for pollution in Beijing, we're offering you some extra relief from the smog by lifting the cap on our Airpocalypse discount for the rest of December—20% off at 200 AQI, and an extra 10% off for every additional 100 points on the US Embassy's scale. Yes, that means FREE BEER if the AQI passes over 1000 and we don't all drop dead!

If drinking Airpocalypse IPA, especially free of charge, is not enough to make a dark day brighter, perhaps leaving the city behind will, and travel agencies make that convenient. Since 2014 they have been promoting "lung-washing tours," known also as "smog-escaping tours." For those interested in booking one, the *Financial Times* reports that the hot lung-washing destinations these days are Sanya on Hainan Island, Lhasa in Tibet, and Zhoushan in the East China Sea.[26]

What Explains the Frequency of Environmental Protests in the 21st Century?

Yang Chaofei, vice-chair of the Chinese Society for Environmental Sciences, estimates that since 1996 the number of environmental protests in China has increased on average 29% annually.[27] In 2011 alone, there was an increase of 120%. Until recently, these protests have occurred mostly in the countryside, among angry, impoverished peasants. But the past decade has seen a shift, as cities have become the scene of more and more environmental protests.

A few factors taken together help account for the increasing frequency of protests. As noted above, social media outlets like Sina Weibo, Renren, and WeChat enable widespread dissemination of information about environmental conditions that simply was not readily available to the public previously. Graphic photographs of air, water, and soil pollution posted on social media can leave a powerful impression, bringing home to people the severity of China's pollution. And, of course, social media outlets make possible the almost instantaneous assembling of protestors.

The heightened visibility of the pollution itself has intensified people's awareness and anxiety. Pollution can become deeply disquieting when people see with their own eyes the thick, soupy concoction that makes daytime night and shuts down roads, schools, and airports; or bright green algal blooms that make water undrinkable and turn fish-rich areas into dead zones; or pig carcasses bobbing up and down in a river that provides a bustling city with drinking water; or crops turning black in the ground from toxins in the water and soil.

Knowledge of the effects of pollution on human health makes people more personally invested. When, for example, "smog" was just "fog," and an irritant to the throat, nose, and eyes, the public found it inconvenient and unpleasant, but their tolerance was higher. However, once "fog" became PM2.5, and once it was shown that PM2.5 could lead to death and reduce life expectancy by more than five years, dirty air became a far more personal affront requiring urgent action. As Ma Jun told a reporter in February 2017, "The public's tolerance and patience is running out and anxiety is growing because they've now acquired more understanding of the hazardous impact of smog."[28]

With the growing prosperity of the past three decades, the average income in China has quadrupled. The middle class is growing, with economists estimating that 300 million Chinese are now earning middle incomes. Even as this middle class, with its greater discretionary income, consumes more and so contributes heavily to the country's environmental problems—just as the middle class in the United States and Europe does—it has at the same begun to take serious measure of quality-of-life issues. Increasingly, people are demanding that the government take responsibility for ensuring not only material prosperity, but blue skies, clean water, and safe food as well.

It is also important to keep in mind that participation in protests over the environment, in general, does not carry the same risk as participation in protests over more politically sensitive issues might. After all, the Beijing government itself has made environmental protection a high priority, proclaiming that a transition from "industrial civilization" to ecological civilization" is now in order, and even vowing to fight a "war on pollution" and requesting the public's support in that war. Additionally, with the promulgation of the Environmental Impact Assessment law, the government—on paper at least—has invited greater public involvement in environmental protection. Thus, the environment is viewed by many Chinese as a relatively "safe space" for civil society to express its views, so long as that expression remains peaceful and orderly and does not pose a challenge to the Communist Party's political authority. Indeed, protests in the name of environmental protection are commonly framed by participants as demonstrations that share—and advance—the values and goals of the regime itself.[29]

Consider, too, that "successful" protests breed more protests. The apparent success of the Xiamen protest in 2007 against the building of the PX plant gained tremendous notoriety through social media (Figure 10.2). That the Xiamen municipal government and the Fuzhou provincial government relented in the face of the "stroll" has done much to inspire environmental protests elsewhere, especially in opposition to the building of PX plants. Since Xiamen, anti-PX street protests have occurred in Chengdu (2008); Dalian (2011); Ningbo (2012); Kunming (2013); Maoming (2014); Jinshan (2015), which attracted between 40,000 and 50,000 protestors at its height; and Longkou in Shandong (2016). The role that successful protests have played in inspiring further protests, the "Xiamen effect," is

Figure 10.2 Protesting a proposed PX plant in Jinshan, a suburb of Shanghai, in 2015

suggested in a comment made by one Maoming protestor in 2014:

> I heard that they tried to build PX plants in Xiamen, Dalian, and Ningbo, and all were stopped after public protests. The Maoming PX plant was driven out of those places. The government intends to kill Maoming people, as if lives in other cities are more valuable and the health of people in Maoming has to suffer. If the PX plant is not toxic, as the government says, it should be built someplace else. If the PX plant can be successfully removed from Xiamen, Maoming people can do the same.[30]

What Is It That People Protest?

Proposals to build PX plants have probably been the most common target since 2007, but they are certainly not the only target. Recent years have seen notable street protests—some turning violent—over the following:

- The building of waste-incineration plants (e.g., Boluo county in Guangdong, 2014; Hangzhou, 2014; Wuxi, 2014; Luoding county in Guangdong, 2015; Xiantao in Hubei, 2016)
- The building of copper-alloy–processing plants (e.g., Shifang, Sichuan, 2012)
- The building of coal-fired power plants or expanding already existing plants (e.g., Hainan Island, 2012; Heyuan in Guangdong, 2015)
- The building of pipelines carrying toxic wastewater into the sea (e.g., Qidong in Jiangsu, 2012)
- Iron and steel plants thought to be carcinogenic (e.g., Gegu township in Tianjin, 2015)
- Industrial parks thought to be poisoning local land and water (Huaxi, 2005; Leping in Jiangxi, 2015)
- The building of nuclear power plants (Shengli in Anhui, 2012; Jiangmen in Guangdong province, 2013)
- Solar plants thought to be polluting (e.g., Haining city in Zhejiang, 2011)

What environmental protests in China have had in common to date is that they have been localized, meaning that participants have been locals, neighbors of the project or proposed project, anxious about the direct consequences the project might have for them (i.e., their physical and economic well-being). These are essentially the NIMBY (not in my backyard) protests familiar to us in the West. The Chinese themselves use the term *linbi* (鄰避), meaning "avoid the neighborhood," to describe them.

As different as the protests may be in their particulars, their etiology follows a similar pattern. Local officials, eager to boost the local economy, attract some revenue-generating project to the region. Word gets out to the local populace that a plant will soon be built, or perhaps one day a construction site suddenly springs up. Little or no consultation with the affected public over the environmental impact of the project has likely occurred. Talk and rumors now spread among the public, aided by social media. Anger and frustration grow: why haven't they been involved in the impact assessment process, as required by the national law? At this point the local community and local officials can find themselves at loggerheads that may result in public protest. As Li Ganjie, current minister of the Ministry of Environment Protection, acknowledged in 2014 (when he was still vice minister): "If the public doesn't participate in the process, and is unable to get explanations and timely answers to their questions, this generates mistrust and suspicion."[31]

How Effective Are the Environmental Protests?

As Minister Li's comment suggests, the protests have been effective in drawing attention to the government's failure to ensure public participation in environmental impact assessment. In fact, in 2015, in response to public pressure, the ministry issued an updated and expanded "Measures on Public Participation in Environmental Protection." Whether the updated "Measures" will be any better implemented or better enforced than the original set, of course, is still a question.

Environmental protests have often achieved their immediate aim of shuttering a polluting factory or prohibiting the construction of a PX plant or a wastewater pipeline. However, that's not always the end of the story: there is nothing preventing the proposed or displaced plant from being relocated in a nearby town or city, one on a lower rung of the socioeconomic ladder and with fewer resources to mount effective opposition. That is, an inherent limitation of the country's environmental protests has been their localized aims. When, for example, the now-famous Xiamen stroll put a stop to the building of a PX plant, the plant was simply relocated and built at Gulei in neighboring Zhangzhou prefecture. (This plant suffered a massive explosion, injuring 14, in April 2015.)

The victories can also be ephemeral. For instance, the Dalian protest succeeded in closing down the local PX plant in August

2011, but it reopened in December, when the media glare had died down.

But whatever the limitations of the protests, they represent the efforts of a burgeoning civil society eager to play a role in shaping the country's environmental future. And the fact that the public has become demonstrably engaged environmentally over the past decade has lent added urgency to the national discussion over how best to balance economic growth and environmental protection.

Are There Environmental NGOs in China?

In 1991 China's first environmental NGO, the Society for Protecting Black-Beaked Gulls, was founded in Liaoning province in the northeast. Three years later, Liang Congjie (1932–2010), the grandson of Liang Qichao (1873–1929), a prominent scholar and political reformer, and the son of Liang Sicheng (1901–1972), an architect often called "the father of modern Chinese architecture," together with three of his colleagues at the Academy for Chinese Culture, established Friends of Nature. Liang's pedigree, intelligence, and political sensibility gave Friends of Nature stature and heft and helped win the support and cooperation of the Chinese government. The organization's early efforts were dedicated to protecting the endangered Tibetan antelope and conserving the habitat of the snub-nosed monkey in Yunnan province in the southwest. Friends of Nature remains one of the most influential and active of China's environmental NGOs.[32]

Ma Jun, director of the Institute for Public and Environmental Affairs (see below), credits Liang Congjie with having "incubated the first generation of environmentalists in China."[33] Friends of Nature nurtured the development of many of the grassroots environmental organizations throughout the country. By 2005 there were estimated to be 2,700 registered environmental NGOs, and today, there are approximately 7,000, a far cry from the 1990s. And these numbers include only those organizations that have applied for formal NGO status, a cumbersome process that requires an organization to gain the sponsorship of a government agency—a real obstacle, as most governmental departments are reluctant to take on the responsibility. Consequently, many environmental organizations forgo the licensing process and instead register as nonprofit businesses, a much simpler process. It is estimated that there are as many environmental organizations operating as nonprofit businesses as there are registered NGOs.

Finally, there exist in China the bizarrely named "government-organized nongovernmental organizations," or GONGOs. GONGOs were environmental organizations established by government agencies themselves, beginning in the 1980s. Two of the largest and best known are the All-China Environment Federation and the China Environmental Protection Foundation. Analysts seem to agree that these GONGOs, which are organized and funded from the top down, were created in part to provide jobs for retired staff at the government agencies and to attract funding, especially from international organizations eager to promote the spread of civil society and NGOs in China. Over the years, as independent NGOs have grown in number, and as they have cultivated closer relationships with the government, the number and importance of GONGOs have declined.

Well-known and active Chinese NGOs today, in addition to Friends of Nature (Beijing), include the Center for Legal Assistance to Pollution Victims (Beijing), Global Village of Beijing, Green Beagle (Beijing), Green Camel Bell (Gansu), Green Earth Volunteers (Beijing), Green Han River (Hubei), Green Volunteer League of Chongqing, Green Watershed (Yunnan), Huai River Guardians (Henan), Sichuan Greenriver Environment Protection Promotion Association, and Xiamen Green Cross Association. The full-time staff at most of these NGOs is less than 10 (owing partly to lack of funding), though Friends of Nature has as many as 20.

What Are Some of the Activities of the NGOs?

These NGOs, and others, support a wide range of activities, as listed in their mission statements, such as:

- Environmental education
- Species and nature conservation
- Energy conservation
- River, lake, and ocean cleanup and protection
- Pollution monitoring
- Pollution impact assessment
- Uncovering pollution violations
- Environmental accidents monitoring
- Advice and legal support for victims of pollution
- Environmental law development
- Trash cleanup and recycling
- Tree planting
- Sustainable development

NGOs have been especially important in recent years in focusing the public's and state's attention on the plight of the country's cancer villages. NGOs like Green Anhui, Chongqing Green Volunteer League, Guardians of the Huai River, and the Center for Legal Assistance of Pollution Victims have worked (1) to gather evidence showing causal links between polluting factories and local cancers, (2) to engage the media in publicizing the existence of these villages, and (3) to provide legal assistance to cancer victims. *The Warriors of Qiugang: A Village Fights Back,*[34] a riveting documentary, tells the story of how residents of the hamlet of Qiugang, together with the NGO Green Anhui, waged a five-year battle to curb pollution from the local chemical factories.

Of China's environmental NGOs, the Beijing-based Institute for Public and Environmental Affairs has a particularly high profile these days. In part, it is because its director, Ma Jun, is widely respected; he was named by *Time* magazine in 2006 as one of the 100 most influential people in the world. It is also because of what Ma and his colleagues have done since 2006. Collecting data recorded by environmental protection bureaus all over the country, they have created nationwide air- and water-pollution maps that pinpoint where pollution levels are excessive, and they name the responsible parties (Figure 10.3). The maps, posted on the group's website and freely available to the public, are constantly updated. Ma describes these maps as "tools of transparency" that enable people to track the country's air and water pollution for themselves and to identify the plants and corporations operating in violation of environmental regulations. The group's aim is to make polluters accountable not just to the law, but also to the citizens whose lives are directly affected. As environmental awareness grows and citizens become more invested in anti-pollution efforts, industries do not savor the prospect of being "named and shamed" publicly on these maps.[35]

While the Beijing government views environmental NGOs positively and recognizes their capacity to assist the state in improving the country's environment, the government retains the power to register and de-register them. And, of course, the Communist Party, mindful that these NGOs have the potential to become spaces that nurture societal discontent and its public expression, has made clear that it does not tolerate activities that could undermine or challenge its authority. Ma Jun observed that, as a consequence, NGOs must always be gauging where the permissible limits of their activities lie: "Every day we have to think, 'How much space do we have?' 'Where are the red lines?' "[36]

This explains why China's NGOs tend to be relatively nonconfrontational in their approach, doing work that is compatible with the priorities and policies of the government. Unlike their counterparts in the West, China's NGOs are not apt to sponsor or stage street protests; they are even cautious about participating in them, for their well-being and influence depend to a considerable degree on building a constructive working relationship with the government.[37] Whether the

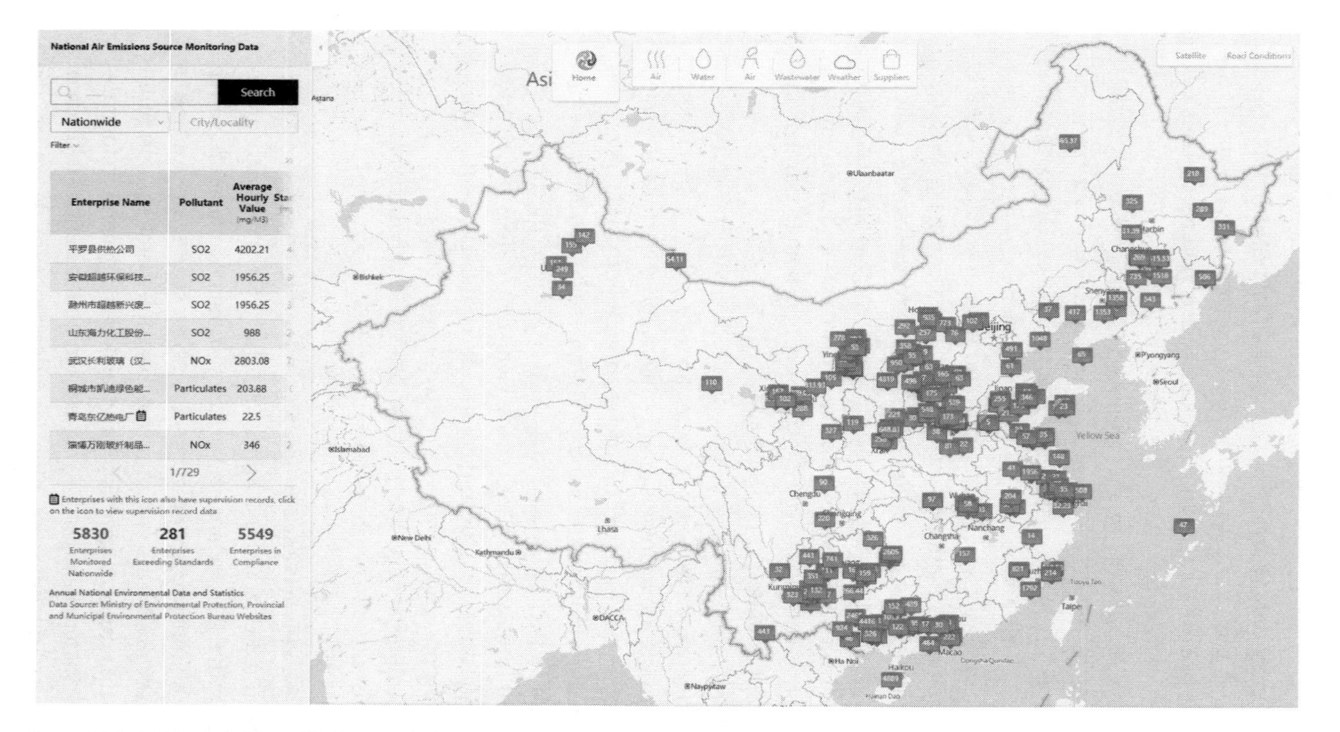

Figure 10.3 Institute for Public and Environmental Affairs map tracking polluting factories across the country and their emission levels

government in coming years will show itself willing to open up more space for environmental NGO activity, and whether the next generation of NGO leaders will be more willing to advocate for positions that put them at odds with the leadership, are open questions.

A brief word about international environmental NGOs. Many now have a presence in China; some of the best known are Greenpeace, the World Wide Fund for Nature, the Nature Conservancy, and the National Resources Defense Council. Smaller and less well known is the Berkeley-based International Rivers Organization, a group that is active in river conservancy, especially in China's southwest. Groups like these have played an important role in assisting in the development of China's NGOs. They have served as models for China's budding NGOs, provided funding and organization-building expertise, and aided in the transfer of information and technology.

In 2016 the Chinese government introduced a new law requiring international NGOs to find an official Chinese sponsor, register with the Ministry of Public Security, and submit to police inspection of all aspects of their operations. This measure, which represents an effort by Beijing to keep close tabs on, and tight control over, the activities of the international NGOs and their relationships with domestic NGOs, has sent a chill down the spine of the international NGOs. We await the law's implementation to see what effect it will have in practice.[38]

Why Does a One-Party Government Allow NGO Activity?

Although the government clearly wants to maintain a relatively high degree of control over the activities of environmental NGOs, the stunning proliferation of the groups in the past two decades suggests that the Beijing leadership tolerates their existence and may even recognize the benefits they provide. The government, after all, understands the severity of the country's environmental crisis and acknowledges that it does not alone have the capacity to resolve it. NGOs might be of some help. For example:

- At little or no expense to the government, NGOs educate people about what they as individuals might do to improve and protect the environment (e.g., recycle waste, plant trees, ride bicycles and public transportation, clean up rivers and lakes, conserve energy, and live sustainably). The government has long insisted that improving environmental conditions depends on a better-informed public.
- The Chinese government has been working over the past decade to unburden itself from some of the heavy costs of social welfare (e.g., health, education, environmental protection, elderly care) and to transfer them to the private sector. NGOs can help pick up some of the costs related to environmental protection.
- The Ministry of Environmental Protection in Beijing has expressed considerable frustration with the failure of many local governments to implement and enforce environmental regulations, claiming that because of their preoccupation with economic development, local officials commonly turn a blind eye to pollution emitted by industries that contribute to the local economy. In keeping watch on local air and water pollution, NGOs are assisting the efforts and interests of the ministry, perhaps even spurring derelict local governments into action.
- NGOs provide a sanctioned channel for people's participation in environmental matters. As such, they may help prevent public displeasure with environmental conditions from boiling over.
- Visible and active NGOs promote goodwill toward China, signaling to the international community the government's growing tolerance of civil society.

11

THE STATE AND ENVIRONMENTAL POLLUTION

Has the Chinese Government Been Responsive to the Challenges Posed by Pollution?

Premier Li Keqiang's 2014 declaration of "war on pollution" was meant to signal to the Chinese people that Beijing recognizes the full scope of the country's pollution crisis as well as the public's expectation that it is the government's responsibility to address it. The motives for Beijing's concern are many: the consequences of air, water, and soil pollution on public health are severe; the economic costs of pollution, as a percentage of the GDP, are steep; and public displeasure with pollution and its effects—reflected especially in street protests—is a threat to the country's social stability as well as the Communist Party's legitimacy.

The government's responsiveness is reflected not only in Li's verbal declaration of war but also in the concrete steps it has taken. For instance:

- Since 2013 it has committed more than $600 billion to air and water "action plans."
- It has been monitoring and publicizing air quality hourly throughout the country and making data collected by environmental bureaus available to the public and organizations like the Institute of Public and Environmental Affairs.

It has been conscientiously updating environmental legislation and actively introducing new legislation intended to promote fuller public participation in environmental matters, to strengthen enforcement of environmental regulations, and to hold officials more strictly accountable for protection of the environment.
It has made China into the world's largest investor in renewable energy.
It has announced that by 2017 it will implement a nationwide carbon trade policy and by 2020 will place a nationwide cap on coal consumption.

This is by no means to suggest that Beijing has been altogether successful in addressing the country's pollution crisis, but I would like to counter the impression held by too many in the West, and especially in the United States, that authorities in China care only about economic development, no matter the cost to the environment. This impression is outdated.

While it is only in recent years that the state's concern with environmental protection has truly deepened, state concern actually goes back a number of decades. What follows is a selective chronology of events that reflect the state's evolving interest in the environment:[1]

1972: Premier Zhou Enlai sends a Chinese delegation to the United Nations Conference on Human Environment in Stockholm. It is said that delegates return home with a better awareness of China's growing environmental problems.
1979: The Standing Committee of the National People's Congress issues the "Environmental Protection Law (Trial Implementation)," outlining for the first time the principles of environmental protection.
1988: As a result of efforts by Qu Geping, a delegate at the 1972 Stockholm conference and a "founding father" of China's environmentalism, the National Environmental

Protection Agency (NEPA) becomes independent of the Ministry of Urban and Rural Construction and becomes a vice-ministerial agency under the State Council.

1989: The "trial" version of the Environmental Protection Law of 1979 is made permanent.

1994: The Friends of Nature becomes a legally registered NGO.

1998: The National Environmental Protection Agency is raised from a vice-ministerial agency to a full ministerial agency—the State Environmental Protection Agency (SEPA).

2002: The Standing Committee of the National People's Congress promulgates the Environmental Impact Assessment Law requiring that any new construction undergo an environmental impact review. It becomes effective on September 1, 2003.

2008: The State Environmental Protection Agency is raised to a cabinet-level ministry, the Ministry of Environmental Protection, and thereby becomes a member of the State Council, the highest executive organ in the country.

What Plans Has the State Proposed for Clearing the Country's Air?

Li Keqiang's "war on pollution" did not explicitly target air any more than water or soil, but it is on air that much of the state's attention has been focused. Attention to water and, especially, soil pollution has lagged by comparison. No doubt, the "airpocalypse" of 2013 did much to move air to center stage; its blanketing descent on Beijing and much of northern China was impossible to ignore. So, too, were the results of prominent international studies quantifying the effects of polluted air on the lives of Chinese people.

By September 2013 China's State Council had issued the "Air Pollution Prevention and Control Action Plan," allocating $277 billion in government funding to it.[2] The "Action Plan" set three air-quality targets, to be reached by

2017: (1) a reduction in the levels of PM10 in all cities above the prefectural level by at least 10% from 2012 levels; (2) a reduction of the finer, more hazardous particulate matter, PM2.5, in the Beijing–Tianjin–Hebei area (also called Jingjinji) by 25%, the Yangtze River Delta by 20%, and the Pearl River Delta by 15%, from their 2012 levels; and (3) a reduction in the annual concentration of PM2.5 in Beijing to 60 μg/m^3.

To achieve these air-quality targets, the 2013 "Air Action Plan" proposed a number of specific measures:

- Reducing the percentage of coal in the country's total energy mix from 67% in 2012 to less than 65%
- Banning new coal-fired power plants in the three key regions (Jingjinji, Yangtze River Delta, Pearl River Delta)
- Increasing the percentage of non-fossil energy sources to 13% from 9.1% in 2012
- Eliminating aging, high-polluting vehicles from the country's roads

These measures reflect what has become for the state the three major pathways for achieving clean air: reducing coal consumption, developing non-fossil fuel energy, and reducing vehicle emissions. Laws and policies issued since the "Action Plan" (e.g., the revised Environmental Protection Law of 2015, the Intended Nationally Determined Contributions submitted in 2015 to the UN, the 2016 Air Pollution Prevention and Control Law, the 13th Five-Year Plan 2016–2020, and a host of official reports) have put forward a range of steps and policies intended to promote each of these pathways.

Steps and policies proposed by the state since 2013 for reducing coal consumption and emissions and developing clean energy are as follows:

- Improving energy efficiency by capping energy consumption at 5 billion tons of coal equivalent by 2020,

reducing energy intensity (energy consumption per unit of GDP) from 2015 levels by 15% by 2020, and reducing carbon intensity (carbon emissions per unit of GDP) from 2015 levels by 18% by 2020
- Reducing coal consumption in Beijing from 23 million tons in 2013 to 10 million tons by 2017, closing Beijing's major coal-fired power plants and replacing them with gas-fired power plants, shutting down 50,000 small, inefficient coal-fired furnaces throughout the country, and banning the construction of new coal power plants until 2018 at least
- Setting up seven trial regional pilot carbon emissions-trading programs in anticipation of a nationwide carbon emissions-trading program by 2017
- Reaching peak CO_2 emissions no later than 2030
- Cutting the country's steel production capacity by 100 to 150 million tons in order to lower carbon emissions
- Increasing the percentage of non-fossil fuels in the country's total primary energy mix to 15% by 2020 and 20% by 2030
- Increasing forest cover by 50 to 100 million hectares (two to four times the size of the United Kingdom), creating an additional 1-gigaton carbon sink

There are now roughly 250 million cars on China's roads (5.5 million in the capital alone). It is estimated that in urban areas vehicle emissions account for 25% to 30% of the PM2.5 in the air. To reduce these emissions, state and municipal governments have enacted or proposed a wide range of measures:

- Eliminating all "yellow label" vehicles from China's roads by 2017. (High-polluting gasoline vehicles that fall below the National I emission standard bear yellow stickers; the estimates I have seen for the number of yellow label cars run between 10 million and 20 million.)
- Limiting the number of new cars on city roads by limiting the availability of new licenses. Through lottery or auction

big cities like Beijing, Shanghai, Shenzhen, and Guangzhou have severely restricted the number of licenses they issue. For instance, Beijing limited the number of yearly licenses to 240,000 in 2011, 150,000 in 2014, and just 90,000 in 2017. In 2016 the competition in Beijing's lottery was such that the odds of winning were 1 in 693.
- Limiting the number of driving days per week per vehicle, with programs like alternate-day driving, based on the license plate number, or banning the vehicle from the road one day per week, again based on the license plate number.
- Imposing congestion fees and increasing parking fees to discourage driving. (Average travel speed in Beijing now is 7.5 mph or 12.1 km/hour.)
- Requiring China VI grade fuel (equivalent to Euro VI) in Beijing by 2016 and nationwide by 2017. China calculates that the lower sulfur content will reduce vehicle emissions by 40% to 50% compared to China V over time. The goal is for 50% of cars on the road to meet the China VI standard by 2020.
- Mandating an average minimum fuel consumption of 47 miles per gallon for passenger cars by 2020.

There has been a big national push to promote the adoption of electric vehicles (including all-electric and plug-in hybrid vehicles) and to reduce the use of cars powered by fossil fuel. That push has included the following:

- Providing subsidies of up to $16,000 for the purchase of an e-vehicle
- Exempting e-vehicles from lotteries and auctions for licenses, a purchase tax, blackout days, and parking fees
- Expanding fast-charging stations for e-vehicles (30-minute charge). The State Grid just added 50 stations along the 780-mile route between Beijing and Shanghai (one every 15.5 miles), and plans to place stations along another 11,800 miles of road by 2020

President Xi Jinping has set a goal of 5 million e-vehicles on the country's roads by 2020. Thus far, however, e-vehicles have had only moderate success in China. Their limited range is one reason; the other is that China's city dwellers live largely in high rises, with limited access to garages and chargers. But with all of the government incentives and the investment in e-vehicle infrastructure, sales between 2014 and 2015 increased about 350%, from 75,000 units to 331,000 units, according to the China Association of Automobile Manufacturers.

At the same time China is building up its mass transit capacity. Cities are developing their subway systems. Beijing, for instance, added 235 miles of new routes between 2007 and 2014 and plans to add six new lines and extend six existing ones between 2014 and 2020. By 2020 the capital will have 27 subway lines (vs. 2 lines in 2002), totaling just less than 620 miles. There will be metro lines in at least 38 of the country's cities, with a total of 3,850 miles of track. The country already has the longest high-speed rail system in the world, extending 12,000 miles, which some people estimate to be longer than all the high-speed rail systems in the world combined. The present plan is to add another 7,000 miles by 2020 and integrate 80% of the country's cities into the network. Finally, as city bus rapid transit expands, so has the proportion of buses powered by electricity. Already in 2014, of the 500,000 municipal buses on the roads, 80,000 were e-powered. The Ministry of Transport now proposes to have 200,000 new-energy buses and 100,000 new-energy taxis on China's roads by 2020.

What Measures Has the Government Proposed to Address Water Pollution and Water Scarcity?

In April 2015, the State Council issued the "Water Pollution Prevention and Control Action Plan," known also as the "Water Ten Plan," committing $330 billion to protect China's water resources. The plan is quite comprehensive, evidence of the government's growing concern over the quality and scarcity of the country's water supply. Among the key objectives are the following:[3]

- Reducing pollution in seven key rivers, including the Yangtze, Yellow, and Pearl; by 2020, 70% of the water in these river systems is to be grade III or above.
- Improving the quality of drinking water in the cities; by 2020, 93% of the urban drinking water is to be grade III or above.
- Counties and "key towns" are to be equipped with wastewater collection and treatment facilities by 2020.
- The country's water consumption is to be capped by 2020 (at 670 billion m^3) and groundwater extraction is to be strictly supervised (to prevent against overexploitation).
- Small-scale paper and pulp mills, tanneries, textile dyeing factories, pesticide producers, and oil refiners are to be closely monitored; if in violation of water-pollution standards, they will be shut down by the end of 2016.

Typical of the plans that come out of Beijing, it lays out broad aims and objectives but does not detail how they are to be achieved or who the responsible agencies are.

In Chapter 6, I indicated that water scarcity is at least as grave a problem as water pollution, since China holds more than 20% of the world's population but has only 7% or so of its freshwater resources. Thus, the annual per capita availability of fresh water is 2,000 m^3, compared to the global per capita availability of 6,000 m^3. Because of the aridity of the north, per capita availability there is much lower still; Beijing has but 100 to 150 m^3/person, not quite 1/40th of the global average and well below the UN's threshold of "absolute scarcity" (500 m^3). This, of course, is why the government has given such high priority to water-transfer projects like the South-North Water Diversion Project (which brings to the north 6 trillion gallons each year from the Yangtze and its tributaries). Moving water from regions of abundance to regions of need is, for Beijing, a possible partial fix to a desperate problem.

In 2011 the average price of water in 25 major Chinese cities was $0.46/m^3$, while the global average was $2.03/m^3$. Deutsche Bank calculated that the Chinese spent 0.5% of their disposable income on water tariffs, compared to the 2.8% spent by Americans. In 2014, the Chinese government reformed its pricing structure, reducing its subsidy on water, raising prices, especially for heavy consumers, and introducing a three-tiered pricing system—all in an attempt to promote water conservation. Under this system, the heaviest users (the top 5%) will pay roughly three times the base rate for water, the second tier (the next 15%) will pay 1.5 times the base rate, and the remaining 80% will see little or no change in their water bills. This reform has met with some pushback, particularly among heavy users (e.g., industry and agriculture), but it seems to be moving forward as planned.[4]

In 2014, the government also proposed pilot markets for trade in water rights in seven provinces. In this program, provinces issue allocations of water and recipients who use less can sell their surplus in the market.[5] In tackling the country's desperate water scarcity, it seems that the government is increasingly relying on market-based solutions (a point the government makes in the "Water Action Plan").

In addition to *moving* water and *conserving* water, Beijing wants to *make more* water. As a result, the government is going all in on desalination. It is an expensive process and an energy-intensive one, so there is considerable debate about its pros and cons. Nonetheless, some authorities see removing salt from seawater as a ready answer to China's water scarcity and are developing technologies that will make the process cheaper and more efficient. Bloomberg reports, "The central government's Special Plan for Seawater Utilization calls for producing three million tons (807 million gallons) a day of purified seawater—roughly quadruple the country's current capacity [0.77 million m^3]."[6] Today, Beijing is building a huge desalination plant in the city of Tangshan, on the shores of Bohai Bay, which by 2019 is expected to supply Beijing with 1 million tons of water per day (one-third of the city's tap water).[7] The costs: $1.1 billion for the plant and $1.4 billion for the 170-mile pipeline to Beijing. Additionally, there are the energy costs associated with the daily operations of the plant.

Finally, there is China's "artificial weather" program, which promises to produce an addition 60 billion m^3 of rain (more than 1.5 times the volume of water in the Three Gorges Reservoir) each year by 2020. "Cloud seeding," the popular term for this controversial geo-engineering technique, launches chemicals, such as silver iodide, into the clouds to induce rain. The government claims that with existing technologies the country could potentially produce 280 billion m^3 of additional rain each year.[8]

What Progress Has the Government Made in the Battle Against Soil Pollution?

The government-sponsored land survey released in 2014 revealed that at least 20% of the country's arable land is contaminated, and some experts estimate that the figure is much higher. But perhaps because polluted soil is less visible and obvious than polluted air and water, it has received less attention. Zhuang Guotai, head of the Ministry of Environmental Protection's Department of Nature and Conservation, remarked, "In comparison with efforts to clean up air and water pollution, we've hardly got started with soil."[9]

Only in mid-2016 did the government finally issue an action plan for soil, and it still has yet to issue a pollution prevention and control law for soil, as it has for air and water. This is not simply because the leadership has been slower to focus on soil pollution; it is also because in the case of air and water, China has been able to draw on the experience of other countries in formulating "action plans" and laws. In the case of soil, however, no other country offers a comparable experience. So extreme is the contamination that China has had no ready models to adopt.

The action plan contains a number of key targets:

1. Cleaning up 90% the country's polluted farmland and industrial sites by 2020, and 95% by 2030
2. Completing a nationwide soil-pollution survey by 2018 that identifies all polluted land and classifies it by level of contamination
3. Establishing a uniform monitoring system that tracks soil quality throughout the entire country by 2020[10]

The scope and severity of the country's soil contamination will make cleanup an enormous challenge and a very costly one, with estimates ranging from $1.1 trillion to $1.6 trillion. Who will pick up the costs? Given that $1.1 trillion is the equivalent of more than one-third of all China's foreign-exchange reserves, the government is not a likely candidate. (Consider too that thus far its funding for soil cleanup has been a very limited $451 million, to be divided among 30 cities between 2015 and 2018.) Some hope that private developers might take on some of the responsibility, especially in cities, since rehabilitation of the soil would increase the value of their property.

Research is under way to develop remediation techniques that can be successfully and inexpensively applied over large land areas. Technologies from overseas that are effective on small plots of land, and often quite expensive, do not serve China's very different needs. Chinese scientists have begun experimenting with cheaper, easier-to-use technologies, like microorganisms that can "change the ionic state of heavy metals in the soil, deactivating the pollutants so they do not harm crops" and Mont SH6, a mineral that when applied to the soil absorbs heavy metals such as cadmium and copper and reduces their toxicity and activity levels.[11] More research and more testing, it is hoped, will result in remediation methods and techniques capable of nursing the country's compromised soil back to good health.

What Are Some of the Specific Environmental Measures Outlined in the Government's Most Recent Five-Year Plan?

Since 1953, every five years the Chinese government has issued a so-called five-year plan, which lays out goals and policies—economic, political, social, and environmental—intended to guide the course of the nation for the next half-decade. These goals and policies signal to the country's officials and people the priorities of the leadership and the direction the leadership would like China to take in the following five years.

The 13th Five-Year Plan (2016–2020), officially adopted in March 2016, reflects the considerable importance the government now attaches to improving the country's environmental conditions. Observers all agree that this Five-Year Plan gives more comprehensive attention to environmental matters than any previous plan. While I have covered some of the measures proposed in the 13th Five-Year Plan in earlier questions in this chapter, it would be helpful here to bring together the targets for 2020 outlined in the plan, as in the aggregate they demonstrate the seriousness and comprehensiveness of the government's environmental planning today:

- Capping annual total energy consumption, for the first time, at 5 billion tons of standard coal equivalent
- Reducing energy intensity from 2015 levels by 15%
- Reducing carbon intensity from 2015 levels by 18%
- Increasing the use of non-fossil fuels from 12% of the primary energy mix in 2015 to 15%
- Approving the construction of six to eight nuclear reactors annually through 2020 in order to reduce the country's consumption of coal

- Increasing the country's forest coverage from 21% in 2015 to 23%
- Instituting a nationwide carbon emissions trading system built on the seven regional trial programs introduced since 2013
- Requiring that 80% of the country's waterways meet grade III or better standards (up from the current 76.7% requirement)
- Requiring that 95% of cities and 85% of counties have proper sewage treatment
- Promoting the establishment of a "green finance system," the aim of which is to expand capital flow (e.g., bonds, loans, development funds) for investment in energy-efficient and green initiatives
- Investing in the construction of 14,500 miles of new high-speed rail lines, which will cover more than 80% of China's major cities (at an estimated cost of $422 billion).

What Are the Country's Major Environmental Administrative Entities?

The country's main environmental regulatory body is the Ministry of Environmental Protection, one of 27 ministries and commissions under the direct control of the State Council (China's cabinet). It is the youngest of all the ministries, created in 2008.

In 1998, the National Environmental Protection Agency was elevated to ministerial-level status, becoming the State Environmental Protection Agency. In 2008, the State Environmental Protection Agency became a full ministry, meaning that its minister serves as a full-time member of the State Council with full voting rights.[12] The Ministry of Environmental Protection's website lays out its general mission (article 1 of "Mandates"): "Be responsible for establishing a sound basic system for environmental protection. Draw up and organize the implementation of national policies, programs, and plans for environmental protection, draft out laws and regulations, and formulate departmental rules." The ministry is divided into 14 departments and has a staff of roughly 300 people.[13] Funding for its operations comes almost entirely from the State Council.

Other ministries with sizable environmental responsibilities include the Ministry of Water Resources, the Ministry of Agriculture, the Ministry of Housing and Urban–Rural Development, the Ministry of Land and Resources, the Ministry of Health, the Ministry of Transport, and the National Development and Reform Commission.[14]

Enforcement of environmental laws and policies falls to the local Environmental Protection Bureaus. There are about 3,000 of these bureaus throughout China, at the various territorial levels, provincial, prefectural, county, and, sometimes, township, employing a total of 175,000 people. Each local bureau is responsible to two authorities: the bureau at the next higher administrative level and the local government within its jurisdiction. It is the local government that provides the local bureau with its annual budget, hires its head, and pays the salaries of its employees.

The chief responsibilities of the local bureaus are (1) to implement the policies and enforce the regulations established by the central Ministry of Environmental Protection and (2) to draft policies and regulations that address the particular local conditions and needs of the area within its jurisdiction. Staff of the local bureau are responsible for inspecting local factories and industries, ensuring compliance with environmental regulations, and imposing fines and penalties on those violating pollution standards.[15]

One final environmental entity to consider is the environmental court. In 2007, Guiyang municipality in Guizhou province opened what was one of the country's first specialized environmental courts. Serious pollution in the municipality's main sources of drinking water—Hongfeng Lake, Baihua Lake, and Aha Reservoir—prompted the action. Establishment of this environmental court, authorized to hear civil, criminal, and administrative cases relating to the region's environment, was intended, in part, to signal to the local population the determination of Guiyang's officials to protect the environment. In May 2008, officials in Wuxi (Jiangsu province) opened an environmental court there when a major algae outbreak turned the waters of Lake Tai into a blanket of shimmering emerald green. And, in December 2008, arsenic pollution in Yangzong Lake in Kunming led to the creation of an environmental court in Yunnan.

Today there are 130 or so city- and district-level environmental courts throughout the country. How useful they have been is unclear. One legal scholar has remarked, "It is too early to draw any conclusions about the efficacy of these courts in improving the enforcement of environmental laws, but it is hard to see any downside to their creation."[16]

What Are Some of the Main Challenges in Enforcing Environmental Regulations?

Since the "trial" Environmental Protection Law was issued in 1979, China has actively legislated environmental standards and promulgated environmental policies. A World Bank study reported that "In the last four decades, more than 28 environmental and resource laws, 150 national administrative environmental regulations, 1300 national environmental standards, and 200 departmental administrative regulations have been issued."[17]

Thus, it is not the lack of environmental protection laws and policies that explains the country's pervasive pollution; rather, it is that the laws and policies are not effectively implemented and enforced. There is an "implementation gap" between environmental laws and policies issued by the state and the state's enforcement of them. As Ma Tianjie, formerly of Greenpeace East Asia and now editor at China Dialogue, put it, "If you look at China's air pollution control laws, they're pretty good compared to global standards . . . But no matter how good [the laws] look on paper, the true test will always be the willingness of local authorities to enforce them."[18] A number of factors have been suggested to explain this gap—and the country's weak record of environmental enforcement.

Weakness of the Ministry of Environmental Protection

The Ministry of Environmental Protection is the youngest of the state ministries and appears to carry less weight in the State Council than the more established ministries (e.g., the National Development and Reform Commission, the Ministry of Water Resources, and the Ministry of Agriculture). Its authority is further limited by the fact that responsibility for environmental protection in the country is divided among a number of state ministries. But, perhaps most seriously, the ministry is understaffed (300 employees) and underfinanced: its relatively meager resources, human and financial, limit its reach and influence at the local level and restrict its ability to supervise the nation's network of environmental protection bureaus effectively.

Tension Between Local and National Interests

The local environmental protection bureaus are expected to answer to both the ministry and the local government within the area of their jurisdiction. In practice, however, each bureau is guided more by the priorities of the local government, since it is the local government that provides most of the bureau's annual budget, appoints the head, pays the employees, evaluates the staff, and even distributes resources like office buildings, cars, and employee housing. Abigail Jahiel summed the matter up nicely: "Since environmental organs are so dependent on local governments, they must take these governments' concerns into account when regulating industry. It is the local government, therefore, that is the more powerful of the environmental agencies' two administrative leaders."[19]

And local governments have tended to favor economic development over environmental protection. A major reason is that the performance evaluations of local officials have been tied almost exclusively to the economic growth of the regions for which they are responsible. Environmental protection has counted for little. A second reason is that since local industry is a major source of revenue for local governments, governments strongly favor industrial growth, often at the expense of the environment.

Third, local industry often provides employment for much of the local population. While shuttering coal-fired power plants, steel mills, cement factories, and other energy-intensive operations may be good for the environment, reining in the toxic air, the consequences for the local economy can be devastating. Fining or shutting down local industry risks putting people out of jobs and so encourages social—and political—instability. For example, Hebei province, which was the home to 7 of 10 of the country's most polluted cities in 2013, cut iron and steel production by 30 million tons in 2014. The result: economic growth declined from 7.7% in 2013 to 6.5% in 2014. The challenge in places like Hebei is to find new, alternative sources of economic growth. In March 2015, operations at 57 companies—steel, ceramic, glass, and coke plants—in the city of Linyi in Shandong province were suspended as part of the province's fight against air pollution. Linyi's PM2.5 level dropped a full 24.3% by May, but reports claimed that some 60,000 residents of Linyi lost their jobs, and local police claimed that the crime rate increased as a result. As one local legislator observed, "In retrospect, [Linyi] might have made too abrupt a turn to transform its economy."[20]

The fourth reason why local governments have tended to favor economic development over environmental protection is that local officials may have personal ties to local industry or industrial leaders. Finally, officials can be bought by polluting industries. All of these reasons suggest why local governments might turn a blind eye to local industry and factories polluting the air, water, and soil.

Insufficient Punishments and Fines for Environmental Violations

The punishments and fines for environmental violations are too slight and inconsequential to deter polluters, rendering laws and regulations toothless. Owners of businesses and industries calculate that it is cheaper and more profitable to pay the fines than to take the measures necessary to comply with the environmental regulations.

Environmental Courts Remain a Work in Progress

The local environmental courts are intended to give added weight to a region's environmental enforcement capacity, but by most accounts they are still suffering from a number of growing pains. Most seriously, perhaps, is that lawyers and judges only recently have begun to receive systematic training in environmental matters and the relevant bodies of laws and regulations. A related problem is that the courts thus far have been slow to accept and to hear cases. The lack of expertise, no doubt, contributes to much of the hesitation, but so too does a lack of systematic procedures and regulations governing the courts. Finally, the courts are not necessarily bodies acting independently; as with the environmental protection bureaus, they tend to be heavily guided by the local governments within their jurisdiction.

Many measures for making environmental enforcement more effective are either under discussion in China or in the very early stages of implementation. The most promising ones, in my view, are as follows:

- Merging the environmental responsibilities of the Ministries of Environmental Protection, Water Resources, Agriculture Land Resources, and the State Forestry Administration into one ministry, a sort of super-Ministry of Environmental Protection
- Making local authorities more responsive to the aims and priorities of the Ministry of Environmental Protection by giving the ministry more responsibility for the budgets of

the local environment bureaus and authorizing it to send inspection teams to the provinces and regions throughout the country. The Deputy Director of the Research Center on Environmental Economics at Fudan University called this a shift to a "vertical management system," "whereby an agency works via an internal hierarchical structure, with lower departments reporting directly to higher ones instead of to outside local governments."[21]

- Holding local officials more accountable for environmental protection by giving stronger consideration to their environmental performance—that is, their effectiveness in protecting the region's natural resources (through a natural resources audit, for example)—in the official evaluation and promotion process, and by cracking down on those who do not dutifully enforce environmental regulations and standards. For instance, in June 2016, in a case that received wide media attention, provincial prosecutors in Shandong successfully sued the local environmental protection bureau in Qingyuan county for failing to punish the Qingshun Chemical Technology Company for producing dyes without the appropriate safety measures.[22] Cases like this receive considerable publicity in the press these days, as if to signal to the people—and local officials themselves—the government's new determination to rein in the laxness and corruption of local environmental officials.[23]
- Increasing investment in environmental protection. China now spends roughly just 1% of its GDP on environmental protection; experts suggest that the investment be increased to somewhere between 2% and 4% of the GDP, which is more in line with what high-income European countries spend. Increased investment could be put toward hiring skilled staff, improving available testing and monitoring technologies, and buying much-needed inspection vehicles.[24]
- Toughening penalties against polluters. Until recently, the cost of compliance with environmental regulations

has been higher than the cost of noncompliance. Fines for pollution have been so insignificant that companies would sooner pay the fines than take the anti-pollution measures required to become compliant. In a 2014 session of the National People's Congress Standing Committee, one lawmaker calculated that operating a 100,000-kilowatt generator in compliance with environmental standards would cost the company $80,000/year in environmental protection fees, while operating it in violation of those standards would cost a mere one-time fine of $1,600.[25] With the revised 2015 Environmental Protection Law (see below), the penalties have become heavier and the deterrent effect stronger. And no longer is the fine a one-off; it is to be assessed daily and cumulatively— without limit—until the company addresses the violation.

What Is the Significance of China's 2015 Revised Environmental Protection Law?

China implemented its first Environmental Protection Law in 1979 on a trial basis, and in 1989 the country formally passed the trial law into legislation. In 2011, lawmakers began revising the law for the first time. After three years and four drafts, they agreed on an amended version in April 2014, which became effective on January 1, 2015.[26] This is an extremely important document. Its articles, in my view, reflect a Chinese government that fully recognizes the severity of its environmental crisis and is committed to bringing about change.

That it took three years and four drafts to come to an agreement indicates that the negotiation process was challenging and that competing priorities and interests of various ministries and party leaders needed sorting out. For one, the National Development and Reform Commission was at times quite outspoken about its worry that environmental measures would take too big a bite out of the country's economic growth.

In any event, what emerged in the revised law was no mere tweaking of an article here and there. The 1989 law contained 47 articles; the 2015 law is much expanded, containing 70 articles, including one entirely new chapter on "Information Disclosure and Public Participation" (articles 53–58). Environmentalists and lawyers find especially promising the revised law's call for stronger penalties, greater public participation, and stricter official accountability for environmental protection.

Stronger Penalties

- Fines may be imposed "consecutively on a daily basis," without any limitation (removing the previous cap of $75,000) and "the coverage of types of violation activities to be subject to the daily-based fine" may be extended (article 59).
- For certain non-criminal violations of the pollution law, the "person directly in charge and other personnel subject to direct liabilities" may be detained for a period of up to 15 days (article 63).
- Local authorities may suspend or shut down operations of an enterprise discharging "pollutants in excess of emission standards, or in excess of the total emission quota of major pollutants" (article 60).

Greater Public Participation

- The ministry "shall release national environmental quality, monitoring data of key pollutant sources and other major environmental information"; local environmental agencies shall do the same. Additionally, citizens and social organizations "shall have the right to obtain environmental information, participate and supervise the activities of environment protection in accordance with the law" (articles 53 and 54).
- Environmental protection agencies above the county level must keep a list of enterprises, institutions, and business operators that violate environmental standards

and "disclose the list of lawbreakers to the public" (article 54). (These articles promoting transparency have helped make possible the pollution mapping of Ma Jun and the Institute of Public and Environmental Affairs.)

- "The project owner of a construction project . . . shall explain relevant situations to the potentially-affected public when preparing the environmental impact report, and solicit public opinions." The environmental impact assessment must be done *before* construction begins (articles 19 and 56).
- A so-called whistleblower article guarantees the right of "citizens, legal persons and other organizations" to report "environmental pollution and ecological damage activities of any units to the appropriate environmental protection administration." If local governments and their environmental protection bureaus fail to fulfill their legal responsibilities, they may be reported to the next higher level of government or the supervisory department. The whistleblower's name and information shall be kept confidential (article 57).
- Grassroots organizations, social organizations, and environmental protection organizations are to be encouraged by "the people's government at various levels . . . to carry out the publicity of environmental protection laws, regulations and knowledge, so as to facilitate a favorable atmosphere for environmental protection" (article 9).
- In an article that was especially welcomed by environmental activists, social organizations meeting the following conditions may take legal action against pollution violations on behalf of the public interest: they are registered at or above the municipal level, have specialized in environmental protection public-interest activities for five years, and have no legal violations (article 58).[27]

Holding Officials More Environmentally Accountable

- People's governments at or above the county level are to assess the environmental protection record of officials—and not simply their economic achievements—in evaluating their performance and considering them for promotion (article 26).

- "The total discharge quota of key pollutants is assigned by the State Council, and allocated to provincial, autonomous region, and provincial municipality government for implementation." Regions that fail to meet the assigned quotas will not be permitted to grant approvals for new construction that might contribute further to the levels of the key pollutants (article 44).
- Officials are to guide agricultural producers in their area in the rational application of fertilizers and pesticides, in proper waste management, and in the "prevention of non-point sources of agricultural pollution" (article 49).
- Higher levels of government are to exercise oversight of the environmental protection works of the "people's governments at lower levels and their relevant departments" (i.e., implementation of vertical management system). Article 67 goes on to say, "Where competent environmental protection departments fail to issue administrative punishments despite being so required in accordance with the law, the competent environmental protection departments may directly make the decision on administrative punishments." This article should be viewed as protection against ineffectual environmental protection bureaus.
- Local officials who commit unlawful environmental-related acts (nine general offenses are listed) can be given a demerit, demoted, removed from office, or dismissed from government, depending on the severity of the violation and its consequences (article 68).

The revised Environmental Protection Law has given environmentalists in China hope. It demonstrates a sound understanding on the part of the government of where and how the environmental regulatory system of the past has fallen short. And, it shows a very real desire to address that system's greatest weaknesses. But, in the end, the success of the revised law depends, as China's environmental law always has, on how conscientiously and effectively authorities implement and enforce it.

12

THE SEARCH FOR CLEANER ENERGY

Where Is China's Coal Consumption Trending?

Coal has been the primary energy source driving China's recent "economic miracle." In 2000 the country went through 1.5 billion tons of coal, and as energy demands have continued to skyrocket, so too has the consumption of coal. By 2013, coal use in China, having grown annually about 12%, had almost tripled to more than 4 billion tons, an amount equal to that consumed by the rest of world combined.

Inexpensive and plentiful, coal has supplied about 70% of China's total energy mix annually since 2000 (by comparison, coal accounted for 18% of the US energy mix in 2013). While generating the energy that has propelled the country's economy, coal has also generated much of the pollution that poisons its air, water, and soil and most of the greenhouse gases that make China the world's leading contributor to global warming (almost 30% of the world's total).

In 2014, for the first time in the 21st century, China's consumption of coal unexpectedly declined, by 2.9% year-over-year from the previous year. The next year, 2015, witnessed a still greater decline of 3.7%. China, of course, remains by far the world's largest user of coal, but some analysts, looking at the recent energy figures, have begun to argue that "history will likely show that 2013–2014 marked the peak in Chinese coal consumption."[1] If these analysts prove to be correct—if history does in fact show that China experienced peak coal consumption in 2013–2014—the country will have achieved that watershed a full decade earlier than most students of China's environment thought possible.

By 2015 coal's share in the country's total energy mix dropped from 70% to 64%. The drop in coal consumption, both in absolute tonnage and in the share of the total energy mix, can be explained, in some part, by the slowing economy of the 2010s (especially in the manufacturing and construction sectors) and the related slowdown in the growth of energy demand. However, in larger, more significant, part, it can be explained by the country's resolve to diversify its energy resources and to speed up the decarbonization of its total energy supply. As recently as 2011, when coal's share of China's energy consumption was still over 70%, non-fossil fuel's share was just 8.4%, but as coal's share has been dropping, non-fossil fuel's share has climbed, reaching 12% in 2015. The most recent available figures show that in the first half of 2016, as the country's consumption of coal continued to decline year-over-year, the use of non-fossil fuel rose steeply—solar by 28%, nuclear by 25%, wind by 14%, and hydropower by 13%.

Will "Cleaner Coal" Have a Place in China's Energy Plans?

Coal may be dirty, but it is cheap. Given China's vast energy needs, it reasonable that the country would be looking at ways to make use of the abundant resource without doing significant harm to the environment. China has considered a number of technologies that would produce cleaner energy from coal. One is carbon capture and storage (CCS), a process that can capture up to 90% of the carbon dioxide that is emitted from fossil fuel power plants. There are CCS technologies that can capture the CO_2 before or after combustion. Once captured it must then be transported and deposited in a storage site, normally underground in a depleted gas or oil field, a saline aquifer, or the deep ocean. China and the United States signed an agreement in 2015 allowing them to share the results of their research into technologies to capture greenhouse gases.

CCS technology and use have developed more slowly globally and in China than expected. A major issue is expense. Coal itself is cheap, but the cost of capturing the CO_2 it emits, transporting it, and injecting it safely underground has discouraged research investment and efforts in CCS. Environmentalists argue that any funding supporting the development of CCS is funding that would be better spent on developing renewable energy technologies. They also stress that CCS is designed to protect against carbon emissions alone; other pollutants, like nitrogen oxide and mercury, continue to be emitted into the atmosphere, contributing to acid rain, smog, toxic air, and soil degradation.

Additional concerns have arisen over CCS, especially over storage. Once injected into underground rock formations, how secure will the CO_2 gases be? Might they escape into the air? Or might they leak from deep storage underground to contaminate drinking water? Could injection into rock formations trigger earthquakes; conversely, might earthquakes disturb the storage sites and permit the escape of CO_2?[2] The future of CCS in China is uncertain, but scientists agree that meaningful deployment of the technology will not, in any event, be feasible until well into the 2020s.

Another coal-related technology of interest in China is gasification, a process whereby coal is mixed with oxygen, heated at ultra-high temperatures, and thereby converted into synthetic natural gas (SNG). When burned, SNG discharges very few local pollutants into the air—many fewer than coal (perhaps 99% fewer)—which appeals to a leadership and people eager to curtail the deadly smog that routinely fills the skies. China in 2014 announced plans to build 50 coal gasification plants, mostly in the north and northwest—Inner Mongolia, Xinjiang, Gansu, and Ningxia—by 2020, though recently it has slowed down construction and scaled back the projected number.

Gasification is attractive in China for any number of reasons: (1) it makes use of a domestic resource that is inexpensive and abundant; (2) it strengthens the country's energy security; (3) it props up a coal industry in decline, and offers it some protection from a hard landing; and (4) SNG burns much cleaner than coal.

Still, enthusiasm for gasification plants has moderated somewhat since 2014, and the role they ultimately will play in the country's energy future is uncertain. Building a coal-to-gas plant is costly; so too is the process of converting coal to gas. As the price of natural gas, and oil too, has declined globally, the economic rationale for the deployment of gasification technology has become less clear to many in China.

But it is not the financial cost alone that has slowed the country's development of a gasification infrastructure; it is also, importantly, the growing awareness of the severe impact that gasification plants have on the environment. An important Duke University study, "China's Synthetic Natural Gas Revolution," concluded that an SNG plant emits seven times more greenhouse gases than a conventional natural gas plant and nearly twice as much as a coal-fired power plant. Thus, the argument continues, a turn by China to SNG may well be a boon to the country's local air quality, but it would be a disaster for global climate change.

The same study also contends that the production of SNG is water-intensive, requiring 50 to 100 times the amount of water needed to produce shale gas. Given that SNG plants would be located mostly in the coal-rich but arid and already water-stressed provinces of the north and northwest, SNG production would risk aggravating the country's water crisis in the region that could least afford it. The area's farmers and herders would be especially vulnerable to any reduction in water resources. In their conclusion, the authors of the Duke study advised that "Chinese policymakers should delay implementing their SNG plan to avoid a potentially costly and environmentally damaging outcome. An even better decision would be to cancel the program entirely."[3]

Can Shale Gas with Its Plentiful Reserves Replace Coal as the Country's Major Source of Energy?

In efforts to reduce its dependence on coal, China has looked increasingly to natural gas. Like coal, natural gas is a fossil fuel, but when burned it emits 43% less carbon and 66% less nitrogen oxide than coal. Between 2005 and 2013 the country's natural gas production doubled, yet it was still unable to keep up with growing demand. To supplement the domestic supply it turned to imports, which multiplied 10-fold between 2008 and 2013, making China the fifth largest importer of gas in the world.

With the largest recoverable shale gas reserves in the world (more than in the United States and Canada together), China has been talking about its own "shale revolution"—one like the boom in the United States—since 2012, when it announced it would begin hydrofracturing (fracking) its reserves. But that revolution has largely sputtered, and almost all of China's shale reserves remain underground. Exploration efforts, while ongoing, have proved to be challenging.

Fracking is the process whereby chemically treated water is injected at high pressure through seams of rock to force the release of natural gas that is trapped there. In China the shale basins are located in mountainous and difficult terrain, with the shale buried 1.9 to 5 miles (3,000–8000 meters) underground. In the United States shale is found in flatland buried less than 1.86 miles deep (less than 3,000 meters). Additionally, China's geological conditions are tectonically more complex and less stable than geological conditions in the United States. The know-how and technology developed in the US shale fields are largely untransferable to conditions in China. The test for China will be to develop the expertise and technology to access its shale reserves, and to do so in a cost-effective manner. But once it gets to the shale gas, there remains the crucial issue of transporting it: China does not have the pipeline infrastructure to move the recovered gas from the remote regions where it is drilled to the areas of the country where it is most needed—the populous centers of the east coast and southeast. Today China has only 28,000 miles (45,062 km) of pipeline, compared to 310,686 miles (500,000 km) of pipeline in the United States.

The costs and challenges aside, many people in China have been reluctant to embrace a "shale revolution." For them, a number of environmental concerns loom. Fracking is water-intensive, requiring in the vicinity of 19,000 tons of water per well, and of China's seven major shale basins, all except the Sichuan basin are located in the north, in dry and water-stressed areas. Fracking threatens to deplete further the low water tables there. They are anxious too that the chemically treated water that is injected into the rock might leak out and contaminate the groundwater. Finally, fracking elsewhere, including the United States, has been associated with methane leaks; a far more potent greenhouse gas than carbon dioxide, methane contributes to global warming and poses a health risk to the population exposed to it.

China has not altogether given up hope of a shale revolution, but, according to energy experts, the obstacles in its way have postponed it for another decade at least.

What Is the Role of Renewable Non-Fossil Energy Sources in China's Energy Mix?

Fossil fuels today constitute 88% of China's total primary energy mix: coal holds the largest piece of the consumption pie (64%), followed by oil (18.1%), and then by gas (5.9%). While fossil fuels have been declining as a percentage of the total, non-fossil fuel energies have been scaling up. From 2010 to 2015, renewable energy (i.e., wind, solar, and hydropower) and nuclear energy (not a renewable source of energy, since uranium is a finite resource) increased their share from 8.3% of the total to 12%, and their combined wattage capacity jumped from 257 gigawatts (GW) to 534 GW, a 100% increase.[4] In 2015 alone, as China's consumption of coal fell 3.7%, its wind capacity increased 27% year-over-year (30.5 GW) to 145 GW—more than the combined capacity of the United States, Germany, and India—and its solar capacity increased 62% (16.5 GW) to 43 GW.[5]

The 13th Five-Year Plan lays out Beijing's ambitious plans to expand the country's non-fossil fuel energy capacity to 15% of the total energy mix by 2020. This chart lists the actual installed capacity of each fuel in 2015 and the 2020 target set for it in the 13th Five-Year Plan:

	Wind	**Solar**	**Hydro**	**Nuclear**
2015 levels	145 GW	43 GW	320 GW	26 GW
2020 targets	210–250 GW	110–150 GW	340 GW	58 GW

If we focus on renewable sources and leave nuclear aside for the moment, in 2015 China already led the world in installed wind power, solar power, and hydropower. And total renewable capacity was easily the largest in the world at more than 500 GW, followed by the United States with less than half that (220 GW). The recent Five-Year Plan makes emphatically clear that China intends to maintain its momentum in renewable energy growth. Indeed, for the past few years, China has invested more, by far, than any other country in renewable energy capacity. In 2015, for example, China put $102 billion to $111 billion into renewable energy (up from $39 billion just five years earlier), more than one-third of the world's total ($286 billion) for the year, and more than the United States ($44 billion), Japan ($36.2 billion) and the United Kingdom ($22.2 billion) combined.

One hotbed of renewable energy construction is in the country's northwest, home of the Gobi Desert. While much of this region is arid and inhospitable to agriculture, it is at the same time rich in both wind and sun. Since the late 2000s, companies eager to expand the country's supply of wind energy have built large-capacity wind farms there. In fact, the Gansu Wind Farm in Jiuquan prefecture just outside of the city of Dunhuang is the largest wind farm in the world. In 2013 it had a capacity of 6.8 GW, more than all of the United Kingdom's wind capacity at the time. By 2020, this one farm is expected to generate 20 GW of wind, just a little shy of what the whole of the United Kingdom and Spain together generate today.[6]

The abundance of wind in the Gobi is matched by the abundance of sun. The surrounding area of Gansu, Qinghai, and Xinjiang provinces has thus appealed equally to the solar industry and, indeed, is fast becoming the solar capital of the world. Qinghai is home to the world's largest solar farm, the 850-MW Longyangxia Dam Solar Park, capable of powering 200,000 households (Figure 12.1).

Bear in mind that the northwest, where wind and solar resources are especially great, is the area of the country where

Figure 12.1 Longyangxia Dam Solar Park in Qinghai province, the largest solar farm in the world

coal is king and water resources, required for the production of coal power, are scarce. Building a strong wind and solar power presence there—and allowing for reduced reliance on coal-generated power—will bring both environmental and economic benefits to the region.

To preserve its limited land resources, China has also begun building wind farms in the water, along the country's east coast. Currently, offshore farms represent only a very small percentage of the country's wind power capacity—approximately 1 GW—but there are plans to ramp up capacity to 30 GW by 2020.

Turning to hydropower: since the establishment of the People's Republic, China has been constructing dams at a torrid pace. For the Communist Party hydroelectricity has been the go-to alternative to fossil-fuel–generated power, a critical source of energy driving the country's economic growth. There are today more than 87,000 hydropower stations in the country, the majority (77%) in the water-rich south. Of these, 23,000 are classified as large dams (dams exceeding 15 meters high), constituting a major chunk of the 57,000 large dams worldwide.

The country's hydropower capacity is around 320 GW, the largest in the world by a large margin, 3.6 times the capacity of Brazil, the world's number two producer (89 GW). This 320 GW represents the lion's share of China's renewable energy capacity of 508 GW. In 2015, hydropower was the third largest contributor to the country's entire primary energy mix (8%), just after coal and oil.

With China's pledge to increase the share of non-fossil fuels in its total energy mix to 15% by 2020 and 20% by 2030, hydropower's installed capacity is sure to grow. The 2020 target for 2020 is 340 GW, a number the country is expected easily to exceed; estimates have it that 2050 could see the capacity climb to as high as 500 GW, though many environmental groups are calling for curbing development sooner. Much of this hydro buildup is proposed for the country's southwest, Yunnan and

Sichuan provinces, and the Qinghai–Tibetan Plateau, where rivers from glacier runoff take form.

The Three Gorges Dam in Hubei province perhaps best exemplifies China's longstanding hydroelectric ambitions (Figure 12.2). Spanning the Yangtze River in Hubei, it is the largest hydroelectric station in the world. Begun in 1994, it took about 14 years to complete. Its massive concrete structure is 1.45 miles (2.33 km) long and 607 feet (185 meters) tall, some five times larger than the Hoover Dam. Its energy capacity is a walloping 22 GW, more than 3 times the capacity of the Grand Coulee Dam (6.8 GW), America's largest, and 20 times that of the Hoover Dam (2.1 GW). The reservoir behind the dam is 410 miles (660 km) long, more than two-thirds the length of the United Kingdom, and 0.7 miles (1.12 km) wide, with a total surface area of 420 square miles (1,088 km^2).

Government sources proudly proclaim that a thermal power plant generating the energy produced by the Three Gorges Dam would burn 50 million tons of coal and emit 100 million tons of carbon dioxide annually.

Figure 12.2 Three Gorges Dam in Hubei province, the largest hydroelectric project in the world

And it is not only within China's borders that Chinese are building hydropower plants. They are aggressively exporting their dam-building experience globally, with more than 300 projects in more than 70 countries in Africa, Asia, the Middle East, Latin America, and Europe. Today, China is the dominant player in the world's hydropower market.[7]

Biomass power plays but a very small role in the country's total energy mix, accounting for just 5.5 GW in 2010 and 10 GW in 2015. While China has abundant biomass resources—in the form of farm and forestry byproducts and residential and industrial waste—the "utilization rate," according to experts, is low, at about 5%. A report in the *China Daily* explains that the "vast majority is not harnessed as the proper technology is not fully in place." In December 2016, however, the National Energy Administration of China announced plans to develop the biomass energy industry over the next five years in order to reduce coal use and clean the air.[8]

A number of motives explain Beijing's efforts these days to build a strong renewable energy infrastructure. Reducing the reliance on coal consumption is no doubt at the top of the list. After all, reduced coal use is expected to result in better, cleaner air, greater availability of freshwater, improved public health, and a more secure energy future. But it should not be lost on us that China also sees clean energy and green technology as central to tomorrow's global economy, and it wants to assume global leadership in that economy. Today, China already is the leading manufacturer in the world of solar photovoltaic panels and wind turbines, and home to the world's largest turbine manufacturer, Goldwind Science and Technology, and the world's largest solar module manufacturer, Trina Solar.

What Are Some of the Limitations of Wind and Solar Energy Use in China?

China expects its renewable energy resources to represent an increasingly large share of its total energy supply over the next couple of decades. The development of wind and solar capacity has been phenomenal in recent years, and projections through the mid-21st century show no letup. Already, the country has both the largest wind and the largest solar capacity in the world.

But a considerable portion of that capacity goes unused each year. In 2015, for example, 12% of the country's energy from solar and 15% of the energy from wind sat idle. A number of factors help to explain this waste. The rapid expansion of wind and solar energy resources has far outpaced the ability of the grid to absorb and transmit the power they generate. Transmission lines are not yet sufficiently extensive or powerful to accommodate the swelling electrical load. A related consideration is the remote location of the production centers of wind and solar energy. North and west China, home to much of the renewable industry, are too far from the urban and industrial hubs of the east and south, where power demand is highest, to allow for the bulk transmission of their wind and solar energy supply. A system of high-voltage power lines is needed to carry wind- and solar-produced electricity across the country.

Without connectivity to the grid, wind and solar energy producers obviously cannot hope to distribute their supply of power. Still, connectivity to the grid does not alone ensure distribution. Grid operators, looking ahead a day or so at the weather forecast (e.g., wind, rain, sun, heat) and the respective availability of different sources of energy, decide which power plants their grid networks will draw on. But for decades the state has made clear that it expects grid operators to give priority access to coal power, with the intention of encouraging the building of coal-fired power plants to drive China's economic development. And this expectation has suited grid operators just fine since coal is predictable and reliable, not to mention inexpensive and abundant.

The end result, however, has been that wind and solar plants, capable of producing considerable amounts of power, stand idle much of the time, since the country's grids have been unable, or slow, to accept their electricity. For example, in the sun-drenched provinces of Xinjiang and Gansu, unused or "curtailed" solar power represented 26% and 31%, respectively, in 2015; in wind-rich Gansu, Xinjiang, and Jilin, wind curtailment rates all exceeded 30%. The grids' preference for coal-fired power helps explain why today China generates less electricity from wind power than the United States despite having almost double the wind power capacity.

President Xi's pledge in September 2015 at a meeting at the White House to implement "green dispatch" is giving hope to the country's environmentalists that China is, in fact, shifting gears and henceforth will give priority grid access to renewable and clean energies, thereby reducing what is now a significant waste of clean energy that could be replacing coal-generated power. Xi's words are worth quoting:

> China's "green dispatch" system will prioritize power generation from renewable sources, and establish guidelines to accept electricity first from the most efficient and lowest-polluting fossil fuel generators. This approach will accelerate the phase down of high-polluting, energy-intensive power while supporting the deployment of renewable and non-fossil sources, and will better utilize China's rapidly growing solar and wind capacity while supporting its ambitious non-fossil energy targets of 15 percent by 2020 and around 20 percent by 2030.[9]

A final limitation of wind and solar energy that must be taken into account is that until a convenient and economic means of storing wind and solar power is developed, both solar photovoltaics and wind turbines will be capable of providing power only when the weather cooperates. This "intermittency" means that at the moment neither wind nor solar can serve as a reliable stand-alone source of power.

Are There Concerns over the Deployment of Hydropower in China?

Few in China would dispute that hydropower is cleaner and less damaging to the planet than coal-fired power, but over the years, awareness of problems associated with the buildout of hydroelectric facilities has grown. Whether these problems, in the end, outweigh the benefits of hydropower use is a matter of some debate. The problems that generate the greatest concern are the following.[10]

Ecological Effects of Dams

Dams interrupt river flow, alter the river's velocity, temperature, and chemical balance, and trap silt, all of which, in turn, affects plant and fish life, fish population, fish migrations, soil health downstream, downstream water resources, and the health of downstream rivers and lakes.

Consider, for instance, that the Yangtze carries about 500 million tons of silt each year to the Three Gorges area; most of it is trapped by the dam there and deposited in the reservoir. The downstream area of the Yangtze is consequently deprived of this sediment, and the effects of this are (1) a deficit in nutrient load downriver, (2) growing coastal erosion, and (3) changes to the ecology of the East China Sea, the outlet for the Yangtze. The dam has also been blamed for having disrupted the habitat of the Chinese sturgeon, the sturgeon, and the paddlefish; all three are now considered endangered. The famous rare freshwater dolphin that once lived in the Yangtze, the *baiji*, was recently declared extinct. Overfishing, water pollution, and the dam have been held responsible. Since the completion of the dam, the two largest freshwater lakes in China, Dongting and Poyang, downstream in Hunan and Jiangxi respectively, have shrunk dramatically, much of their areas having gone dry. Experts attribute the conditions of these lakes to the much-reduced river flow resulting from the damming.

Population Resettlement

It is estimated that in the past half-century more than 23 million people have been forced to resettle to make way for dams. They are promised housing and resettlement cash in return but often receive less than full compensation. The land available to them for farming is typically degraded, and their lack of skills, training, and education makes them poorly suited for most other jobs, even if they are available. Of the 23 million people displaced by the dam-building frenzy, 8 million are said to be living below the poverty line.[11] Finally, there is also the often-high emotional cost of being uprooted from all that they have ever known. The Three Gorges dam alone necessitated the resettlement of a government-estimated 1.3 million people, though the actual figure is likely closer to 2 million.

Loss of Farmland

When the Three Gorges reservoir was filled, according to official reports, 13 cities, 140 towns, and 1,350 villages were submerged, forever lost. So, too, were 74,131 acres (30,000 hectares) of agricultural land, which experts regard as some of China's most fertile. In a country where land resources have been chipped away and food security has become a state priority, flooding vast swaths of arable, cultivated land represents a considerable sacrifice.

Greenhouse Gas Emissions

Hydroelectric is often described as a zero-emissions energy source, but this is not the full story. The flooding reservoir water swallows up plant life and inundates trees and forests; as the vegetation and soil rots with time, the surface water of the reservoir releases into the air carbon dioxide and methane, a greenhouse gas far more potent than carbon dioxide. Earlier, scientists believed that the surface of reservoirs may account for 20% of all human-made methane emission, but recent research suggests that it is still higher, although the researchers themselves say that the issue needs more study. Still, there is now a strong scientific consensus that dam reservoirs release a considerable burden of greenhouse gases into the air and are major contributors to climate change.[12]

Earthquakes and Landslides

Much of China is geologically unstable and seismically active. This is especially true in western and southwestern China, where the current hydro expansion is taking place. Looking at dams that have been built, are under construction, or are planned in the region, a Probe International 2012 study concluded that 1.4% are located in "zones of low seismic hazard," 48.2% are in "zones of high to very high seismic hazard," and the remaining 50.4% are in "zones of moderate hazard." The upshot here—that 98.6% of these dams are located in zones of moderate to very high seismic hazard—is worrisome to geologists and environmentalists. Structural damage to a dam, or a dam's collapse, could lead to massive and uncontrollable flooding downstream.[13]

But recent studies have begun to indicate that the dams themselves, with the weight of the impounded water, can place tremendous pressure on the underlying geological plates and activate movement. This is called "reservoir-induced seismicity." There is a growing belief among scientists that the 2008 Wenchuan earthquake outside of Chengdu, which killed almost 90,000 people, may have been set off by smaller quakes triggered by the nearby Zipingpu Dam. The 2014 earthquake in Ludian county in Yunnan, responsible for over 600 deaths, has been tied by some geologists to two dams within 10 kilometers, both of whose reservoirs were being filled at the time of the quake. Research into reservoir-induced seismicity is still in its early stages, but thus far it suggests that caution should be taken in constructing dams in seismically active areas of China.[14]

A 2010 study by seismologists at the China Earthquake Administration has added to concerns: researching the seismic activity in the Three Gorges area during the 6.5-year period

(2003–2009) in which the reservoir was being filled, they found that the area around the reservoir registered 3,429 small earthquakes, a 10-fold increase in frequency over the era before the Three Gorges Dam was built.[15]

With dams also comes the worry of landslides. The fluctuation of water levels in their reservoirs makes for quick changes in water pressure, which, in turn, weaken and destabilize the surrounding terrain. Seismic activity—a tremor or a quake—can set a perilous landslide in motion. So, too, can heavy rains, as the May 2016 Fujian landslide, which took more than 40 lives, reminds us.

Climate Change

Of concern, too, is how climate change might affect the country's future hydropower capacity. The Qinghai–Tibetan Plateau region is the source of 10 of Asia's major rivers, including those on which China today is building, or planning to build, new hydropower plants—Jinsha River (upper reaches of Yangtze River), Nu River, Lancang River, and Yarlung Zangbo River. Owing to rising temperatures (3.42°F [1.9°C] since 1961), the glaciers in the plateau region, which feed the headwaters of these rivers, have shrunk 33% in the past century. Some scientists warn that two-thirds of these glaciers could be entirely gone as early as 2050. The effect that this magnitude of glacial melt would have on China's water resources—and on the country's hydropower capacity—is, literally, incalculable.[16]

The frequency and severity of droughts are expected to increase in the coming decades as the climate changes. Droughts will affect river flow, which in turn will create greater variability in the capacity of hydropower plants to generate electricity.[17]

Geopolitics

The Chinese government has targeted 10 rivers as key to their plans for large-scale hydro expansion. Three of these rivers, located in China's southwest, are the Lancang, the Yarlung Zangbo, and the Nu. But building dams on these rivers entails geopolitical risks, as they are all transboundary: the Lancang starts in Qinghai, flows into Tibet and Yunnan, and then makes its way to Southeast Asia as the Mekong River, streaming through Myanmar (Burma), Laos, Thailand, Cambodia, and Vietnam; the Yarlung Zangbo has its headwaters in Tibet, snakes its way into India, where it becomes the Brahmaputra, and then merges with the Ganges and flows out to sea through Bangladesh; and the Nu, which has its source in Qinghai, flows into Tibet and Yunnan, and then streams into Myanmar and Thailand as the Salween.

Tensions arise when China builds dams on, or diverts water from, the length of these rivers within its borders. After all, dam building and water diversion there mean changes to river flow, sediment and nutrient load, pollution levels, and aquatic life downstream, across its borders. Agriculture, especially rice and wheat production, and fisheries, wild and farmed, are profoundly affected; so too is the supply of drinking water, for a large and growing population. And the more water China draws to generate hydropower for its use, the less is available to its riparian neighbors to develop their hydropower resources. The crux of the problem is that there exist no international treaties that govern the use of these transboundary waters.[18] And China has not shown an eagerness to participate in any such treaties.

By controlling the headwaters of the Lancang/Mekong, Yarlung Zangbo/Brahmaputra, and Nu/Salween, China, in effect, exercises considerable power over more than 1 billion people living in countries to the south. In the coming years, as China moves forward with plans to expand its hydropower capacity, the risk of skirmishes with neighboring peoples over water use and rights looms. To ensure stability in the region, China should proceed with care and in a spirit of cooperation.

What Are China's Plans for the Development of Nuclear Power?

Nuclear energy, which has lost favor globally, is enjoying a boom in China. Nuclear first entered the picture in the 1970s when the Chinese government targeted it as a "developing industry." In 2004, the government called for accelerated development of nuclear energy, from "moderate development" to "positive development." The Fukushima disaster in 2011 slowed the growth of nuclear energy around the world; the Chinese government suspended the construction of all nuclear reactors to ponder the future of nuclear power. But a year later it lifted the suspension, intent again on forging ahead, and by the end of 2012 the country had 14 nuclear reactors in operation, with an installed capacity of 11 GW. By 2015, the number of reactors had more than doubled to over 30, another 20 were under construction, and nuclear capacity had more than doubled to 26 to 28 GW.

Since lifting the suspension, then, China has become a big-time player in nuclear energy (Figure 12.3). In 2015, only the United States (99 GW), France (63 GW), and Japan (40 GW) had more nuclear power capacity than China. And while these three countries—along with many others—have curtailed construction of nuclear power plants, China is building capacity. The 13th Five-Year Plan target is to construct 6 to 8 new plants annually through 2020—a total of 30 to 40 additional plants—which would bring the number of reactors to 60 to 70 and the nuclear capacity to at least 58 GW (with another 30 GW under construction). This would likely put China just behind the United States as the world's leading producer of nuclear energy.

The country's plans for nuclear power extend beyond 2020: the government recently announced that the post-2020 goal is to construct 10 new plants each year. The China Nuclear Energy Association has thus projected that by 2030 China's installed nuclear capacity will be 160 GW, and by 2050 it will

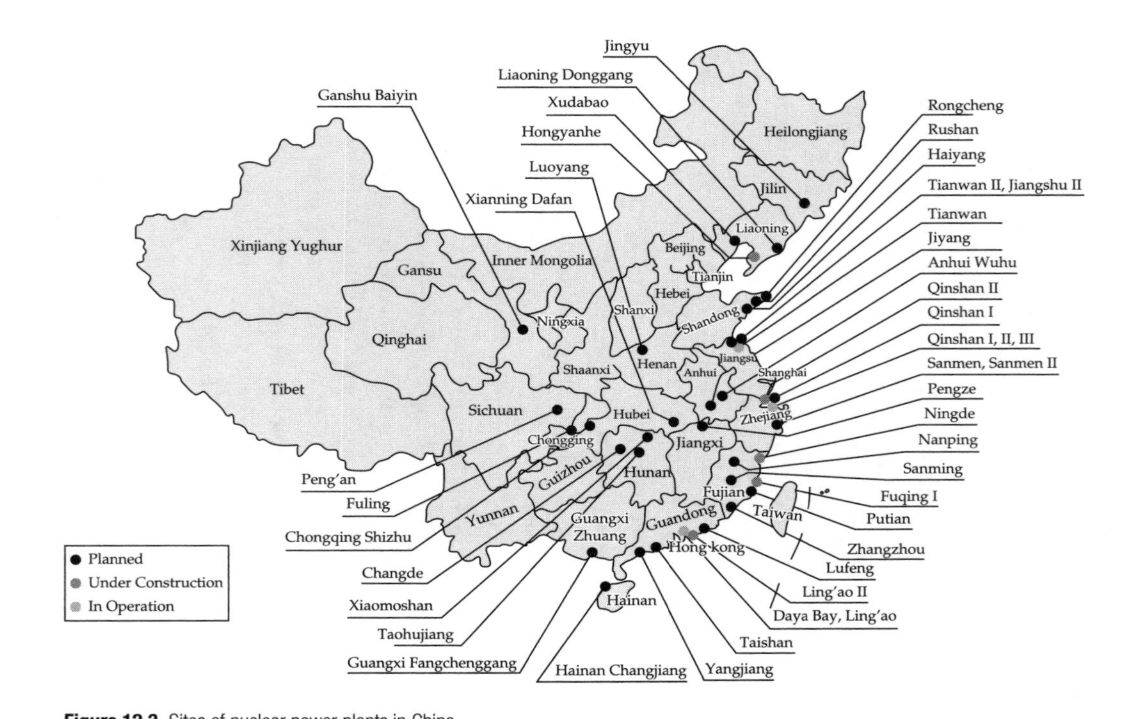

Figure 12.3 Sites of nuclear power plants in China

Source: Research Institute of Tepia (as of Nov. 2008)

reach 240 GW, 10 times the country's present capacity and 2.5 times more than the capacity of the United States today.[19] Some experts think the capacity in 2050 will be closer to 400 GW, generated by what would be 400 to 500 new nuclear reactors.[20]

As of early 2016 China's nuclear agenda also includes building, by 2020, 20 floating nuclear power plants, which could sail to remote sites wherever power is needed.[21] Construction of the first such floating reactor began in 2017. It is believed that the main uses of China's floating nuclear plants will be to generate power for offshore oil and gas exploration and for building and operating artificial islands on reefs in the South China Sea. Tensions over what is viewed in the region as China's aggressive behavior are already high, and China's plan to build a fleet of floating nuclear plants is intensifying them.

The Beijing leadership views nuclear energy as a clean alternative to fossil fuels, a source of power that emits many fewer pollutants and much less carbon. But as with wind and solar energy, Beijing believes that the country's investment in nuclear energy will benefit more than the environment alone. Already, today, China is helping to build reactors in countries around the world: Pakistan, Argentina, Britain, and Romania, to name a few.[22] China is positioning itself to be the leader of what it is convinced will be the economy of tomorrow, an economy based on clean energy and green technology.

Is There Opposition to the Government's Plan to Promote Nuclear Power?

There has been some vocal opposition by those who worry that the country may be ramping up its nuclear capacity far too quickly, and that in its eagerness to develop the economy and new sources of energy the government is putting the people's safety at risk. One prominent nuclear physicist at the Chinese Academy of Science, He Zuoxiu, called the rush to build another 30 to 40 nuclear plants by 2020 "insane," and predicted that China will "most probably" suffer from a nuclear disaster by 2030.[23] "China has to have nuclear energy—we need the power," He Zuoxiu acknowledges, "but we need to slow down and take a more measured approach, and really learn the lessons of Fukushima."[24]

The nuclear plants operating today are situated mostly along the east and south coast, where energy is in highest demand and where there is ready availability of water, which is essential for cooling the reactors. But as space along these coasts is running out, the government is building, and planning to build, reactors inland, locating them near rivers and lakes that can supply cooling water. Many question the wisdom of expanding nuclear sites inland. Nuclear power plants require more water—for cooling purposes—than coal-fired power plants producing the same amount of electricity. The country's fresh water is already in short supply, with groundwater drying up and rivers and lakes even disappearing. Will inland nuclear plants be competing with local farmers and inhabitants for limited water resources? Will there be enough water to keep the reactors running (in the summers between 2003 and 2009 plants across Europe were forced to stop operations owing to limited water availability)? Will climate change, with the heat waves and droughts that are expected to result, make matters still worse?

China—especially the central and western parts—is a country of intense seismicity and, as a consequence, highly vulnerable to destructive earthquakes. Since 1900, more earthquakes have struck China than any other country in the world. According to the China Earthquake Administration's Institute of Geology, nearly 800 of them were of magnitude 6 or above. For some, like Wang Yi'nan, a student and colleague of He Zuoxiu, building nuclear facilities in a region of such known tectonic instability is irresponsible: "Nuclear power is not yet controlled, not yet tamed, not yet safe . . . China cannot take the enormous risks of building nuclear power plants inland."[25]

While the above experts, and others like them, have expressed concerns about China's intention to go all-in on nuclear, the general public has seemed, until recently, largely amenable to—or at least silent about—Beijing's efforts to build the country's nuclear capacity. Likely, anxiety over the health-threatening smog has inclined the public to look favorably on a nuclear alternative that promises clean energy. This was especially true before 2011 and the Fukushima nuclear meltdown. Since then, criticism of nuclear development appears to be growing, and with the criticism have come some protests. Local residents, worried principally about the effects on their health, have gathered to express opposition to plans to build a nuclear power plant in Pengze county in Jiangxi (2012), a uranium processing facility in the city of Heshan in Guangdong (2013), and a nuclear fuel reprocessing plant in the city of Lianyungang in Jiangsu (2016). Thus far, the protests have been localized and have shown little sign of expanding into a countrywide anti-nuclear movement.

EPILOGUE

THE ENVIRONMENTAL CHALLENGE IN THE 21ST CENTURY

How Serious Is China Today About Addressing Its Environmental Problems?

In the late 1970s, just after the death of Chairman Mao (1976), paramount leader Deng Xiaoping launched a series of liberal market reforms. Few observers then would have imagined what the next four decades would bring. China's GDP has grown almost 10% annually since, and its economy is now the second largest in the world. Forty years ago, the single-speed Flying Pigeon bicycle ruled the roads; today, China is the world's largest car market. And, if 40 years ago, you looked out across the Huangpu River from the Bund in Shanghai, you would have seen farmland and a few warehouses and wharves; now you look up from the Bund and see the stunning, futuristic cityscape of Pudong. The material progress of the past 40 years has been breathtaking—a source of pride for the Chinese people, as well as a source of legitimacy for the ruling Chinese Communist Party.

But that progress has come at great cost to China's environment and the health of the Chinese people. There are 1.4 million or so premature deaths in China annually owing to ambient air pollution. More than 60% of China's groundwater and 50%

of the water in the country's rivers and lakes are classified as "poor" or "very poor." Some 300 million people do not have access to safe drinking water. And, in a country where arable land is precious, 20% of it is contaminated with heavy metal; some environmentalists say that the actual figure may be as high as 70%.

Public awareness of the pollution crisis has grown. The subject of pollution now gets a lot of airtime in China's social media. More telling, and certainly more ominous for the ruling Communist Party, has been the rise of environmental protests, as citizens have taken more freely to the streets to express opposition to the building of coal-fired power plants, petrochemical plants, waste incinerators, oil refineries, battery manufacturers, and the like. Environmental protests have increased an average of 29% annually since 1996, and pollution is now the leading cause of social unrest in China.

The year 2013 marks what in the future, I think, will be viewed as a turning point in modern China's environmental policies and attitudes. Whether driven by an increasing realization of the toll that environmental degradation was taking on the country's air, water, and land, or of the toll that it was taking on the nation's GDP (authoritative estimates pegged it at 8–12% of the GDP), or of the toll it was taking on the people's patience (and thus the ruling party's legitimacy), China's leadership in that year promised a new ecological direction for the country. In May, the just-appointed president, Xi Jinping, convened a study session with members of the Politburo on "promoting ecological progress," promising that China will no longer "sacrifice the environment for temporary economic growth" but "will consciously promote a green, sustainable and low-carbon development pattern" and "carefully balance economic development and environmental protection."[1] A few months later, in November, the Central Committee of the Communist Party met and, echoing Xi Jinping's words, "vowed to pursue a green and sustainable path to balanced economic, ecological and social development."[2]

With the efficiency that only an authoritarian, one-party state can muster, the government took a number of immediate and decisive steps, no doubt both to give substantive expression to its environmental pledge and to tamp down the people's growing frustration over the worsening pollution. In 2013, China's leadership committed $277 billion through the end of 2017 to an air pollution "action plan" and $333 billion to a water pollution "action plan." In the next year, declaring "war on pollution," it shuttered hundreds of small and inefficient coal plants, banned the building of new coal-fired power plants in the country's so-called three key economic regions, and limited the growth of energy-intensive industries (e.g., cement, glass, steel, and aluminum). More recently, in anticipation of the 2015 climate change talks in Paris, it announced plans to cap the nation's energy consumption nationwide by 2020, "peak" carbon emissions by 2030, introduce a nationwide carbon cap-and-trade program in 2017, and increase the share of non-fossil fuel resources to 20% of its primary energy mix by 2030. Today, China is the world's largest consumer of wind energy and the world's second largest consumer of solar energy, and it is by far the world's largest investor in renewable energy.

How successful China ultimately will be in addressing its environmental crisis, in cleaning up its polluted air, water, and soil, is uncertain. But to doubt the determination with which Beijing is tackling the so-called war on pollution would be a mistake. There exists today a growing awareness, among the leaders and public alike, of just how much is at stake—China's environment, economy, health, and political and social stability.

What Is the "Ecological Civilization" Campaign?

With the establishment of the People's Republic in 1949, China has pursued an aggressive, no-holds-barred policy of economic development, summed up neatly in the slogan *xian wuran hou zhili* ("pollute first, clean up later"). By all accounts, as we have seen throughout this book, China's economic development has been nothing short of staggering. But so, too, have been the effects on the country's environment. The "clean up later" stage has apparently now arrived. Chinese leaders and media no longer talk of the "pursuit of growth at all costs." Since 2013 they have spoken of a new policy, of building an "ecological civilization" (生态文明 *shengtai wenming*), proclaiming that the country's economic growth must henceforth be balanced by equal concern for protecting the environment and the people's "quality of life."[3]

The campaign is meant to mobilize everyone, the public and government officials alike. To the public the campaign's message is: "We, the Party, have heard you and are taking every measure possible to ensure your quality of life. But alone we cannot protect the environment against harm from anthropogenic sources; we call on everyone's 'legal and orderly' participation, and also on everyone's understanding and patience, should efforts to build an ecological civilization slow our country's economic growth." To officials—at the national, the provincial, and the local levels—the message is: "In the name of economic growth you have been lax in implementing and enforcing our country's environmental regulations. Worse still, many of you have been guilty of corruption, taking bribes from polluters. Such laxness and corruption will no longer be tolerated."

Launching a campaign is one thing but selling it is another, requiring a range of rhetorical strategies. To win support for the Party's eco-civilization project, officials and state media regularly resort to a language of nationalism, explaining that "industrial civilization"—a civilization that has its roots in the post–Industrial Revolution West—is unworkable in the 21st-century world of strained natural resources and unequal wealth distribution. A "civilization revolution" is required, turning away from today's outmoded model to a new model that takes account of the inherent value of the natural world, the reciprocal relationship between nature and humankind, and the obligation humankind has to preserve the planet's resources for future generations.

And China, the leadership and the media claim, has in its native tradition precisely the cultural resources needed to construct this new civilization in place of "industrial civilization." As Pan Yue, former Deputy Minister of Environmental Protection, explained: "Ecological thinking is one of the main essences of Chinese traditional civilization, which makes it possible for us to reflect on and transcend the material civilization that has dominated mankind since the Renaissance."[4] More specifically, he maintained that it is the so-called Three Teachings—Confucianism, Daoism, and Buddhism—that furnish the conceptual and linguistic resources for constructing a meaningful native-based eco-civilization:

> One of the core principles of traditional Chinese culture is that of harmony between humans and nature. Different philosophies all emphasize the political wisdom of a balanced environment. Whether it is the Confucian idea of humans and nature becoming one, the Daoist view of the Dao reflecting nature, or the Buddhist belief that all living things are equal, Chinese philosophy has helped our culture to survive for thousands of years. It can be a powerful weapon in preventing an environmental crisis and building a harmonious society.[5]

This raises a series of fascinating questions: Can, in fact, Confucianism, Daoism, and Buddhism make a genuine contribution to the development of a "post-industrial" eco-philosophy and eco-civilization, as Pan Yue and others assert? Are the resources they offer more than superficial, or is the reference to them in the campaign just a nationalistic prop to help win people's cooperation as the state shifts direction and marches into an unsure economic and ecological future? The next couple of decades may offer some answers.

As China Aims to Build an Ecological Civilization in the 21st Century, What Are Some of the Challenges It Faces?

Urbanization

Beijing has begun pursuing a policy of aggressive urbanization, aiming to move 250 million people from the countryside to the cities by 2025. The state's expectation is that by urbanizing, it will promote the growth of the middle class, and that this growing middle class, in turn, will help transform the country's economy from one based on low-value-added, high-polluting manufactured products, much of it for export, to one based on higher-value products (especially in green and high-tech industries), services, and domestic consumption. Economically, this may be a reasonable policy, but, environmentally, the challenges it poses are considerable. They include urban spread at the expense of arable land; extensive construction of buildings and roadways; higher demand for housing, large appliances, and air conditioning and heating systems; increased use of automobiles; greater consumption of laptops, computers, microwaves, and other electronic goods; and higher concentrations of sewage, wastewater discharge, and solid waste requiring treatment. And then, of course, there is the air pollution that results from urban industry, power plants, cars, transportation sources, housing and utilities, and so forth.

Environmental degradation need not be the inevitable outcome of China's "hyper-urbanization" policy. It brings with it an opportunity to engage in the thoughtful planning of smart, sustainable, people-friendly cities, with green systems of public transportation, energy-efficient buildings, and communities that intelligently integrate work life, residential life, and recreational life. Such cities could serve as models to the rest of the world, especially developing countries.

A Rising Middle Class and Civil Society

A growing urban, middle class likely means higher levels of consumption—and more pollution. But it also means a wealthier, better-informed citizenry, more deeply invested in protecting the environment and in safeguarding the health of their families. It is this urban middle class that has already begun taking to social media, and to the streets, to register displeasure with environmental conditions. The targets of displeasure, thus far, have been local, directed at threats posed to the immediate environment by this particular plant or that particular incinerator. If, however, McKinsey's estimates are accurate, and by 2022 a full 75% of China's urban households will be middle and upper middle class, we, and leaders in Beijing, might expect a growing civil engagement with the environment, one with the potential to evolve into an organized national movement.[6]

A growing civil engagement that partners with the government and assists in advancing its goals could be a huge benefit to the ruling party and its environmental efforts. However, a growing engagement that sees the government as ineffectual in addressing the country's environmental crisis or, still worse, as responsible for generating the crisis can threaten sociopolitical stability, and ultimately the very legitimacy of the Communist Party. If the country's civil society continues to expand, as is expected, Beijing will continue to face a knotty question: How much latitude should civil society be given in building the country's ecological civilization?

Climate Change

Climate change, in which, of course, China's burden of carbon emission plays an increasingly large role, has resulted in a 1°C rise in temperature over the past 40 years. The future promises further warming, with scientists predicting severe consequences for China's environment: a rise in sea levels, accelerated glacial melt, and an increase in extreme weather events. A rise in sea levels will affect China's eastern coastal area in particular, which accounts for 40% of the country's population and 56% of its GDP. The megacities of Shanghai and Tianjin, with populations of 23 million and 11 million respectively, are thought to be especially vulnerable. According to the Coastal City Flood Vulnerability Index, Shanghai is the most vulnerable city in the world to serious flooding from climate change.[7]

Mountain glaciers in the Qinghai–Tibet region and the Himalayas are the major source of the Yellow River and the Yangtze River, China's two largest rivers. But these glaciers have shrunk by 15% in the last 30 years alone. Their retreat, scientists argue, threatens to lower river runoff levels, lower groundwater levels, reduce water supplies for drinking and irrigation, and shrink the crop yield. Throw in extreme weather events like floods, droughts, and typhoons, and climate change clearly does not augur well for a healthy Chinese eco-civilization.

International Relations

If the world has become increasingly "globalized," no place is it more obvious than in matters environmental. The United States and the European Union outsource their manufacturing to China, China dirties its air, and then winds send that air to Korea, Japan, and even the west coast of the United States, where it deposits particulate matter and mercury. China experiences a drought and buys grain on the world commodities market, and the price of bread in Egypt goes up, contributing to political destabilization. A more affluent Chinese population moves from a semi-vegetarian diet to a meat diet, resulting in a greater demand for livestock, but since China does not have adequate land resources to harvest livestock feed, the country imports it (mainly soybeans and maize) from the Amazon, which clears the region's rainforests to grow it.

Looking ahead, as China weans itself from coal and looks for cleaner sources of energy, it continues to develop hydroelectric power. This, as we know, has meant constructing huge hydropower dams in China's southwest, at the headwaters of rivers that flow into other countries—the Lancang (Mekong), the Nu (Salween), and the Yarlung Zangbo (Brahmaputra)—affecting river flow (rate and amount), river ecology, sedimentation, fishing, aquaculture, and agriculture in Southeast Asian countries and India. Turning to a cleaner source of energy may thus prove beneficial to China's eco-civilization project, but it also makes for tense relations with neighboring countries.

Then there is logging. Since logging has been tied to widespread erosion, desertification, and flooding in the country, the Chinese government has outlawed it. The result: China is now the largest importer of timber in the world, in effect outsourcing its deforestation. And much of that timber, it turns out, is unlawfully cut in Indonesia, Malaysia, Myanmar, Siberia, and parts of Africa, to the dismay of authorities in these places, and smuggled into China.

China's pursuit of a new kind of eco-civilization, where economic growth and environmental protection achieve a balanced accord, will have implications beyond its own boundaries. China runs a risk of losing the patience and goodwill of the international community if, in fashioning a healthier, more harmonious society for itself, it appears to ignore the ecological and economic well-being of other countries.

Much is at stake as China attempts to make an "environmental turn" in the 21st century—and not only for China. If today's economic system is global, even more so is today's ecological system. Just as manufactured products, technology, food, currency, and the like routinely make their way across countries and continents, so, too, do air and water and the pollutants they carry. When any one country warms the atmosphere with its greenhouse emissions, there is no place on the planet that is not affected. What happens to China environmentally in the 21st century matters deeply—for everyone.

NOTES

Chapter 1

1. "Greenpeace: China Saw Average PM2.5 Levels Fall by 10% in 2015, But 80% of Cities Still Fail to Meet National Air Quality Standards," Greenpeace.org, January 1, 2016. For a fuller discussion of PM2.5 see Chapter 5 in this volume.
2. See the Institute for Health Metrics and Evaluation, "Global Burden of Disease Study, 2010," *Lancet*, Vol. 380, No. 9859 (December 2012); and Richard A. Rohde and Richard A. Muller, "Air Pollution in China: Mapping of Concentrations and Sources," *PLoS One*, Vol. 10, No. 8 (August 20, 2015).
3. Fergus Green and Nicholas Stern, "China's Changing Economy: Implications for Its Carbon Dioxide Emissions," *Climate Policy*, March 16, 2016.
4. Jonathan Kaiman, "Beijing Smog Makes City Unliveable, Says Mayor," *The Guardian*, January 28, 2015.
5. Jonathan Kaiman, "China's Toxic Air Pollution Resembles Nuclear Winter, Say Scientists," *The Guardian*, February 25, 2014.
6. "Thirsty Beijing to Raise Water Prices in Conservation Push," Reuters, April 29, 2014.
7. "2013 State of Environment Report Review," China Water Risk, July 9, 2014.
8. Barry van Wyk, "The Groundwater of 90% of Chinese Cities is Polluted," Danwei.com, February 18, 2013 (http://www.danwei.com/the-groundwater-of-90-of-chinese-cities-is-polluted/).
9. *OECD Economic Surveys: China, 2013* (Paris: OECD Publishing, 2013), pp. 115–116.

10. Jin Xiangcan, Xu Qiujing, and Huang Changzhu, "Current Status and Future Tendency of Lake Eutrophication in China," *Science in China*, Ser. C, Life Sciences, Vol. 48, Supplement (September 2005) [in Chinese].
11. Beth Walker, "Most of China's Coastal Waters Heavily Polluted," ChinaDialogue.net, March 11, 2015.
12. Laura Lin, "Chinese Countryside Facing More Serious Drinking Water Crisis Than Cities," ChinaDialogue.net, May 7, 2014.
13. Edward, Wong, "One-fifth of China's Farmland is Polluted, State Study Finds," *New York Times*, April 17, 2014.
14. "China Says Over 3 Mln Hectares of Land Too Polluted to Farm," Reuters, December 30, 2013.
15. "China's Soil Heavily Polluted by Mining, Industry: Report," Radio Free Asia, April 17, 2014.
16. "*Xinhua* Insight: China Alerted by Serious Soil Pollution, Vows Better Protection," *Xinhua*, April 17, 2014.
17. "Guiyu: An E-Waste Nightmare," Greenpeace East Asia, August 11, 2009; Ivan Watson, "China: The Electronic Wastebasket of the World," CNN, May 30, 2013.
18. Michael Standaert, "China's Notorious E-Waste Village Disappears Almost Overnight," Bloomberg BNA (www.bna.com), December 17, 2015.

Chapter 2

1. Mark Elvin, *The Retreat of the Elephants: An Environmental History of China* (New Haven, CT: Yale University Press, 2004), pp. 42–44.
2. Arthur Waley, *The Book of Songs* (New York: Grove Press, 1960), p. 162 (Mao Ode #290).
3. Qu Geping and Li Jinchang, *Population and the Environment in China*, translated by Jiang Baozhong and Gu Ran (Boulder, CO: Lynne Rienner Publishers, 1994), p. 25.
4. Mark Elvin, "Three Thousand Years of Unsustainable Growth: China's Environment from Archaic Times to the Present," *East Asian History*, Vol. 6 (1993), pp. 36–37 (slightly revised).
5. Qi Feng, Hua Ma, Xuemei Jiang, Xin Wang, and Shixiong Cao, "What Has Caused Desertification in China," Nature.com (Scientific Reports), November 3, 2015; and "Desertification and Land Degradation in China," Geocases (http://www.geocases1.co.uk/printable/Desertification%20and%20land%20degredation%20in%20China.htm).

6. Peter Hays Gries, Chapter 3, "A 'Century of Humiliation'" in *China's New Nationalism: Pride, Politics, and Diplomacy* (Berkeley: University of California, 2004), and Zheng Wang, *Never Forget National Humiliation: Historical Memory in Chinese Politics and Foreign Relations* (New York: Columbia University Press, 2012).
7. See Judith Shapiro, *Mao's War Against Nature: Politics and Environment in Revolutionary China* (Cambridge, UK: Cambridge University Press, 2001).
8. Yang Jisheng, *Tombstone: The Great Chinese Famine, 1958–1962*, translated by Stacy Mosher and Jian Guo (New York: Farrar, Straus and Giroux, 2012); and Frank Dikötter, *Mao's Great Famine: The History of Mao's Most Devastating Catastrophe, 1958–1962* (New York: Walker and Co., 2010).
9. "Jiang Zemin's Speech Marking Yangtze-Damming for Three Gorges Project," Embassy of the People's Republic of China in the United States of America (http://www.china-embassy.org/eng/zt/sxgc/t36514.htm).
10. William Theodore de Bary and Irene Bloom, eds., *Sources of Chinese Tradition*, Volume 1, 2nd ed. (New York: Columbia University Press, 1999), p. 300.
11. See Daniel K. Gardner, *Confucianism: A Very Short Introduction* (New York: Oxford University Press, 2014).
12. Shapiro, *Mao's War Against Nature*, p. 8.

Chapter 3

1. China's GDP in 2015 was $11.007 trillion, US GDP was $18.036 trillion, and Japan's GDP was $4.124 trillion.
2. Again, membership in the WTO provided an enormous boost. Within the first three years, FDI in China grew almost 30%. For more on China and the WTO, see Abigail Jahiel, "China, the WTO and Implications for the Environment," *Environmental Politics*, Volume 15, No. 2 (April 2006), pp. 310–329.
3. Oliver Wainwright, "Santa's Real Workshop: The Town in China that Makes the World's Christmas Decorations," *The Guardian*, December 19, 2014.
4. Marc Bain, "These Chinese Textile Mills Are Going Green—and Saving Millions," *Quartz*, April 16, 2015 (https://qz.com/383562/these-chinese-textile-mills-are-going-green-and-saving-millions/).

5. Jintai Lin, Da Pan, Steven J. Davis, et al., "China's International Trade and Air Pollution in the United States," *Proceedings of the National Academy of Sciences USA*, Vol. 111, No. 5 (February 4, 2014), pp. 1736–1741.
6. Li Jing, "670,000 Smog-Related Deaths a Year: The Cost of China's Reliance on Coal," *South China Morning Post*, November 5, 2014.
7. Angel Hsu and William Miao, "28,000 Rivers Disappeared in China: What Happened," *The Atlantic*, April 29, 2013.
8. United Nations Environment Program (UNEP), "The Songhua River Spill China, December 2005 (Field Mission Report)," December 2005.
9. "Shoots, Greens and Leaves," *The Economist*, June 16, 2012 (http://www.economist.com/node/21556904).
10. John Vidal, "Air Pollution Costs Trillions and Holds Back Poor Countries," *The Guardian*, September 8, 2016; and *The Cost of Air Pollution: Strengthening the Economic Case for Action*, The World Bank and Institute for Health Metrics and Evaluation (Washington, DC: World Bank, 2016).
11. On urban expansion, see Xuemei Bai, Peijun Shi, and Yansui Liu, "Society: Realizing China's Urban Dream," *Nature*, Vol. 509, Issue 7499 (May 7, 2014), pp. 158–160; and Kaifang Shi, Yun Chen, Bailiang Yu, et al., "Urban Expansion and Agricultural Land Loss in China: A Multiscale Perspective," *Sustainability*, Vol. 8, Issue 8 (August 2016), pp. 1–16.
12. See, for example, Peiyue Li, Hui Qian, and Jianhua Wu, "Environment: Accelerate Research on Land Creation," *Nature*, Vol. 510, Issue 9503 (June 4, 2014), pp. 29–31.
13. "Beijing May Face Waste Crisis in Four Years," Crienglish.com, December 30, 2009 (http://english.cri.cn/6909/2009/12/30/2001s538914.htm). The film *Beijing Besieged by Waste* (Beijing: Wang Jiuliang Studio Production, 2011) graphically documents Beijing's waste problem.
14. "Full Text of Hu Jintao's Report at the 18th Party Congress," *Xinhua*, November 17, 2012 (http://news.xinhuanet.com/english/special/18cpcnc/2012-11/17/c_131981259.htm).
15. "Communiqué of the Third Plenary Session of the 18th Central Committee of the Communist Party of China," China.org.cn, January 15, 2014 (http://www.china.org.cn/china/third_plenary_session/2014-01/15/content_31203056.htm).

16. Rafael Halpin, "Hebei is Warning for Whole Chinese Economy," *Financial Times* (blogs.ft.com), April 25, 2014 (http://blogs.ft.com/beyond-brics/2014/04/25/guest-post-hebei-is-warning-for-whole-chinese-economy/).
17. Li Jing, "60,000 Jobs: The Cost of One Chinese City's Cleaner Air," *South China Morning Post*, July 2, 2015.

Chapter 4

1. Dominic Barton, Yougang Cheng, and Amy Jin, "Mapping China's Middle Class," *McKinsey Quarterly*, June 2013.
2. Bin Zhao, "Consumerism, Confucianism, Communism: Making Sense of China Today," *New Left Review*, I/222 (March–April 1997), pp. 43–59.
3. Xinye Zheng, Chu Wei, Ping Qin, et al., "Characteristics of Residential Energy Consumption in China: Findings from a Household Survey," *Energy Policy*, Vol. 75 (2014), pp. 126–135.
4. Barton, Cheng, and Jin, "Mapping China's Middle Class."
5. "Survey on China's Middle-Class Consumers (Executive Summary)," HKTDC Research, August 1, 2013 (http://economists-pick-research.hktdc.com/business-news/article/Research-Articles/Main/rp/en/1/1X000000/1X09U5RU.htm).
6. For a general discussion of China's new consumerism, see Lianne Yu, *Consumption in China: How China's New Consumer Ideology is Shaping the Nation* (Cambridge, UK: Polity Press, 2014); and Arthur R. Kroeber, *China's Economy: What Everyone Needs to Know* (Oxford: Oxford University Press, 2016), Chapter 10, "The Emerging Consumer Economy."
7. Adam Minter, "China's War on Golf Courses," Bloomberg View, April 6, 2015.
8. AECOM, "China Theme Park Pipeline Report 2013," inparkmagazine.com, December 19, 2013 (http://www.inparkmagazine.com/wp-content/uploads/2013/12/AECOM-China-Theme-Park-Pipeline-Report-2013.pdf).
9. Kelli Barrett, "Is China's Demand for Rosewood Turning Africa's Forests into Furniture?," Ecosystem Marketplace, December 2, 2015; Laurence Caramel, "China's Rosewood Craving Cuts Deep into Madagascar Forests," *The Guardian*, February 16, 2015.
10. Karl Gerth, "Lifestyles of the Rich and Infamous: The Creation and Implications of China's New Aristocracy," *Comparative*

Sociology, Vol. 10, Issue 4 (2011), pp. 488–507; "To the Piste," *The Economist*, January 24, 2015.

11. "Beijing Bans High-Emission Vehicles in Anti-Smog Move, Xinhua," Reuters, February 13, 2017.
12. Maureen Fan, "Creating a Car Culture in China," *Washington Post*, January 1, 2008.
13. On cars and car culture in China today, see Karl Gerth, *As China Goes, So Goes the World* (New York: Hill and Wang, 2010), Chapter 1, "No Going Back?"; and Peter Hessler, *Country Driving: A Journey Through China from Farm to Factory* (New York: Harper, 2010).
14. Tania Branigan, "China and Cars: A Love Story," *The Guardian*, December 14, 2012.
15. Adam Taylor, "A Luxury Car Club is Stirring Up Class Conflict in China," *Business Insider*, April 15, 2013.
16. "Porsche Vs. Bicycle in Modern-Day Tortoise and Hare," Bloomberg, October 2012 (https://www.bloomberg.com/news/videos/b/4d1526ab-4cec-463c-8f13-87c18bc45093).
17. Philip M. Fearnside, and Adriano M. R. Figueiredo, "China's Influence on Deforestation in Brazilian Amazonia: A Growing Force in the State of Mato Grosso," BU Global Economic Governance Initiative, Discussion Paper 2015-3 (http://www.bu.edu/pardeeschool/files/2014/12/Brazil1.pdf); and Beth Hoffman, "How Increased Meat Consumption in China Changes Landscapes Across the Globe," *Forbes*, March 26, 2014.
18. Arjen Y. Hoekstra, "The Hidden Water Resource Use Behind Meat and Dairy," *Animal Frontiers*, Vol. 2, No. 2 (April 2012), pp. 3–8.
19. Gideon Eshel, Alon Shepon, Tamar Makov, and Ron Milo, "Land, Irrigation Water, Greenhouse Gas, and Reactive Nitrogen Burdens of Meat, Eggs, and Dairy Production in the United States," *Proceedings of the National Academy of Sciences USA*, Vol. 111, No. 33 (August 2014), pp. 11996–12001.
20. Damian Carrington, "Giving Up Beef Will Reduce Carbon Footprint More than Cars, Says Expert," *The Guardian*, July 21, 2014.
21. In June 2016, the Chinese government urged people to reduce their consumption of meat by 50%, to 40 to 70 grams daily.

Chapter 5

1. According to the WHO, India's mean annual PM2.5 exposure in 2015 was 73 $\mu g/m^3$; China's was 54 $\mu g/m^3$.

2. Greta Anand, "India's Air Pollution Rivals China's as World's Deadliest," *New York Times*, February 14, 2017.
3. Christine Ottery, "Air Pollution Increases Risk of Premature Death in Chinese Cities," Greenpeace Energydesk, February 4, 2015.
4. Xin Ling, "Tracking Down China's Haze Pollution," *Bulletin of the Academy of Sciences*, Vol. 27, No. 3 (2013), pp. 140–144; and Dabo Guan and Zhu Liu, *Tracing Back the Smog: Source Analysis for PM2.5 Pollution in Beijing–Tianjin–Hebei*, Greenpeace East Asia, December 2, 2013.
5. Zachary Davies Boren, "Beyond Beijing: 190 Cities Have Hazardous Air Pollution Amidst New Targets," Energy Desk Greenpeace, January 26, 2015.
6. David Roberts, "How the US Embassy Tweeted to Clear Beijing's Air," *Wired*, March 6, 2015.
7. Patti Waldmeir, "China Pollution: Fears Over Poor Air Exacerbate Healthcare Concerns," *Financial Times*, March 1, 2013.
8. Teo Cheng Wee, "Beijing's Anti-Smog Domes," *The Strait Times*, January 11, 2016.
9. See Oliver Wainwright, "Inside Beijing Airpocalypse—a City Made 'Almost Uninhabitable' by Pollution," *The Guardian*, December 16, 2014; Virginia Mangin, "Return of 'Airpocalypse': Beijing's Expats Flee Smog," BBC Capital, March 21, 2014; and Edward Wong, " 'Airpocalypse' Smog Hits Beijing at Dangerous Levels," *New York Times*, January 16, 2014.
10. Li Jing, "670,000 Smog-Related Deaths a Year: The Cost of China's Reliance on Coal," *South China Morning Post*, November 5, 2014.
11. E.g., Fergus Green and Nicholas Stern, "Managing Economic Change and Mitigating Climate Change: China's Strategies, Policies, and Trends," in *China's New Sources of Economic Growth: Reform, Resources and Climate Change*, Vol. 1, ed. by Ligang Song, Ross Garnaut, Cai Fang, and Lauren Johnston (Canberra: Australian National University, 2016); and Ye Qi, Nicholas Stern, Tong Wu, Jiaqi Liu, and Fergus Green, "China's Post-Coal Growth," *Nature Geoscience* (online), July 25, 2016. Anders Hove of the Paulson Institute is less sure: "What Do Beijing's Blue Skies Really Mean? It's Too Soon to Say," Paulson Institute, May 27, 2015.

12. Su Song, "China's Clean Air Challenge: The Health Impacts of Transport Emssions," *WRI China* (online), November 28, 2014.
13. Heping Jia, "Pollution Research Sparks Car Control Debate in China," *Chemistry World* (online), January 23, 2014.
14. "Air Pollution in China," UNDP Issue Brief, April 23, 2015.

Chapter 6

1. Ting Feng, "Water, the Origin of Life," Center for Sustainable Development (Earth Institute, Columbia University), Policy Brief Series, June 23, 2015.
2. Elizabeth Carlton, Song Liang, Julia Z. McDonell, et al., "Regional Disparities in the Burden of Disease Attributable to Unsafe Water and Poor Sanitation in China," *Bulletin of the World Health Organization*, Vol. 90, No. 8 (August 2012), pp. 578–587.
3. Ibid.
4. "Allen G. P. Ross, Adrian C. Sleigh, Yuesheng Li, et al., "Schistosomiasis in the People's Republic of China: Prospects and Challenges for the 21st Century," *Clinical Microbiology Reviews*, Vol. 14, No. 2 (April 2001), pp. 270–295.
5. Nadya Ivanova, "Toxic Water Across Much of China, Huge Harvests Irrigated with Industrial and Agricultural Runoff," Circle of Blue, January 18, 2013 (http://www.circleofblue.org/2013/world/toxic-water-across-much-of-china-huge-harvests-irrigated-with-industrial-and-agricultural-runoff).
6. Avraham Ebenstein, "The Consequences of Industrialization: Evidence from Water Pollution and Digestive Cancers in China," *Review of Economics and Statistics*, Vol. 94, No. 1 (2012), pp. 186–201.
7. Peter H. Gleick, "China and Water," in *The World's Water 2008–2009*, ed. by Peter H. Gleick (Washington, DC: Island Press, 2009).
8. Jinxia Wang, Jikun Huang, Scott Rozelle, et al., "Understanding the Water Crisis in Northern China: What the Government and Farmers are Doing," *International Journal of Water Resources Development*, Vol. 25, Issue 1 (2009), pp. 141–158.
9. Feng Hu, "Groundwater Under Pressure," China Water Risk, May 14, 2015.
10. Stuart Leavenworth, "Beijing Has Fallen: China's Capital Sinking by 11cm a Year, Satellite Study Warns," *The Guardian*, June 23, 2016.
11. *Bulletin of First National Census for Water* (http://www.mwr.gov.cn/2013pcgb/merge1.pdf) (in Chinese); and Angela Hsu

and William Miao, "28,000 Rivers Disappeared in China: What Happened?" *The Atlantic*, April 29, 2013.

12. Yurong Hu. Shreedhar Maskey, and Stefan Uhlenbrook, "Trends in Temperature and Rainfall Extremes in the Yellow River Source Region, China," *Climatic Change*, Vol. 110, No. 1 (2012), pp. 403–429.
13. "China's Water Crisis Part II—Water Facts at a Glance," China Water Risk, March 2010.
14. "China Coal-Fired Economy Dying of Thirst as Mines Lack Water," Bloomberg News, July 24, 2013.
15. On the South-North Water Diversion Project and some of its challenges, see Britt Crow-Miller, "Diverted Opportunity and What the South-North Water Transfer Project Really Means," Global Water Forum, March 4, 2014; and Lily Kuo, "China is Moving More than a River Thames of Water Across the Country to Deal with Water Scarcity," *Quartz*, March 6, 2014.
16. Edward Wong, "Plan for China's Water Crisis Spurs Concern," *New York Times*, June 1, 2011.
17. Brett Guerringue, "South-North Water Transfer Project," *ICE Case Studies*, No. 277, May 2013.
18. Susanne Wong, "China Bets on Massive Water Transfers to Solve Crisis," *International Rivers* (online), December 15, 2007.

Chapter 7

1. "China's Soil Heavily Polluted by Mining, Industry," Radio Free Asia (Report), April 17, 2014.
2. Chris Buckley, "Rice Tainted with Cadmium is Discovered in Southern China," *New York Times*, May 21, 2013; and Didi Kirsten Tatlow, "After 'Cadmium Rice,' Now 'Lead' and 'Arsenic Rice,'" *New York Times*, April 25, 2014.
3. "Soil Contamination," *China Daily*, June 14, 2013.
4. Samuel S. Myers, Anotnella Zanobetti, Itai Kloog, et al., "Increasing CO_2 Threatens Human Nutrition," *Nature*, Vol. 510, Issue 7503 (June 5, 2014), pp. 139–142.
5. G. Ma, Y. Jin, Y. Li, F. Zhai, et al., "Iron and Zinc Deficiencies in China: What is a Feasible and Cost-Effective Strategy," *Public Health Nutrition*, Vol. 11, Issue 6 (June 2008), pp. 3184–3211.
6. Yuxuan Li, Weifang Zhang, Lin Ma, et al., "An Analysis of China's Fertilizer Policies: Impacts on the Industry, Food Security, and the Environment," *Journal of Environmental Quality*, Vol. 42, No. 4 (June 2014), pp. 972–981.

7. Xiao-tang Ju, Guang-xi Xing, Chen Xin-ping, et al., "Reducing Environmental Risk by Improving N Management in Intensive Chinese Agricultural Systems," *Proceedings of the National Academy of Sciences USA*, Vol. 106, No. 9 (March 2009), pp. 3041–3046.
8. Yuxuan Li et al., "An Analysis of China's Fertilizer Policies."
9. Xiao-tang Ju et al., "Reducing Environmental Risk by Improving N Management."
10. Sheng Li, Yaoqi Zhang, Denis Nadolnyak, et al., "Fertilizer Industry Subsidies in China: Who Are the Beneficiaries?," *China Agricultural Economic Review*, Vol. 6, Issue 3 (2014), pp. 433–451.
11. Yuxuan Li et al., "An Analysis of China's Fertilizer Policies."
12. Richard Wike and Bridget Parker, "Corruption, Pollution, Inequality Are Top Concerns in China," PEW Research Center, September 24, 2015.
13. Gong Jing, Zheng Cui, and Wang Qingfeng, "Food in China: A Chemical Age," ChinaDialogue.net, August 6, 2012.
14. "Chinese Sprout an Interest in Organic Farming Amid Concerns Over Food Safety," *South China Morning Post*, September 27, 2015.
15. "White Paper—The Grain Issue in China," Information Office of the State Council of the People's Republic of China, October 1996 (http://www.iatp.org/files/Grain_Issue_in_China_White_Paper_The.htm).
16. Quoted in Elizabeth Economy and Michael Levi, *By All Means Necessary: How China's Resource Quest Is Changing the World* (New York: Oxford University Press, 2014), p. 31. For a recent report, see "How is China Feeding Its Population of 1.4 Billion?" Center for Strategic and International Studies, China Power Project, Washington, DC, January 2017.
17. "China's Farmland Well Above 'Red Line,'" *Xinhua*, April 22, 2015.
18. Nadya Ivanova, "Toxic Water: Across Much of China, Huge Harvests Irrigated with Industrial and Agricultural Runoff," Circle of Blue, January 18, 2013; and Xiangbin Kong, "China Must Protect High-Quality Arable Land," *Nature*, Vol. 506, Issue 7486 (February 5, 2014), p. 7.
19. Climate change is likely to have a strong impact here. The Asian Development Bank estimates that climate change—and the resulting severe storms, floods, droughts, subsidence, and landslides—could induce crop failure on 39.17 million hectares

of the country's 120 million hectares (31.5%) of arable land. See *Addressing Climate Change Risks, Disasters, and Adaptation in the People's Republic of China* (Asian Development Bank, 2015).

20. *China Economic Update: Special Topic—Changing Food Consumption Patterns in China; Implications for Domestic Supply and International Trade* (Beijing: World Bank, 2014).
21. Barbara Demick, "China Looks Abroad for Greener Pastures," *Los Angeles Times*, March 29, 2014.
22. "China Seeks Food Security with $43 Billion Bid for Syngenta," Reuters, February 4, 2016.
23. Wang Xuan, "Can Ecological Agriculture Feed China," ChinaDialogue.net, July 10, 2014.

Chapter 8

1. Alyssa Abkowitz, "Inside Scoop: In Beijing Offices, the Air is Just as Bad Inside as Outside," *Wall Street Journal*, December 31, 2015.
2. Meng Si, "Special Report: Rural Villages in China Hit by Fluorine Poisoning from Coal-burning," ChinaDialogue.net, July 3, 2014.
3. Javier C. Hernández, "Chinese Parents Outraged After Illnesses at School Are Tied to Pollution," *New York Times*, April 18, 2016.
4. "China Releases First Plan to Protect Environment from Toxic Chemicals," China Briefing, February 26, 2013.
5. Jonathan Kaiman, "Inside China's 'Cancer Villages,'" *The Guardian*, June 4, 2013.
6. Hon-ming Lam, Justin Remais, Ming-chiu Fung, et al., "Food Supply and Safety Issues in China," *The Lancet*, Vol. 381, No. 9882 (June 8, 2013), pp. 2044–2053.
7. Institute for Health Metrics and Evaluation, "Global Burden of Disease Study, 2010," *The Lancet*, December 2012; Richard A. Rohde and Richard A. Muller, "Air Pollution in China: Mapping of Concentrations and Sources," *PLoS One*, Vol. 10, No. 8 (August 2015), e0135749; J. Lelieveld, J. S. Evans, M. Fnais, et al., "The Contribution of Outdoor Air Pollution Sources to Premature Mortality on a Global Scale," *Nature*, Vol. 525, Issue 7569 (September 17, 2015), pp. 367–371. In a press release, Richard Muller remarked, "When I was last in Beijing, pollution was at the hazardous level: Every hour of exposure reduced my life expectancy by 20 minutes. It's as if every man, woman and child smoked 1.5 cigarettes each hour" (or 36 cigarettes each day).

8. Li Jing, "670,000 Smog-Related Deaths a Year: The Cost of China's Reliance on Coal," *South China Morning Post*, November 5, 2014.
9. Christine Ottery, "Air Pollution Increases Risk of Premature Death in Chinese Cities," Greenpeace Energydesk, February 4, 2015.
10. Yuyu Chen, Avraham Ebenstein, Michael Greenstone, and Hongbin Li, "Evidence on the Impact of Sustained Exposure to Air Pollution on Life Expectancy from China's Huai River Policy," *Proceedings of the National Academy of Sciences USA*, Vol. 110, No. 32 (August 6, 2013), pp. 12936–12941.
11. "Exposure to Air Pollution Increases the Risk of Obesity," Duke Today, February 19, 2016.
12. Jonathan Kaiman, "China's Toxic Air Pollution Resembles Nuclear Winter, Say Scientists," *The Guardian*, February 25, 2014.
13. "Geely Chairman Li Shufu: From an Adventurous Newcomer to an Industry Leader," *Global Times*, July 23, 2013.
14. Liu Hongqiao, *Bottled Water in China: Boom or Bust?* China Water Risk (Beijing), 2015.
15. Andrew Browne. "The Great Chinese Exodus," *Wall Street Journal*, August 15, 2014.
16. E.g., Xiang Liu, Ningxiu Li, Chaojie Liu, et al., "Urban–Rural Disparity in Utilization of Preventive Care Services in China," *Medicine*, Vol. 95, Issue 37 (September 2016), pp. 1–7; and Jianlin Hou and Yang Ke, "Addressing the Shortage of Health Professionals in Rural China: Issues and Progress," *International Journal of Health Policy and Management*, Vol. 4, Issue 5 (May 2015), pp. 327–328.
17. "Health Sector Reform in China," World Health Organization, Western Pacific Region, WHO China Representative Office (http://www.wpro.who.int/china/mediacentre/factsheets/health_sector_reform/en/).
18. See Ethan D. Schoolman and Chunbo Ma, "Migration, Class and Environmental Inequality: Exposure to Pollution in China's Jiangsu Province," *Ecological Economics*, Vol. 75 (March 2012), pp. 140–151; and Chunbo Ma and Ethan Schoolman, "Who Bears the Environmental Burden in China—An Analysis of the Distribution of Industrial Pollution Sources," *Ecological Economics*, Vol. 69, No. 9 (2010), pp. 1869–1876.

19. Edward Wong, "Pollution Leads to Greater Risk of Dementia Among Older Women, Study Says," *New York Times*, February 4, 2017.
20. Lilian Calderón-Garcidueñas, Ricardo Torres-Jardón, Rand J Kulesza, et al., "Air Pollution and Detrimental Effects on Children's Brain. The Need for a Multidisciplinary Approach to the Issue Complexity and Challenges," *Frontiers in Human Neuroscience*, Vol. 8, Article 613 (August 12, 2014), pp. 1–7.
21. Zhiwei Xue, Wenbiao Hu, Yewu Zhang, et al., "Exploration of Diarrhoea Seasonality and Its Drivers in China," *Scientific Reports*, Vol. 5, No. 8241 (February 4, 2015).

Chapter 9

1. "Top Clothing Brands Linked to Water Pollution Scandal in China," ChinaDialogue.net, September 10, 2012.
2. Barbara Finamore, "A New Flank in China's War on Pollution? Controlling Emissions from Ports and Shipping," *Huffington Post*, December 30, 2014.
3. Phillip Stalley is not persuaded of the beneficial effects of global trade on the environment: "The steady drumbeat of pollution cases involving foreign investors casts doubt on the assertions of those that make the strongest case for the environmental benefits of economic globalization. It is apparent that a significant number of foreign-invested companies are not engaging in rigorous self-regulation and that foreign investment is not necessarily 'greening China' . . . Even if most foreign companies do not run afoul of regulators, many appear largely willing to comply with the law of the land rather than expend resources to promote environmental protection. MNCs are not 'exporting environmentalism' as extensively as some depicted . . . Reports published by the IPE and Greenpeace . . . time and time again show MNCs adopting a *de facto* 'don't ask, don't tell' attitude when it comes to the environmental practices of suppliers . . . The overall impression is that MNCs' requests to their suppliers to adhere to environmental regulations are often *pro forma* and not aimed at exerting pressure on suppliers' environmental management." See Stalley, "Mind the Gap: The Role of Foreign-Invested Firms in Narrowing the Implementation Gap in China's Environmental Governance," in *Chinese Environmental*

Governance, ed. by Bingqiang Ren and Huisheng Shou (New York: Palgrave Macmillan, 2013).

4. "Apple Launches New Clean Energy Programs in China to Promote Low-Carbon Manufacturing and Green Growth," Apple.com, October 22, 2015.
5. Jung Min-ho, "Greenpeace Spares China from Blame for Dust," *Korea Times*, March 4, 2015.
6. Kate Galbraith, "Worries in the Path of China's Air," *New York Times*, December 25, 2013.
7. Heping Jia, "China Blamed for Mercury on Iconic Mount Fuji," *Chemistry World*, October 18, 2013.
8. Geoffrey Mohan, "Mercury Levels Rising in Pacific Yellowfin Tuna, Study Says," *Los Angeles Times*, February 2, 2015.
9. Clayton Jones, "Japanese Link Increased Acid Rain to Distant Coal Plants in China," *Christian Science Monitor*, November 6, 1992; and "Acid Rain—A Global Problem," *Library Index* (http://www.libraryindex.com/pages/1144/Acid-Rain-GLOBAL-PROBLEM.html).
10. Jenna R. Jambeck, Roland Geyer, Chris Wilcox, et al., "Plastic Waste Inputs from Land into the Ocean," *Science*, Vol. 347, Issue 6223 (February 13, 2015), pp. 768–771.
11. "FY 2014 Survey Results of Marine Litter in Coastal Areas," Ministry of the Environment (Government of Japan), June 3, 2015.
12. "China's Fuel-Fired Power Plants Cause Air Pollution in Northern Vietnam: Study," *Tuoi Tre News*, October 8, 2015 (http://tuoitrenews.vn/society/30873/chinas-fuelfired-power-plants-cause-air-pollution-in-northern-vietnam-study).
13. "Japan, China Officials Unite on Environmental Measures as Ties Warm," *Japan Times*, December 28, 2014.
14. "Japan, China, S. Korea to Jointly Tackle PM2.5 Problem," *Japan Times*, April 30, 2014.
15. "Kitakyushu, Prefecture to Help China Tackle PM2.5," Fukuoka-now.com, June 13, 2014.
16. "China, Japan, ROK Sign 5-Year Environmental Pact," *Xinhua*, April 30, 2015.
17. David Kirby, "Made in China: Our Toxic, Imported Air Pollution," *Discover Magazine*, April 2011.
18. Marissa Fessenden, "China's Smog Might be to Blame for the East Coast's Rough Winter," Smithsonian.com, March 9, 2015.

19. Christina Nelson, "Air Pollution Impedes Executive Hiring in China," *China Business Review*, June 10, 2014.
20. Suzanne Goldenberg, "US Energy Secretary Warns of 'Sputnik Moment' in Green Technology Race," *The Guardian*, November 29, 2010.
21. Jintai Lin, Da Pan, Steven J. Davis, et al., "China's International Trade and Air Pollution in the United States," *Proceedings of the National Academy of Sciences USA*, Vol. 111, No. 5 (February 4, 2014).
22. Christopher L. Weber, Glen P. Peters, Dabo Guan, and Klaus Hubacek, "The Contribution of Chinese Exports to Climate Change," *Energy Policy*, Vol. 36 (2008), pp. 3572–3577.
23. See Yanmei Li, Jiafeng Fu, and Bo Yang, "Sources and Flows of Embodied CO_2 Emissions in Import and Export Trade of China," *Chinese Geographical Science*, Vol. 24, Issue 2 (April 2014), pp. 220–230; Bin Shui and Robert C. Harris, "The Role of CO_2 Embodiment in US–China Trade," *Energy Policy*, Vol. 34 (2006); Anna Swanson, "Here's One Thing the U.S. Does Export to China: Carbon Dioxide," *Forbes*, November 12, 2014.
24. Frank Ackerman, "Your iPhone Causes China's Pollution," *Huffington Post*, February 13, 2014.
25. See, for instance, Zhongxiang Zhang, "Who Should Bear the Cost of China's Carbon Emissions Embodied in Goods for Exports?," *East-West Center Working Papers* (Economic Series), No. 122, November 2011.
26. Michael Forsythe, "China's Emissions Pledges Are Undercut by Boom in Coal Projects Abroad," *New York Times*, December 11, 2015.
27. Chinese steel, cement, and glass producers are setting up operations overseas as well. See, for instance, Dexter Roberts, "China's Plan to Export Pollution," *Bloomberg BusinessWeek*, November 27, 2014.
28. Beth Walker, "China Stokes Global Coal Growth," ChinaDialogue.net, September 23, 2016.

Chapter 10

1. Maria Repnikova and Kechang Fang, "Behind the Fall of China's Greatest Newspaper," *Foreign Policy*, January 29, 2015.
2. See http://www.caixin.com/.
3. For a convenient listing of government-issued reports, see China Water Risk, "China Government Reports" (http://

chinawaterrisk.org/resources/research-reports/china-government-reports/).

4. Samuel Kay, Bo Zhao, and Daniel Sui, "Can Social Media Clear the Air? A Case Study of the Air Pollution Problem in Chinese Cities," *Professional Geographer*, Vol. 67, Issue 3 (2015), pp. 351–363.
5. Janice Hua Xu, "Communicating the Right to Know: Social Media in the Do-It-Yourself Air Quality Testing Campaign in Chinese Cities," *International Journal of Communication*, Vol. 8 (2014), pp. 1374–1393.
6. C. Custer, "Deng Fei Launches Weibo Campaign to Share Images of Water Pollution," TechinAsia, February 15, 2013.
7. Leslie Hook, "China's Environmental Activists," *FT Magazine*, September 20, 2013.
8. "Outrage Over Polluted Yangtze River with Excrement and Urine," *China Daily*, January 5, 2015.
9. Feng Yongfeng, "China's Citizen Journalists Leading Fight Against Polluters," ChinaDialogue.net, May 29, 2014. For more on environmental bloggers and their efforts to engage the public, see Feng Yongfeng, "Citizen Journalists in China," ChinaDialogue.net, April 11, 2012.
10. "Chinese Residents Force Relocation of Chemical Plant in Xiamen, 2007," Global Nonviolent Action Database, Swarthmore College (http://nvdatabase.swarthmore.edu/content/chinese-residents-force-relocation-chemical-plant-xiamen-2007).
11. Chang Cheng, "20 Years of Public Voice," ChinaDialogue.net, June 20, 2012.
12. Monica Tan, "Social Media, China, and the Environment," *The Diplomat*, July 25, 2012.
13. Hook, "China's Environmental Activists."
14. Daniela Yu and Anita Pugliese, "Majority of Chinese Prioritize Environment Over Economy," Gallup, June 8, 2012.
15. Wang Hongyi, "Protecting Environment Tops Public Concerns in Poll," *China Daily*, May 16, 2014.
16. *Flash Report: The Different Faces of Sustainability in China, USA and Europe* (Amsterdam: Motivaction International, 2014).
17. Cynthia Shahan, "China's Citizens Overwhelmingly Want Renewable Energy," CleanTechnica, September 29, 2016.

18. Daniel K. Gardner, "China's 'Silent Spring' Moment?: Why 'Under the Dome' Found a Ready Audience on China," *New York Times*, March 18, 2015.
19. Paul G. Harris, "Environmental Perspectives and Behavior in China: Synopsis and Bibliography," *Environment and Behavior*, Vol 38, No. 1 (January 2006), pp. 5–21.
20. Wei-jie Guan, Xue-nan Zheng, Kian Fan Chung, and Nan-shan Zhong, "Impact of Air Pollution on the Burden of Chronic Respiratory Diseases in China: The Time for Urgent Action," *The Lancet*, Vol. 388 (October 15, 2016), pp. 1939–1951; and Josh Ye, "Chinese, U.S. Scientists Invent Air Filter that Blocks 99.94pc of PM2.5 Pollutants—and It's Made of Soya Beans," *South China Morning Post*, January 16, 2017.
21. "Measures on Open Environmental Information (for Trial Implementation)" (http://www.sustainability-fj.org/pdf/091120_07.pdf).
22. "Cutting Through the Fog with China's First Pollution Information Transparency Index (PITI)," National Resources Defense Council, November 2009; Barbara Finamore, "A Step Forward for Environmental Transparency in China," National Resources Defense Council, March 30, 2013.
23. "Environmental Impact Assessment Law of the People's Republic of China" (http://www.cecc.gov/resources/legal-provisions/peoples-republic-of-china-environmental-impact-assessment-law-2003).
24. For example, see Yuhong Zhong, "Assessing the Environmental Impact of Projects: A Critique of the EIA Legal Regime in China," *Natural Resources Journal*, Vol. 49 (Spring 2009): 485–524.
25. Tan, "Social Media, China, and the Environment."
26. Patti Waldmeir, "Shanghai Notebook: Bronchial Set Seek Blue Sky Breathing in China," *Financial Times*, November 24, 2014.
27. Jie Feng and Tao Wang, "Officials Struggling to Respond to China's Year of Environment Protests," ChinaDialogue.net, December 6, 2012.
28. Nectar Gan, "China Firing Blanks in 'War on Pollution' as Smog Worsens," *South China Morning Post*, February 2, 2017.
29. These are what Kevin J. O'Brien and Lianjiang Li call protests of "rightful resistance." See their book *Rightful Resistance in Rural China* (Cambridge, UK: Cambridge University Press, 2006).

30. Kingsyhon Lee and Ming-sho Ho, "The Maoming Anti-PX Protest of 2014," *China Perspectives*, No. 2014/3, pp. 33–39.
31. Zhang Chun and Luna Lin, "Flawed Planning Process Partly to Blame for Mass Protests, Admits MEP Official," ChinaDialogue.net, June 11, 2014.
32. On Friends of Nature, see Judith Shapiro, *China's Environmental Challenges*, 2nd ed. (Malden, MA: Polity Press, 2016); and Elizabeth Economy, *The River Runs Black: The Environmental Challenge to China's Future*, 2nd ed. (Ithaca: Cornell University Press, 2010). For a study of environmental NGOs in China, see Joy Y. Zhang and Michael Barr, *Green Politics in China: Environmental Governance and State–Society Relations* (London: Pluto Press, 2013).
33. Michael Wines, "Liang Congjie, Chinese Environmental Pioneer, Dies at 78," *New York Times*, October 29, 2010.
34. Ruby Yang (director), *Warriors of Qiugang* (Beijing: Thomas Lennon Films and Chang Ai Media Project, 2010).
35. For the IPE maps, go to http://wwwold.ipe.org.cn/en/pollution/index.aspx.
36. Hook, "China's Environmental Activists."
37. Here, for example, is how one NGO, the Chongqing Green Volunteer League, describes itself: "We are the government's friend, partner, officer, and assistant; we are the government's connection to the people. We work to advance dialoguing and collaboration in the field of environmental protection between the government, the public, and enterprise" (http://chinadevelopmentbreif.cn/directory/the-chongqing-green-volunteer-league/).
38. Edward Wong, "Clampdown in China Restricts 7,000 Foreign Organizations," *New York Times*, April 28, 2016; and Zheping Huang, "NGOs are Under Threat in China's Latest Crackdown Against 'Foreign Forces,'" *Quartz*, January 4, 2017.

Chapter 11

1. For a more complete chronology see Charles R. McElwee, *Environmental Law in China: Mitigating Risk and Ensuring Compliance* (Oxford: Oxford University Press, 2011), pp. 17–30.
2. For an English version of the "Air Pollution Prevention and Control Action Plan," see the October 2013 translation by Clean Air Alliance of China (http://en.cleanairchina.org/product/6346.html).

3. The "Action Plan" can be found in Chinese at http://www.gov.cn/zhengce/content/2015-04/16/content_9613.htm.
4. Brian Segele and William Kazer, "To Conserve Water, China Raises Prices for Top Users," *Wall Street Journal*, January 8, 2014.
5. "China to Roll Out Seven Pilot Markets for Trading Water Rights," Reuters, July 24, 2014.
6. Christina Larson, "China Turns to the Sea for Fresh Water," *Bloomberg Businessweek*, April 9, 2015.
7. Beth Walker, "China's Desalination Plans Could Thwart 'War on Pollution,'" ChinaDialogue.net, February 4, 2015.
8. "China Sets 2020 'Artificial Weather' Target to Combat Water Shortages," Reuters, January 13, 2015; and Josh Ye, "China Showers 1.15 Billion Yuan on Rainmaking Project for Parched Northwest," *South China Morning Post*, January 24, 2017.
9. He Guangwei, "The Soil Pollution Crisis in China: A Cleanup Presents Daunting Challenge," Yale Environment 360 (e360.yale.edu), July 14, 2014.
10. For the plan (in Chinese) see http://www.gov.cn/zhengce/content/2016-05/31/content_5078377.htm; a summary in English can be found at "New 'Soil Ten Plan' To Safeguard China's Food Safety and Healthy Living Environment," China Water Risk, May 31, 2016.
11. See He Guangweili, "The Soil Pollution Crisis in China"; and an April 2015 presentation on "Soil Pollution" by Girishma Rastogi (https://prezi.com/l8wianzju4oo/soil-pollution/).
12. Until May 2017, Chen Jining was Minister of Environmental Protection, having replaced Zhou Shengxian, who in 2015 reached the mandatory retirement age of 65. In May, Chen was named Acting Mayor of Beijing and then Mayor. Li Ganjie, the former Vice Minister of the Ministry of Environmental Protection, has since replaced Chen as minister.
13. For a description of these departments see McElwee, *Environmental Law in China*, pp. 82–90.
14. For more on these ministries, see McElwee, *Environmental Law in China*, pp. 91–99; and Table 2 in Genia Kosta, *Barriers to the Implementation of Environmental Policies at the Local Level in China*, Policy Research Working Paper (7016), World Bank Group, August 2014, p. 24.
15. As Abigail Jahiel, a China environmental expert, writes, the bureaus have no easy task: "It is the local EPB that must ensure

that factories install pollution prevention technology, operate waste treatment facilities, reduce harmful emissions, or pay fees if these emissions exceed standards—even if the factories view these costs as unreasonable. It is the local EPB, too, that must ensure that city planning agencies reject proposals from heavily polluting foreign and domestic firms seeking to invest in the area or that counties wishing to turn wetlands into farmland conduct environmental impact assessments—even if these projects promise to be lucrative for the local economy" (Abigail R. Jahiel, "The Organization of Environmental Protection in China," *China Quarterly*, No. 156 [December 1998], p. 765).

16. McElwee, *Environmental Law in China.*
17. Kosta, *Barriers to the Implementation of Environmental Policies.*
18. Jonathan Kaiman, "China Strengthens Environmental Laws," *The Guardian*, April 25, 2014.
19. Jahiel, "The Organization of Environmental Protection in China," p. 759.
20. Li Jing, "60,000 Jobs: The Cost of One Chinese City's Cleaner Air," *South China Morning Post*, July 2, 2015.
21. Li Zhiqing, "China Restructures Its Environmental Agencies From the Bottom Up," Sixth Tone, April 28, 2016.
22. "Conflict of Interest to Blame for Degradation of China's Air, Water and Soil," *South China Morning Post*, June 23, 2016.
23. Institute of Public and Environmental Affairs chief Ma Jun was recently quoted as saying that he has been "encouraged by the government's commitment to punish not only just the companies causing pollution, but also local officials who have often ignored environmental crimes" (Jihee Junn, "China Plans 'Greener, Cleaner' Industry but Faces Complex Challenges," *Asia Pacific Report*, June 20, 2016). As recently as February 2016, however, Minister Chen Jining, according to a Reuters report, complained that "not enough pressure was being put on local governments to implement environmental policies, and there was not enough cooperation between government departments" ("China Needs More Power to Crack Down on Polluters—Minister," Reuters, February 18, 2016).
24. Kosta, *Barriers to the Implementation of Environmental Policies*, pp. 27–28
25. "China's Legislature Adopts Revised Environmental Protection Law," *Global Times*, April 24, 2014.

26. See "English Translation of China's New Environmental Law," ChinaDialogue.net, May 20, 2014 (https://www.chinadialogue.net/Environmental-Protection-Law-2014-eversion.pdf).
27. Estimates of the number of qualifying NGOs run between 300 and 700.

Chapter 12

1. E.g., Fergus Green and Nicholas Stern, "Managing Economic Change and Mitigating Climate Change: China's Strategies, Policies, and Trends," in *China's New Sources of Economic Growth: Reform, Resources and Climate Change*, Vol. 1, ed. by Ligang Song, Ross Garnaut, Cai Fang, and Lauren Johnston (Canberra: Australian National University, 2016); and Ye Qi, Nicholas Stern, Tong Wu, Jiaqi Liu, and Fergus Green, "China's Post-Coal Growth," *Nature Geoscience* (online), July 25, 2016.
2. For a discussion of CCS see Joseph Romm, *Climate Change: What Everyone Needs to Know* (Oxford: Oxford University Press, 2016).
3. Chi-en Yang and Robert B. Jackson, "China's Synthetic Natural Gas Revolution," *Nature Climate Change*, Vol. 3 (October 23, 2013), pp. 852–854.
4. One GW is roughly the amount of power generated by one large coal-fired power plant, which can power 700,000 to 1 million houses.
5. For comparison, the same year the United States had a country record for a single year of 8.6 GW of wind power and 7.3 GW of solar power.
6. Jonathan Watts, "Winds of Change Blow Through China as Spending on Renewable Energy Soars," *The Guardian*, March 19, 2012.
7. Frauke Urban and Johan Nordensvard, "China Dams the World: The Environmental and Social Impacts of Chinese Dams," *E-International Relations*, January 30, 2014 (http://www.e-ir.info/2014/01/30/china-dams-the-world-the-environmental-and-social-impacts-of-chinese-dams/).
8. "China to Boost Biomass Energy Development in 2016–2020," *China Daily*, December 6, 2016.
9. "U.S–China Joint Presidential Statement on Climate Change," Obamawhitehouse.archive.gov, September 25, 2015 (https://obamawhitehouse.archives.gov/the-press-office/2015/09/25/us-china-joint-presidential-statement-climate-change).

10. For a good overview, see Charlton Lewis, "China's Great Dam Boom: A Major Assault on Its Rovers," Yale Environment 360, November 4, 2013 (http://e360.yale.edu/features/chinas_great_dam_boom_an_assault_on_its_river_systems).
11. Luan Dong and Jennifer Turner, "Rethinking China's Dam Rush," China Water Risk, June 9, 2014.
12. Warren Cornwall, "Hundreds of New Dams Could Mean Trouble for Our Climate," *Science*, September 28, 2016.
13. John Jackson (pseudonym), *Earthquake Hazards and Large Dams in Western China: A Probe International Study* (Toronto: Probe International, April 2012).
14. Xiao Fan, *Did the Zipingpu Dam Trigger China's 2008 Earthquake? The Scientific Case: A Probe International Study* (Toronto: Probe International, December 2012).
15. Patricia Adams, "Chinese Study Reveals Three Gorges Dam Triggered 3,000 Earthquakes, Numerous Landslides," Probe International, June 1, 2011.
16. Joydeep Gupta, "Melting Glaciers May Impact Hydropower Plans," The Third Pole, September 2, 2016 (https://www.thethirdpole.net/2016/09/02/studies-of-melting-glaciers-urgently-needed/).
17. Chris Sall, *Climate Trends and Impacts in China*, The World Bank, September 2013, notes (p. 16), "The drought that hit southern China in the winter and spring of 2011, for example, lowered water levels in reservoirs and forced dam operators to cut back on electricity generation by as much as 48 percent in some provinces at a time when electricity demand from manufacturers in coastal areas was spiking."
18. There is the Mekong River Commission (MRC), an advisory body whose mission is to promote cooperation among its four members, Cambodia, Laos, Thailand, and Vietnam; China and Myanmar, two critical players in the region, are not members but so-called Dialogue Partners.
19. "Nuclear Power in China," World Nuclear Association, February 2017 (http://www.world-nuclear.org/information-library/country-profiles/countries-a-f/china-nuclear-power.aspx).
20. E.g., James Conca, "China Shows How to Build Nuclear Reactors Fast and Cheap," *Forbes*, October 22, 2015.
21. Michael Forsythe, "China to Develop Floating Nuclear Power Plants," *New York Times*, April 22, 2016.

22. Jost Wübbeke and Guan Ting, "China's Nuclear Industry Goes Global," *The Diplomat*, February 11, 2016.
23. He Zuoxiu, "Chinese Nuclear Disaster 'Highly Probable' by 2030," ChinaDialogue.net, March 19, 2013.
24. Emma Graham-Harrison, "China Warned Over 'Insane' Plans for New Nuclear Power Plants," *The Guardian*, May 25, 2011; and Leslie Hook, "China Nuclear Protest Builds Steam, " *Financial Times*, February 22, 2012.
25. Wang Yi'nan, "Drought and Earthquake Pose 'Enormous Risk' to China's Nuclear Plans," ChinaDialogue.net, February 27, 2013.

Epilogue

1. "President Xi Jinping Pledges Not to Sacrifice Environment," *CCICED Update*, Issue 6 of 2013, May 31, 2013 (http://english.mep.gov.cn/Resources/publications/CCICED_updates/201606/P020160601415968232223.pdf).
2. Chang Meng, "China's Top Leaders Prescribe Eco-Civilization for Balanced Growth," *Global Times*, November 14, 2013.
3. See, especially, "Opinions of the CPC Central Committee and the State Council on Further Promoting the Development of Ecological Civilization, April 25, 2015," Environmental-partnership.org (http://environmental-partnership.org/wp-content/uploads/download-folder/Eco-Guidelines_rev_Eng.pdf); and "Integrated Reform Plan for Promoting Ecological Progress," issued by the Party on September 22, 2015 (http://english.gov.cn/policies/latest_releases/2015/09/22/content_281475195492066.htm).
4. Hu Kanping, "Pan Yue's Reflections on the Environment," in *The China Environment Yearbook: Changes and Struggles*, Vol. 2, edited by Yang Dongping (Leiden: Brill Academic Publishers, 2008) (online version, "Pan Yue's Thoughts on the Environment," http://www.fon.org.cn/uploads/attachment/97691361766594.pdf).
5. Pan Yue, "Green China and Young China (Part Two)," ChinaDialogue.net, July 18, 2007.
6. Dominic Barton, Yougang Cheng, and Amy Jin, "Mapping China's Middle Class," *McKinsey Quarterly*, June 2013.
7. S. F. Balica, N. G. Wright, and F. van der Meulen, "A Flood Vulnerability Index for Coastal Cities and Its Use in Assessing Climate Change Impacts," *Natural Hazards*, Vol. 64, Issue 1 (October 2012), pp. 73–105.

SELECTED READINGS

This book covers a wide range of topics relating to the environment in China. Readers wishing to delve more deeply into a particular topic should consult the endnotes and the list of selected readings here.

Chapter 1: Overview

Albert, Eleanore and Xu Beina. "China's Environmental Crisis." Council on Foreign Relations, January 18, 2016 (http://www.cfr.org/china/chinas-environmental-crisis/p12608).

"The East is Grey." *The Economist*, August 10, 2013 (http://www.economist.com/news/briefing/21583245-china-worlds-worst-polluter-largest-investor-green-energy-its-rise-will-have).

Economy, Elizabeth C. *The River Runs Black: The Environmental Challenge to China's Future*, 2nd ed. Ithaca: Cornell University Press, 2010.

Hill, Marquita. *Understanding Environmental Pollution*, 3rd ed. Cambridge, UK: Cambridge University Press, 2010.

Hilton, Isabel. "The Environment." *The China Story*. Australian Centre on China in the World, May 28, 2014 (https://www.thechinastory.org/lexicon/the-environment/).

"Illicit Trade in Electrical and Electronic Waste (E-waste) from the World to the Region." Chapter 9 in *Transnational and Organized Crime in East Asia and the Pacific: A Threat Assessment*. UNODC (United Nations Office on Drugs and Crime), April 2013, pp. 101–111.

Lewis, Johanna I. and Gallagher, Kelly Sims. "Energy and Environment in China: National and Global Challenges." In *The Global Environment: Institutions, Law and Policy*. Edited by Regina Axelrod and Stacy VanDeveer. Washington: CQ Press, 2014.

Shapiro, Judith. *China's Environmental Challenges*, 2nd ed. Malden, MA: Polity Press, 2016.

Smith, Richard. "China's Communist-Capitalist Ecological Apocalypse." *Real-World Economics Review*, No. 71 (2015): 19–62 (http://www.paecon.net/PAEReview/issue71/Smith71.pdf).

Spangenberg, Joachim H. "China in the Anthropocene: Culprit, Victim, Last Best Hope for a Global Ecological Civilization." *BioRisk*, Vol. 9 (2014): 1–37.

Standaert, Michael. "China's Notorious E-Waste Village Disappears Almost Overnight." Bloomberg BNA, December 17, 2015 (www.bna.com).

Watts, Jonathan. *When a Billion People Jump: How China Will Save Mankind or Destroy It.* New York: Scribner, 2010.

Chapter 2: Historical Background

Dikötter, Frank. *Mao's Great Famine: The History of China's Most Devastating Catastrophe, 1958–1962*. New York: Walker and Co., 2010.

Elvin, Mark. "The Environmental Legacy of Imperial China." *China Quarterly*, No. 156 (December 1998): 733–756.

Elvin, Mark. *The Retreat of the Elephants: An Environmental History of China.* New Haven: Yale University Press, 2004.

Elvin, Mark. "Three Thousand Years of Unsustainable Growth: China's Environment from Archaic Times to the Present." *East Asian History*, Vol. 6 (1993): 7–46.

Elvin, Mark and Liu Ts'ui-jung. *Sediments of Time: Environment and Society in Chinese History*. Cambridge, UK: Cambridge University Press, 1998.

Gries, Peter Hayes. *China's New Nationalism: Pride, Politics, and Diplomacy.* Berkeley: University of California Press, 2004.

Marcuse, Gary. "China: A Vision of Green Democracy." Pulitzer Center on Crisis Reporting, December 2015 (www.pulitzercenter.org/reporting/a-vision-of-green-democracy).

Marks, Robert B. *China: Its Environment and History.* Lanham, MD: Rowman and Littlefield, 2012.

Marks, Robert B. *Tigers, Rice, Silk, and Silt: Environment and Economy in Late Imperial South China*. Cambridge, UK: Cambridge University Press, 1999.

Miller, James. "Humans Must Conquer Nature: Philosophical and Religious Sources of China's Anti-Environmental Ideology." *Journal of the Royal Asiatic Society, Shanghai*, Vol. 74 (2010): 1–20. (Available at http://qspace.library.queensu.ca/bitstream/handle/1974/7252/RAS%20article%20humans%20must%20defeat%20nature.pdf?sequence=1.)

Pietz, David A. *The Yellow River: The Problem of Water in Modern China*. Cambridge, MA: Harvard University Press, 2015.

Qu Geping and Li Jinchang. *Population and the Environment in China*. Translated by Jiang Baozhong and Gu Ran. Boulder, CO: L. Rienner Publishers, 1994.

Shapiro, Judith. *Mao's War Against Nature: Politics and Environment in Revolutionary China*. Cambridge, UK: Cambridge University Press, 2001.

Tucker, Mary Evelyn and Berthrong, John, eds. *Confucianism and Ecology: The Interrelation of Heaven, Earth, and Humans*. Cambridge, MA: Harvard University Press for the Harvard University Center for the Study of World Religions, 1998.

Wang, Zheng. *Never Forget National Humiliation: Historical Memory in Chinese Politics and Foreign Relations*. New York: Columbia University Press, 2012.

Yang Jisheng. *Tombstone: The Great Chinese Famine, 1958–1962*. Translated by Stacey Mosher and Jian Guo. New York: Farrar, Straus, and Giroux, 2012.

Chapter 3: Economic Development and the Environment

"670,000 Smog-Related Deaths a Year: The Cost of China's Reliance on Coal." *South China Morning Post*, November 5, 2014.

Bai Xuemei. "The Urban Transition in China: Trends, Consequences and Policy Implications." In *The New Global Frontier: Urbanization, Poverty and Environment in the 21st Century*. Edited by George Martin, et al. London: Earthscan, 2008.

Bai Xuemei, Shi Peijun, and Liu Yansui. "Realizing China's Urban Dream." *Nature*, Vol. 509, Issue 7499 (May 7, 2014) (http://www.nature.com/news/society-realizing-china-s-urban-ream-1.15151).

"China Produces and Consumes Almost as Much Coal as the Rest of the World Combined." U.S. Energy Information Administration, May 14, 2014.

"China Remains Hot Spot for Foreign Investment." *China Daily*, July 13, 2016. http://www.chinadaily.com.cn/business/2016-07/13/content_26070020.htm.

"China's Reckoning: The Economic Miracle Hits Troubled Times." WSJ.com, 2015 (http://graphics.wsj.com/chinas-reckoning-the-economic-miracle-hits-troubled-times/).

Cui Linli and Shi Jun. "Urbanization and Its Environmental Effects in Shanghai, China." *Urban Climate*, Vol. 2 (2012): 1–15.

Jahiel, Abigail. "China, the WTO and Implications for the Environment." *Environmental Politics*, Vol. 15, No. 2 (April 2006): 310–329.

Kahn, Matthew and Zheng Siqi. *Blue Skies Over Beijing: Economic Growth and the Environment in China*. Princeton: Princeton University Press, 2016.

Kroeber, Arthur R. *China's Economy: What Everyone Needs to Know*. New York: Oxford University Press, 2016.

Li Keqiang. "Li Keqiang Expounds on Urbanization." China.org.cn, May 26, 2013 (http://china.org.cn/china/2013-05/26/content_28934485.htm).

Liu Jianguo and Diamond, Jared. "China's Environment in a Globalizing World: How China and the World Affect Each Other." *Nature*, Vol. 435, No. 30 (June 2005): 1179–1186.

Naughton, Barry. *The Chinese Economy: Transitions and Growth*. Cambridge, MA: MIT Press, 2007.

Peng Xizhe. "China's Demographic History and Future Challenges." *Science*, Vol. 333 (July 29, 2011): 581–587.

Ren Xuefei. *Urban China*. Malden, MA: Polity Press, 2013.

Stalley, Peter. "Mind the Gap: The Role of Foreign-Invested Firms in Narrowing the Implementation Gap in China's Environmental Governance." In *Chinese Environmental Governance: Dynamics, Challenges, and Prospects in a Changing Society*. Edited by Bingqiang Ren and Huisheng Shou. New York: Palgrave Macmillan, 2013.

Zhu Qin and Peng Xizhe. "The Impacts of Population Change on Carbon Emissions in China During 1978–2008." *Environmental Impact Assessment Review*, Vol. 36 (2012): 1–8.

Chapter 4: China's New Consumerism

Caramel, Laurence. "China's Rosewood Craving Cuts Deep into Madagascar Forests." *The Guardian*, February 16, 2015.

"China's Appetite for Meat Swells, Along with Climate-Changing Pollution." *Scientific American*, May 20, 2014.

"China's Plan to Cut Meat Consumption by 50% Cheered by Climate Campaigners." *The Guardian*, June 20, 2016.

"Empire of the Pig." *The Economist*, December 20, 2014.

Eshel, Gidon, Shepon, Alon, Makov, Tamar, and Milo, Ron. "Land, Irrigation Water, Greenhouse Gas, and Reactive Nitrogen Burdens of Meat, Eggs, and Dairy Production in the United States." *Proceedings of the National Academy of Sciences USA*, Vol. 111, No. 33 (August 2014): 11996–12001.

Fearnside, Philip M. and Figueiredo, Adriano M. R. "China's Influence on Deforestation in Brazilian Amazonia: A Growing Force in the State of Mato Grosso." BU Global Economic Governance Initiative, Discussion Paper 2015-3 (http://www.bu.edu/pardeeschool/files/2014/12/Brazil1.pdf).

Feng Kuishuang, Hubacek, Klaus, Guan Dabo. "Lifestyle, Technology and CO_2 Emissions in China: A Regional Comparative Analysis." *Ecological Economics*, Vol. 69 (2009): 149–154.

Gerth, Karl. *As China Goes, So Goes the World*. New York: Hill and Wang, 2010.

Gerth, Karl. "Lifestyles of the Rich and Infamous: The Creation and Implications of China's New Aristocracy." *Comparative Sociology*, Vol. 10 (2011): 488–507.

Hessler, Peter. *Country Driving: A Chinese Road Trip*. New York: Harper, 2010.

Hoekstra, Arjen Y. "The Hidden Water Resource Use Behind Meat and Dairy." *Animal Frontiers*, Vol. 2, No. 2 (April 2012): 3–8.

Kochhar, Rakesh. "Mapping the Global Population: How Many Live on How Much, and Where." PEW Research Center, July 8, 2015 (http://www.pewglobal.org/2015/07/08/mapping-the-global-population-how-many-live-on-how-much-and-where/).

"Mapping China's Middle Class." *McKinsey Quarterly*, June 2013 (http://www.mckinsey.com/industries/retail/our-insights/mapping-chinas-middle-class).

"Nine Important Developments in China's Outbound Tourism 2013." *Forbes*, January 1, 2014.

Ning Hui. "Mozambique Faces Race Against Time to End Illegal Logging." *The Guardian*, August 31, 2016.

Stein, Karen. "Understanding Consumption and Environmental Change in China: A Cross-National Comparison of Consumer Patterns." *Human Ecology Review*, Vol. 16, No. 1 (2009): 41–49.

"To the Piste!" *The Economist*, January 24, 2015.

Yu, LiAnne. *Consumption in China: How China's New Consumer Ideology Is Shaping the Nation*. Malden, MA: Polity Press, 2014.

Zhao Bin. "Consumerism, Confucianism, Communism: Making Sense of China Today." *New Left Review*, I/222 (March–April 1997): 43–59.

Chapter 5: What's Happening to China's Air

"2013 Will be Remembered as the Year that Deadly, Suffocating Smog Consumed China." *Quartz*, December 19, 2013 (http://qz.com/159105/2013-will-be-remembered-as-the-year-that-deadly-suffocating-smog-consumed-china/).

"Air Pollution: Chinese and American Cities in Comparison [Infographic]." *Forbes*, January 23, 2015.

"Air Pollution in China." UNDP Issue Brief, No. 8, April 2015.

Boren, Zachary Davies. "Beyond Beijing: 190 Chinese Cities Have Hazardous Air Pollution Amidst New Targets." Greenpeace Energydesk, January 26, 2015 (http://energydesk.greenpeace.org/2015/01/26/beyond-beijing-190-chinese-cities-hazardous-air-pollution/).

Guan Dabo and Liu Zhu. "Tracing Back the Smog: Source Analysis for PM2.5 Pollution in Beijing–Tianjin–Hebei." Greenpeace East Asia, December 2, 2013 (http://www.greenpeace.org/eastasia/Global/eastasia/publications/reports/climate-energy/2013/Tracing%20back%20the%20smog%20(English%20full%20report.pdf).

Hansen, Mette Halskov and Ahlers, Anna Lisa. "Air Pollution: How Will China Win Its Self-Declared War Against It?" University of Oslo: Department of Culture Studies and Oriental Languages, September 2015 (https://www.academia.edu/15344565/Air_Pollution_How_Will_China_Win_its_Self-Declared_War_Against_it).

Ho, Mun S. and Nielson, Chris P., eds. *Clearing the Air: The Health and Economic Damages of Air Pollution in China*. Cambridge, MA: MIT Press, 2007.

Karplus, V. J. "Double Impact: Why China Needs Coordinated Air Quality and Climate Strategies." Paulson Papers on Energy and the Environment, February 2015.

Kelly, William J. and Jacobs, Chip. *The People's Republic of Chemicals*. Los Angeles: Rare Bird Books, 2014.

Liu Jianyi and Cao Xin. "PM2.5 Pollution in Major Cities in China: Pollution Status, Emission Sources and Control Measures." *Fresenius Environmental Bulletin*, January 2015.

"A Summary of the 2015 Annual PM2.5 City Rankings." Greenpeace East Asia, December 30, 2015 (http://www.greenpeace.org/eastasia/Global/eastasia/publications/reports/climate-energy/2015/GPEA%202015%20City%20Rankings_briefing_int.pdf).

Wainwright, Oliver. "Inside Beijing's Airpocalypse—a City Made 'Almost Uninhabitable' by Pollution." *The Guardian*, December 16, 2014.

West, James. "Airpocalypse Now: Beijing's Toxic Smog Measures 'Beyond Index' Levels." *Mother Jones*, January 15, 2015.

Xin Ling. "Tracking Down China's Haze Pollution." *Bulletin of the Academy of Sciences*, Vol. 27, No. 3 (2013): 140–144.

Zhang Dongyong, Liu Junjuan, and Li Bingjun. "Tackling Air Pollution in China—What Do We Learn from the Great Smog of 1950s in London." *Sustainability*, Vol. 6, No. 8 (August 2014): 5322–5338.

Zhang Yan-lin and Cao Fang. "Fine Particulate Matter (PM2.5) in China at a City Level." *Scientific Reports*, Vol. 5, Article No. 14884 (October 15, 2015) (http://www.nature.com/articles/srep14884).

Chapter 6: Water Contamination and Water Scarcity

Bai Xuemei and Shi Peijun. "Pollution Control in China's Huai River Basin: What Lessons for Sustainability?" *Environment*, Vol. 48 (2006): pp. 22–38.

"Beijing's Water Crisis: 1949–2008 Olympics." Probe International Beijing Group, 2008 (updated 2010).

Carlton, Elizabeth J., Liang Song, McDowell, Julia Z., et al. "Regional Disparities in the Burden of Disease Attributable to Unsafe Water and Poor Sanitation." *Bulletin of the World Health Organization*, Vol. 90, No. 8 (August 2012): 578–587.

Chen Mi, Tomás, Roberto, Li Zhenhong, et al. "Imaging Land Subsidence Induced by Groundwater Extraction in Beijing (China) Using Satellite Radar Interferometry." *Remote Sensing*, Vol. 8, Issue 6, Article 468 (2016).

"China Coal-Fired Economy Dying of Thirst as Mines Lack Water." Bloomberg News, July 24, 2013.

China Urban Water Blueprint. The Nature Conservancy, April 2016.

"China's Thirsty Coal Industry Guzzles Precious Water." *The Seattle Times*, May 16, 2014.

Ebenstein, Avraham. "The Consequences of Industrialization: Evidence from Water Pollution and Digestive Cancers in China." *Review of Economics and Statistics*, Vol. 94, No. 1 (2012): 186–201.

Freeman, Carla. "Quenching the Dragon's Thirst: The South-North Water Transfer Project—Old Plumbing for New China?" Environmental Research Brief: China Environment Forum, January 2011.

Gleick, Peter. "China and Water." *The World's Water 2008–2009*, edited by Peter Gleick, 79–97. Washington, DC: Island Press, 2008.

Guerringue, Brett. "South-North Water Transfer Project." *ICE Case Studies*, No. 277 (May 2013).

Ivanova, Nadya. "Toxic Water Across Much of China, Huge Harvests Irrigated with Industrial and Agricultural Runoff." Circle of Blue, January 18, 2013. (http://www.circleofblue.org/2013/world/toxic-water-across-much-of-china-huge-harvests-irrigated-with-industrial-and-agricultural-runoff/).

Khan, Sulmaan. "Suicide by Drought: How China is Destroying Its Own Water Supply." *Foreign Affairs*, July 18, 2014.

Kuo, Lily. "China is Moving More Than a River Thames of Water Across the Country to Deal With Water Scarcity." *Quartz*, March 6, 2014 (http://qz.com/158815/chinas-so-bad-at-water-conservation-that-it-had-to-launch-the-most-impressive-water-pipeline-project-ever-built/).

Liu Hongqiao. "China's Long March to Safe Drinking Water." China Water Risk, March 2015.

Ma Jun. *China's Water Crisis*. Norwalk, CT: EastBridge, 2004.

Magee, Darrin. "Moving the River? China's South-North Water Transfer Project." *Engineering Earth* (December 30, 2010): 1499–1514.

Magee, Darrin. "The Politics of Water in Rural China: A Review of English-Language Scholarship." *Journal of Peasant Studies*, Vol. 40, No. 6 (2013): 1189–1208.

Mertha, Andrew C. *China's Water Warriors: Citizen Action and Policy Change*. Ithaca: Cornell University Press, 2008.

Moore, Scott. "Issue Brief: Water Resource Issues, Policy and Politics in China." *Brookings Issue Brief*, Brookings Institution, January 2013.

Peng, Jennie. "Market Report: Developing Desalination in China." *WaterWorld*, January 1, 2011.

"Photo Slideshow: China Completes Second Line of South-North Water Transfer Project," Circle of Blue, January 8, 2015 (http://www.circleofblue.org/2015/world/photo-slideshow-china-completes-second-line-south-north-water-transfer/).

Ross, Allen G. P., Sleigh, Adrian C., Li Yuesheng, et al. "Schistosomiasis in the People's Republic of China: Prospects and Challenges for the 21st Century." *Clinical Microbiology Reviews*, Vol. 14, No. 2 (April 2001): 270–295.

Shifflet, Susan Chan, Turner, Jennifer L., Luan Dong, et al. *China's Water–Energy–Food Roadmap: A Global Choke Point Report*. Wilson Center, March 2015.

Turner, Jennifer. *China Environment Series 12* (Special Water and Energy Issue). Wilson Center, 2013.

Turvey, Samuel. *Witness to Extinction: How We Failed to Save the Yangtze River Dolphin*. Oxford: Oxford University Press, 2008.

Walker, Beth. "China's Desalination Plans Could Thwart 'War on Pollution.'" *ChinaDialogue.net*, April 2, 2015.

Wang, Jinxia, Huang Jikun, Rozelle, Scott, et al. "Understanding the Water Crisis in Northern China: What the Government and Farmers are Doing." *International Journal of Water Resources Development*, Vol. 25, No. 1 (2009): 141–158.

Wang, M., Webber, M., Finlayson, B., and Barnett, J. "Rural Industries and Water Pollution in China." *Journal of Environmental Management*, Vol. 86 (2008): 648–659.

Yong, Jiang. "China's Water Scarcity." *Journal of Environmental Management*, Vol. 90 (2009): 3185–3196.

Zhao Xu, Liu Junguo, Liu Qingying, et al. "Physical and Virtual Water Transfers for Regional Water Stress Alleviation in China." *Proceedings of the National Academy of Sciences USA*, Vol. 112, No. 4 (January 27, 2015): 1031–1035.

Chapter 7: Soil Pollution and Agriculture

Brown, Lester. *Who Will Feed China: Wake-Up Call for a Small Planet*. New York: W. W. Norton, 1995.

Buckley, Chris. "Rice Tainted with Cadmium is Discovered in Southern China." *New York Times*, May 21, 2013.

China Economic Update (Special Topic: Changing Food Consumption Patterns in China: Implications for Domestic Supply and International Trade). Beijing: World Bank Office, June 2014.

"China's Farmland Well Above Red Line." *Xinhua*, April 22, 2015 (http://news.xinhuanet.com/english/2015-04/22/c_134175085.htm).

"China's Soil Heavily Polluted by Mining, Industry." Radio Free Asia (RFA), April 17, 2014.

"Chinese Sprout an Interest in Organic Farming Amid Concerns Over Food Safety." *South China Morning Post*, September 28, 2015.

Demick, Barbara. "China Looks Abroad for Greener Pastures." *Los Angeles Times*, March 29, 2014.

Gale, Fred, Hansen, James, and Jewison, Michael. "China's Growing Demand for Agricultural Imports." *USDA-ERS Economic Information Bulletin*, No. 136 (February 2015).

Gong Jing, Cui Zheng, and Wang Qingfeng. "Food in China: A Chemical Age." ChinaDialogue.net, June 8, 2012.

He Guangwei. "China Faces Long Battle to Clean Up its Polluted Soil." ChinaDialogue.net, July 14, 2014.

He Guangwei. "Special Report: The Legacy of Hunan's Polluted Soil." ChinaDialogue.net, July 7, 2014

He Guangwei. "Special Report: The Victims of China's Soil Pollution Crisis." ChinaDialogue.net, June 30, 2014.

Hirsch, Peter. "Infographic: Soil Pollution in China." ChinaDialogue.net, August 4, 2014.

Hu, Elise. "Korea's Air is Dirty, But It's Not All Close-Neighbor China's Fault." NPR.org, June 3, 2016.

Ju Xiao-tang, Xing Guangxi, Chen Xinping, et al. "Reducing Environmental Risk by Improving N Management in Intensive Chinese Agricultural Systems." *Proceedings of the National Academy of Sciences USA*, Vol. 6, No. 109 (March 3, 2009): 3041–3046.

Lam Hon-Ming, Remais, Justin, Fung Ming-chiu, et al. "Food Supply and Food Safety Issues in China." *The Lancet*, Vol. 381, Issue 9882 (June 8, 2013): 2044–2051.

Levitt, Tom. "What Are the Ecological Costs of China's Future Food Imports?" ChinaDialogue.net, September 10, 2012.

Levitt, Tom. "Who Will Feed China's Pigs . . . And Why It Matters to Us and the Planet." ChinaDialogue.net, August 18, 2014.

Li Jianmin and Li Zhaohu. "Physical Limitations and Challenges to Grain Security in China." *Food Security*, Vol. 6, No. 2 (April, 2014): 159–167.

Li Sheng, Zhang Yaoqi, Nadolnyak, Denis, et al. "Fertilizer Industry Subsidies in China: Who Are the Beneficiaries?" *China Agricultural Economic Review*, Vol. 6, Issue 3 (2014): 433–451.

Li Yuxuan, Zhang Weifeng, Ma Lin, et al. "An Analysis of China's Fertilizer Policies: Impacts on the Industry, Food Security, and the Environment." *Journal of Environmental Quality*, Vol. 42, No. 4 (July 2013): 972–981.

Lu Yonglong, Jenkins, Alan, Ferrier, Robert C., et al. "Addressing China's Grand Challenge of Achieving Food Security While Ensuring Environmental Sustainability." *Science Advances*, Vol. 1, No. 1 (February 2015).

McBeath, Jennifer Huang, and McBeath, Jerry. *Environmental Change and Food Security in China*. Springer: New York, 2010.

Meng, Angela. "Heavy Metal Pollution in Hunan Soil Exceeds China's Limits by 1,500 Times." *South China Morning Post*, December 2, 2014.

Myers, Samuel S., Zanobetter, Antonella, Kloog, Itai, et al. "Increasing CO_2 Threatens Human Nutrition." *Nature*, Vol. 510 (June 5, 2014): 139–142.

Myllyvirta, Lauri. "Peabody: Why the World's Largest Private Coal Miner Went Bust—in One Graph." Greenpeace Energydesk, April 15, 2016.

Sanders, Richard, and Xiao Xingji. "The Sustainability of Organic Agriculture in Developing Countries: Lessons from China." *International Journal of Environmental Cultural, Economic, and Social Sustainability*, Vol. 6, No. 6 (2010): 233–243.

Tan, Debra. "The State of China's Agriculture." China Water Risk, April 9, 2014.

Wang Xuan, "Can Ecological Agriculture Feed China?" ChinaDialogue.net, July 10, 2014.

Wang Yue, "Polluted Farmland Leads to Chinese Food Security Fears." ChinaDialogue.net, January 7, 2014.

"White Paper—The Grain Issue in China." Information Office of the State Council of the People's Republic of China, October 1996.

Wong, Edward. "One-Fifth of China's Farmland Is Polluted, State Study Finds." *New York Times*, April 17, 2014.

Wu Linhai and Zhu Dian, *Food Safety in China: A Comprehensive Review*. Boca Raton, FL: CRC Press, 2015.

Chapter 8: Pollution and Public Health

"'Cadmium Rice': Heavy Metal Pollution of China's Rice Crops." Greenpeace East Asia, April 24, 2014.

Chen, Stephen. "Agriculture Feels the Choke as China Smog Starts to Foster Disastrous Conditions." *South China Morning Post*, February 25, 2014.

Chen Yuyu, Ebenstein, Avraham, Greenstone, Michael, and Li Hongbin. "Evidence on the Impact of Sustained Exposure to Air Pollution on Life Expectancy from China's Huai River Policy."

Proceedings of the National Academy of Sciences USA, Vol. 110, No. 32 (August 6, 2013): 12936–12941.

"Dangerous Breathing, PM 2.5: Measuring the Human Health and Economic Impacts on China's Largest Cities," Greenpeace: Beijing, 2012.

Guan Wei-jie, Zheng Xue-yan, Chung Kian Fan, and Zhong Nan-shan. "Impact of Air Pollution on the Burden of Chronic Respiratory Diseases in China: Time for Urgent Action." *The Lancet*, Vol. 388 (October 15, 2016): 1939–1951.

Holdaway, Jennifer. "Environment and Health in China: An Introduction to an Emerging Research Field." *Journal of Contemporary China*, Vol. 19, No. 63 (2010): 1–22.

Holdaway, Jennifer, "Environment and Health Research in China: The State of the Field." *China Quarterly*, Vol. 214 (June 2013): 255–282.

Hu Wei, Downward, George S., Reiss, Boris, et al. "Personal and Indoor PM2.5 Exposure from Burning Solid Fuels in Vented and Unvented Stoves in a Rural Region of China with a High Incidence of Lung Cancer." *Environmental Science and Technology*, Vol. 48 (2014): 8456–8464.

Huo Daishan. "Controlling Pollution in the Huaihe River Basin: Still a Long Way to Go." In *The China Environment Yearbook* (vol. 2): *Changes and Struggles*. Edited by Yang Dongping. Leiden: Brill, 2008.

Institute for Health Metrics and Evaluation. "Global Burden of Disease Study, 2010." *Lancet*, Vol. 380, No. 9859 (December 2012): 2224–2260.

Kaiman, Jonathan. "China's Toxic Air Pollution Resembles Nuclear Winter, Say Scientists." *The Guardian*, February 25, 2014.

Kaiman, Jonathan. "Inside China's 'Cancer Villages.'" *The Guardian*, June 4, 2013.

Kan Haidong, Chen Renjie, and Tong Shilu. "Ambient Air, Climate Change, and Population Health in China." *Environment International*, Vol. 42 (July 2012): 10–19.

Larson, Christina, "Rates of Lung Cancer Rising Steeply in Smoggy Beijing." *Bloomberg News*, February 28, 2014.

Liu, Lee. "Made in China: Cancer Villages." *Environment* (March/April 2010).

Lockwood, Alan H. *The Silent Epidemic: Coal and the Hidden Threat to Health*. Cambridge, MA: MIT Press, 2012.

Lora-Wainwright, Anna. *Fighting for Breath: Living Morally and Dying of Cancer in a Chinese Village*. Honolulu: University of Hawaii Press, 2012.

Meng Si. "Special Report: Rural Villages in China Hit by Fluorine Poisoning from Coal-Burning." ChinaDialogue.net, July 3, 2014.

Phillips, Tom. "China's Toxic School: Officials Struggle to Contain Uproar over Sick Students." *The Guardian*, April 19, 2016.

Rohde, Richard A., and Muller, Richard A. "Air Pollution in China: Mapping of Concentrations and Sources." *PLoS One*, Vol. 10, No. 8 (August 2015).

Schoolman, Ethan D., and Ma, Chunbo. "Migration, Class and Environmental Inequality: Exposure to Pollution in China's Jiangsu Province." *Ecological Economics*, Vol. 75 (March 2012): 140–151.

Smith, Geoffrey. "The Cost of China's Dependence on Coal—670,000 Deaths a Year." *Fortune*, November 5, 2014.

Tan, Debra. "Cancer Villages: Toxic Tipping Point?" China Water Risk, May 9, 2013.

Wang Shunqin, Zhang Jinliang, Zeng Xiaodong, et al. "Association of Traffic-Related Air Pollution with Children's Neurobehavioral Functions in Quanzhou, China." *Environmental Health Perspectives*, Vol. 117, No. 10 (October 2009): 1612–1618.

Wei Yongjie, Zhang Junfeng (Jim), Li Zhigang, et al. "Chronic Exposure to Air Pollution Particles Increases the Risk of Obesity and Metabolic Syndrome: Findings from a Natural Experiment in Beijing." *FASEB Journal*, Vol. 30, No. 6 (June 2016): 2015–2022.

Wong, Edward. "Air Pollution Linked to 1.2 Million Premature Deaths in China." *New York Times*, April 1, 2013.

Wong, Edward. "Pollution Leads to Drop in Life Span in Northern China, Research Finds." *New York Times*, July 8, 2013.

Ye Xibiao, Fu Hua, and Guidotti, Tee. "Environmental Exposure and Children's Health in China." *Archives of Environmental and Occupational Health*, Vol. 62, No. 2 (Summer 2007): 61–73.

Zhang Junfeng, Mauzerall, Denise L., Zhu Tong, et al. "Environmental Health in China: Progress Towards Clean Air and Water." *Lancet*, Vol. 375, No. 9720 (2010): 1110–1118.

Zhao Xiaoli, Zhang Sufang, and Fan Chunyang. "Environmental Externality and Inequality in China: Current Status and Future Choices." *Environmental Pollution*, Vol. 190 (July 2014): 176–179.

Chapter 9: China's Pollution and the World

"China's Smog Polluting Fuji, New Study Says." *The Japan Times*, October 5, 2013.

Doucleff, Michalleen. "Why China's Pollution Could be Behind Our Cold, Snowy Winters." NPR, March 8, 2015 (http://www.npr.org/sections/goatsandsoda/2015/03/08/391056439/why-chinas-pollution-could-be-behind-our-cold-snowy-winters).

"Forecasting China's Smog Seen as Business Opportunity for IBM and Microsoft." *The Guardian*, December 29, 2015.

Forsythe, Michael. "China's Emissions Pledges Are Undercut by Boom in Coal Projects Abroad." *New York Times*, December 11, 2015.

"FY 2014 Survey Results of Marine Litter in Coastal Areas." Ministry of the Environment, Government of Japan, June 3, 2015 (https://www.env.go.jp/en/headline/2167.htm).

Galbraith, Kate. "Worries in the Path of China's Air." *New York Times*, December 25, 2013.

Harner, Stephen. "Japan, China, Korea Cooperation and China's Environmental Clean-up Gold Rush." *Forbes*, May 1, 2014.

Hotz, Robert Lee. "Which Countries Create the Most Ocean Trash?" *Wall Street Journal*, February 12, 2015.

"How Responsible Are Americans for China's Pollution Problem: A *ChinaFile* Conversation." February 27, 2014 (http://www.chinafile.com/conversation/how-responsible-are-americans-chinas-pollution-problem).

Jambeck, Jenna R. "Plastic Waste Inputs from Land into the Ocean." *Science*, Vol. 347, No. 6223 (February 13, 2015): 768–771.

"Japan, South Korea Concerned That China's Smog Will Affect Them." *South China Morning Post*, November 6, 2013.

Kirby, David. "Made in China: Our Toxic, Imported Air Pollution." *Discover Magazine*, March 18, 2011.

"Korea, China, Japan Vow Closer Cooperation on Environment." *Yonhap News*, April 30, 2015 (http://english.yonhapnews.co.kr/national/2015/04/30/0301000000AEN20150430003900315.html).

Lin, Jintai, Pan Da, Davis, Steven J., et al. "China's International Trade and Air Pollution in the United States." *Proceedings of the National Academy of Sciences USA*, Vol. 111, No. 5 (February 4, 2014), pp. 1736–1741.

Moan, Susan. "Nitrogen Pollution Disrupts Pacific Ocean." *Nature*, September 22, 2011(http://www.nature.com/news/2011/110922/full/news.2011.552.html).

Murray, Lisa. "Australian Coal the Loser as China Looks for Cheaper, Greener Options." *Australian Financial Review*, September 30, 2015.

Spegele, Brian. "U.S. Consumers Contribute, Not a Little, to Chinese Air Pollution." *Wall Street Journal*, January 21, 2014.

"Vietnam Affected by Pollution from Local, Chinese Coal Power Plants." VietnamNet Bridge, October 21, 2015 (http://english.vietnamnet.vn/fms/environment/144334/vietnam-affected-by-pollution-from-local-chinese-coal-power-plants.html).

Walker, Beth. "China Stokes Global Coal Growth." ChinaDialogue.net, September 23, 2016.

Warwick, Joby. "U.S. Exports Its Greenhouse-Gas Emissions—as Coal. Profitable Coal." *Washington Post*, October 15, 2015.

Wong, Edward. "China Exports Pollution to U.S., Study Finds." *New York Times*, January 20, 2014.

Chapter 10: Pollution and the Public Response

"10,000 Protest in Chinese City Over Planned Coal-Fired Power Plant." *South China Morning Post*, April 13, 2015.

Chang Cheng, "20 Years of China's Public Voice." ChinaDialogue.net, June 20, 2012.

"China Middle-Class Protests Turn Violent After Petitions Ignored." *Bloomberg News*, May 26, 2014.

"Corruption, Pollution, Inequality are Top Concerns in China." Pew Research Center, September 24, 2015.

Custer, Charles. "Deng Fei Launches Weibo Campaign to Share Images of Water Pollution." TechinAsia, February 5, 2013.

Duggan, Jennifer. "Green China: Why Beijing Fears a Nascent Environmental Protest Movement." *TakePart*, October 9, 2015.

"Environmental Activism Gaining a Foothold in China, DW.com, April 15, 2015 (http://www.dw.com/en/environmental-activism-gaining-a-foothold-in-china/a-18384605).

"Environmental Concerns on the Rise in China." Pew Research Center, September 19, 2013.

"Environmental Impact Assessment Law of the People's Republic of China" (http://www.cecc.gov/resources/legal-provisions/peoples-republic-of-china-environmental-impact-assessment-law-2003).

Fei Sheng. "Environmental Non-Government Organizations in China Since the 1970s." *International Review of Environmental History*, Vol. 1 (2015): 81–101.

Feng Yongfeng. "China's Citizen Journalists Lead Fight Against Polluters." ChinaDialogue.net, May 29, 2014.

Geall, Sam, ed. *China and the Environment: The Green Revolution.* London: Zed Books, 2013.

Gilbert, Skye. "Victory: A Grassroots NGO Empowers a 'Cancer Village' to Take Action." China Environment Forum, Wilson Center, July 7, 2011.

Haddad, Mary Alice. "Increasing Environmental Performance in a Context of Low Governmental Enforcement: Evidence from China." *Journal of Environment and Development*, Vol. 24, No. 1 (2015): 3–25.

Harris, Paul. "Environmental Perspectives and Behavior in China: Synopsis and Bibliography." *Environment and Behavior*, Vol. 38, No. 1 (January 2006): 5–21.

Ho, Peter, and Edmonds, Richard Louis. *China's Embedded Activism: Opportunities and Constraints of a Social Movement.* New York: Routledge, 2008.

Hook, Leslie. "China's Environmental Activists." *Financial Times*, September 20, 2013.

Johnson, Thomas R. "Regulatory Dynamism of Environmental Mobilization in Urban China." *Regulation and Governance*, Vol. 10, Issue 1 (March 2016): 14–28.

Kay, Samuel, Zhao, Bo, and Sui, Daniel. "Can Social Media Clear the Air? A Case Study of the Air Pollution Problem in Chinese Cities." *Professional Geographer*, Vol. 67, No. 3 (2015): 351–363.

Larson, Christina. "The New Epicenter of China's Discontent." *Foreign Policy*, August 23, 2011.

Lauter, David. "In China, App Aims to Shame Polluters by Showing Who is Fouling Air." *Los Angeles Times*, December 30, 2014.

Lee Kingsyhoon and Ho Ming-sho. "The Maoming Anti-PX Protest of 2014: An Environmental Movement in Contemporary China." *China Perspectives* No. 4 (2014): 33–39.

Liu Jianqiang. "China's New 'Middle Class' Environmental Protests." ChinaDialogue.net, January 2, 2013.

Makinen, Julie. "China Seeks to Fight Smog by Brainstorm: All Ideas Welcome." *Los Angeles Times*, September 14, 2014.

Mol, Arthur. "China's Middle Class as Environmental Frontier." *Al Jazeera*, January 11, 2012.

Olesen, Alexa. "Do Chinese NIMBY Protests Actually Work?" *Foreign Policy*, May 13, 2014.

Ramzy, Austin. "Q. and A.: Ma Jun on Using Mobile Phones to Fight Pollution." *New York Times*, April 28, 2015.

Ru Jiang, and Ortolano, Leonard. "Development of Citizen-Organized Environmental NGOs in China." *Voluntas* 20 (2009): 141–168.

Schwartz, Jonathan. "Environmental NGOs in China: Roles and Limits." *Pacific Affairs*, Vol. 77, No. 1 (Spring 2004): 28–49.

Shen Yongdong, "Protest Against Industrial Air Pollution: A Case from Hangzhou City, China." University of Oslo, Middle East Institute, December 10, 2015 (http://www.mei.edu/content/map/protest-against-industrial-air-pollution-case-hangzhou-city-china).

Sima Yangzi. "Grassroots Environmental Activism and the Internet: Constructing a Green Public Sphere in China." *Asian Studies Review*, Vol. 35 (December 2011): 477–497.

Tilt, Bryan. *The Struggle for Sustainability in Rural China: Environmental Values and Civil Society*. New York: Columbia University Press, 2010.

Wainwright, Oliver. "Inside Beijing's Airpocalypse—A City Made 'Almost Uninhabitable' by Pollution." *The Guardian*, December 16, 2014.

Wines, Michael. "Liang Congjie, Chinese Environmental Pioneer, Dies at 78." *New York Times*, October 29, 2010.

Xu, Janet Hua. "Communicating the Right to Know: Social Media in the Do-It-Yourself Air Quality Testing Campaign in Chinese Cities." *International Journal of Communication*, 8 (2014): 1374–1393.

Yang Guobin. "Environmental NGOs and Institutional Dynamics in China." *China Quarterly*, Vol. 181 (March 2005): 46–66.

Yang, Ruby (director). *Warriors of Qiugang* (documentary). Beijing: Thomas Lennon Films and Chang Ai Media Project, 2010.

Zhan Jiang. "Environmental Journalism in China." In *Changing Media, Changing China*. Edited by Susan Shirk. New York: Oxford University Press, 2010.

Zhang, Joy Y., and Barr, Michael. *Green Politics in China: Environmental Governance and State-Society Relations*. London: Pluto Press, 2013.

Zhao Yuhong. "Assessing the Environmental Impact of Projects: A Critique of the EIA Legal Regime in China." *Natural Resources Journal*, Vol. 49 (Spring 2009): 485–524.

Chapter 11: The State and Environmental Pollution

"8 Game-Changing Policy Paths." China Water Risk, February 10, 2015.

"Action Plan for Prevention and Control of Soil Pollution, No. 31 (2016) of the State Council" (unofficial translation). Danish Soil Partnership (http://danishsoil.org/media/test_sites/uploads/Soil%20Ten%20Plan.pdf).

"Action Plan Targets Soil Pollution." State Council, People's Republic of China, June 2, 2016 (http://english.mep.gov.cn/News_service/media_news/201606/t20160602_353072.shtml).

"Beijing to Adopt China's Tightest Fuel Standards by Jan: Xinhua." Reuters.com, May 23, 2016.

Chen Gang. *Politics of China's Environmental Protection: Problems and Progress.* Singapore: World Scientific Publishing Co., 2009.

"China Announces Action Plan to Tackle Water Pollution." State Council, People's Republic of China, April 16, 2015 (http://english.gov.cn/policies/latest_releases/2015/04/16/content_281475090170164.htm).

"China Environment Ministry Given Powers to Inspect Provinces." Reuters, May 12, 2016.

"China Passes New Laws on Foreign NGOs Amid International Criticism." *BBC*, April 28, 2016.

"China Punishes Officials Over Sewage in First Environmental Case of Its Kind." *The Guardian*, June 21, 2016.

"China Said to Consider $16 Billion E-V Charging Fund." *Bloomberg News*, August 26, 2014.

"China Says Half of New State Cars to Be New Energy by 2012: Xinhua." Reuters, May 5, 2016.

"China to Build 30,000 Kilometers High-Speed Railways by 2020." CCTV, January 12, 2016 (http://english.cntv.cn/2016/01/12/VIDExvHxQhfEiwLpNyD5zQIX160112.shtml).

"China's Coal City Replacing Gas Taxis with Electric." *Xinhua*, April 29, 2016.

"China's Legislature Adopts Revised Environmental Protection Law." *Xinhua*, April 24, 2014.

"Climate, Energy and China's 13th Five-Year Plan in Graphics." ChinaDialogue.net, March 18, 2016.

"Efforts to Prevent and Remedy Soil Pollution." State Council, People's Republic of China, May 31, 2016 (http://english.gov.cn/policies/latest_releases/2016/05/31/content_281475361737430.htm).

"Electric Vehicles to Get Free Rein on Beijing Roads." *Wall Street Journal*, May 21, 2015.

Environmental Protection Law of the People's Republic of China. ChinaDialogue.net, April 24, 2014 (https://www.chinadialogue.net/Environmental-Protection-Law-2014-eversion.pdf).

Fialka, John. "China Will Start the World's Largest Carbon Trading Market." ClimateWire (*Scientific American*), May 16, 2016.

Field, Kyle. "Electric Bus Adoption is Taking Off in China." CleanTechnica, November 26, 2015 (https://cleantechnica.com/2015/11/26/electric-bus-adoption-taking-off-china/).

Finamore, Barbara. "New Weapons in the War on Pollution: China's Environmental Protection Law Amendments." NRDC.org, April 24, 2014.

Finnsdóttir, Fifa. "Assembling the Green Dragon: Challenges and Developments in Contemporary Chinese Environmental Politics." Bachelor's Thesis, University of Iceland, 2010.

Forsythe, Michael. "China Curbs Plans for More Coal-Fired Power Plants." *New York Times*, April 25, 2016.

Hart, Melanie, Ogden, Peter, and Gallagher, Kelly Sims. "Green Finance: The Next Frontier for U.S.–China Climate Cooperation." Center for American Progress, June 13, 2016.

Henderson, Geoffrey, Song, Ranping, and Joffe, Paul. "5 Questions: What Does China's New Five-Year Plan Mean for Climate Action." World Resources Institute, March 18, 2016.

Hu Feng. "MEP Reform: From Mountaintop to Ocean?" China Water Risk, March 12, 2014.

Jahiel, Abigail R. "The Organization of Environmental Protection in China." *China Quarterly*, No. 156 (December 1998): 757–787.

Ker, Michelle, and Logan, Kate. "New Environmental Law Targets China's Local Officials." ChinaDialogue.net, April 28, 2014.

Kong, Ada, and Wang Jing. "Is China's New Plan to Tackle Soil Pollution Too Little, Too Late?" Greenpeace East Asia, June 3, 2016.

Kotska, Genia. "Barriers to the Implementation of Environmental Policies at the Local Level in China." World Bank Group, Policy Research Working Paper 7016 (August 2014).

Kumar, Sanjeev, and Thurlow, Hania. "China's 13th Five-Year Plan: The Clean Technology Revolution and Its Implications for Europe." Change Partnership, March 2016.

Kuo, Lily. "China is Building a Great Wall of Trees to Fight Climate Change and the Encroaching Gobi Desert." *Quartz*, April 27, 2015.

Li Jing. "60,000 Jobs: The Cost of One Chinese City's Cleaner Air." *South China Morning Post*, July 3, 2015.

Liu Hongqiao. "Mega-dams in China's Earthquake Zones Could Have 'Disastrous Consequences.'" ChinaDialogue.net, October 29, 2012.

McElwee, Charles. *Environmental Law in China: Managing Risk and Ensuring Compliance*. New York: Oxford University Press, 2011.

McGregor, Dawn, and Liu Hongqiao. "Be Green and Prosper." China Water Risk, February 4, 2016.

Myllyvirta, Lauri, Shen Xinyi, and Lammi, Harri. "Is China Doubling Down on Its Coal Power Bubble?" Greenpeace East Asia, November 11, 2015.

Obrien, Kevin J., and Stern, Rachel. "Politics at the Boundary: Mixed Signals and the Chinese State." *Modern China* Vol. 38, No. 2 (March 2012): 175–199.

"One Out of 693: Beijing Car Plate Lottery Hits New Low." ECNS.cn, April 26, 2016 (http://www.ecns.cn/cns-wire/2016/04-26/208222.shtml).

"PRC Law on Air Pollution Prevention and Control." Clean Air Alliance of China, August 2015 (http://en.cleanairchina.org/product/7332.html).

Rana, Renu. "China's Information Disclosure Initiative: Assessing the Reforms." *China Report*, Vol. 51, No. 2 (2015): 129–143.

Selighson, Deborah, and Hsu, Angel. "How China's 13th Five-Year Plan Addresses Energy and the Environment." ChinaFile, March 10, 2016.

Spegele, Brian, and Kazer, William. "To Conserve Water, China Raises Prices for Top Users." *Wall Street Journal*, January 8, 2014.

"The State Council Issues Action Plan on Prevention and Control of Air Pollution Introducing Ten Measures to Improve Air Quality." State Council, People's Republic of China, September 12, 2013 (http://english.gov.cn/policies/latest_releases/2016/09/06/content_281475435053302.htm).

Stern, Rachel. *Environmental Litigation in China: A Study in Political Ambivalence*. Cambridge, UK: Cambridge University Press, 2013.

Stern, Rachel. "The Political Logic of China's New Environmental Courts." *China Journal* (July 2014): 53–74.

Tan, Debra. "China's Soil Ten." China Water Risk, June 17, 2016.

Tan, Debra. "Water Ten: Comply or Else." China Water Risk, May 14, 2015.

Tan, Debra. "The War on Water Pollution." China Water Risk, March 12, 2014.

Tan Yeling. "Transparency Without Democracy: The Unexpected Effects of China's Environmental Disclosure Policy." *Governance: An International Journal of Policy, Administration, and Institutions*, Vol. 27, No. 1 (2014): 37–62.

Tao Chuanjin. "Rural Society Coping with Pollution." In *The China Environment Yearbook* (Vol. 2): *Changes and Struggles*. Edited by Yang Dongping. Leiden: Brill, 2008.

Wang, Alex. "Environmental Courts and Public Interest Litigation in China." *Chinese Law and Government*, Vol. 43, No. 6 (November–December 2010): 4–17.

Wang, Alex. "The Search for Sustainable Legitimacy: Environmental Law and Bureaucracy in China." *Harvard Environmental Law Review*, Vol. 37, No. 365 (2013): 365–440.

Wong, Edward. "China's Plan to Curb Air Pollution Sets Limits on Coal Use and Vehicles." *New York Times*, September 12, 2013.

Wu Wencong. "Tougher Plan to Reduce Air Pollution." *China Daily*, July 25, 2013.

Xue, Lulu. "4 Lessons from Beijing and Shanghai Show How China's Cities Can Curb Car Congestion." World Resources Institute, April 10, 2015.

Zhang Chun. "Beijing's Car Controls Not Enough to Beat the Smog." ChinaDialogue.net, February 2, 2016.

Zhang Chun, "Pilot Scheme to Grade Officials on Environmental Protection." ChinaDialogue.net, September 28, 2015.

Zhang Xiliang, Karplus, Valerie, Qi Tianyu, et al. "Carbon Emissions in China: How Far Can New Efforts Bend the Curve?" *Energy Economics*, Vol. 54 (2016): 388–395.

Zhao Xingang, et al. "A Critical Analysis on the Development of China Hydropower." *Renewable Energy*, Vol. 44 (2012): 1–6.

Zhao Yuhong. "Assessing the Environmental Impact of Projects: A Critique of the EIA Legal Regime in China." *Natural Resources Journal*, Vol. 49 (Spring 2009): 485–524.

Zheng Xiang, Cheng Di, Wang Qi, and Zhang Zhenxing. "Seawater Desalination in China: Retrospect and Prospect." *Chemical Engineering Journal*, Vol. 242 (2014): 404–413.

Zhuang Pinghui. "Beijing to Build 12 New Subway Lines to Help Support Growth as Chinese Economy Slows." *South China Morning Post*, September 30, 2015.

Chapter 12: The Search for Cleaner Energy

Adams, Patricia. "Chinese Study Reveals Three Gorges Dam Triggered 3,000 Earthquakes, Numerous Landslides." Probe International, June 1, 2011.

Bosshard, Peter. "China Dams the World." *World Policy Journal*, Vol. 26, No. 4 (Winter 2009/2010): 43–51.

"China." U.S. Energy Information Administration, April 11, 2016 (http://energy.gov/sites/prod/files/2016/04/f30/China_International_Analysis_US.pdf.)

"China Nuclear: The Future is Unclear." China Water Risk, April 15, 2015.
"China to Approve Up to Eight More Nuclear Reactors This Year." *South China Morning Post*, April 22, 2015.
"China's Idled Wind Farms May Spell Trouble for Renewable Energy." *Bloomberg News*, June 28, 2016.
Clifford, Mark L. *The Greening of Asia: The Business Case for Solving Asia's Environmental Emergency*. New York: Columbia University Press, 2015.
"Climate, Energy and China's 13th Five-Year Plan in Graphics." ChinaDialogue.net, March 18, 2016.
Crow, James Mitchell. "Has Carbon Capture's Time Finally Come?" *Cosmos*, December 15, 2014.
Cusick, Daniel. "China Blows Past the U.S. in Wind Power." ClimateWire (*Scientific American*), February 2, 2016.
Davidson, Michael. "Transforming China's Grid: Integrating Wind Energy Before it Blows Away." The Energy Collective, August 14, 2013.
Dupuy, Max, and Wang, Xuan. "China's String of New Policies Addressing Renewable Energy Curtailment: An Update." Renewable Energy World, April 18, 2016.
Fan Xiao. "Did the Zipingpu Dam Trigger China's 2008 Earthquake? The Scientific Case." A Probe International Study, December 2012.
Fensom, Anthony. "China: The Next Shale-Gas Superpower?" *The National Interest*, October 9, 2014.
Gallagher, Kelly Sims. *The Globalization of Clean Energy Technology: Lessons from China*. Cambridge, MA: MIT Press, 2014.
Gass, Henry. "China Push into Synthetic Natural Gas Has Pollution Consequences." ClimateWire (*Scientific American*), October 2, 2013.
Gleick, Peter, H. "China Dams." In *The World's Water, Volume 8: The Biennial Report on Freshwater Resources*. Edited by Peter H. Gleick. Washington, DC: Island Press, 2011.
Gleick, Peter H. "Three Gorges Dam Project, Yangtze River, China." In *The World's Water 2008–2009: The Biennial Report on Freshwater Resources*. Edited by Peter H. Gleick and Michael Cohen. Washington, DC: Island Press, 2008.
Granoff, Illmi, Pickard, Sam, Doczi, Julian, et al. *Can Fracking Green China's Growth?* Overseas Development Institute (London), April 2015.
"The Great Water Grab: How the Coal Industry is Deepening the Global Water Crisis." Greenpeace International, March 2016.

Grey, Eva. "China's Energy Revolution." Power-technology.com, August 11, 2015 (http://www.power-technology.com/features/featurechinas-energy-revolution-4643231/).

Gupta, Joydeep. "Melting Glaciers May Impact Hydropower Plans." The Third Pole, September 2, 2016 (https://www.thethirdpole.net/2016/09/02/studies-of-melting-glaciers-urgently-needed/).

Hart, Melanie. "Beijing's Energy Revolution is Finally Gaining Serious Momentum." Center for American Progress, December 3, 2015.

He Zuoxiu, "Chinese Nuclear Disaster 'Highly Probable' by 2030." ChinaDialogue.net, March 19, 2013.

Hove, Anders, and Mo, Kevin. "Going for Gold: Championing Renewable Integration in Jing-Jin-Ji." The Paulson Institute, 2016.

Hvistendahl, Mara. "China's Three Gorges Dam: An Environmental Catastrophe?" *Scientific American*, March 25, 2008 (https://www.scientificamerican.com/article/chinas-three-gorges-dam-disaster/).

"Issue Brief: Why is China Taking Action on Clean Energy and Climate Change." *ChinaFAQs*, May 29, 2013.

Jackson, John (pseudonym). "Earthquake Hazards and Large Dams in Western China." A Probe International Study, April 2012.

Lewis, Charlton. "China's Great Dam Boom: A Major Assault on its Rivers." YaleEnvironment 360, November 4, 2013. (http://e360.yale.edu/feature/chinas_great_dam_boom_an_assault_on_its_river_systems/2706/).

Lewis, Joanna. *China's Wind Power Industry and the Global Transition to a Low-Carbon Economy*. New York: Columbia University Press, 2013.

Li Bo, Yao Songqiao, Yu Yin, and Guo Qiaoyu. "The 'Last Report' on China's Rivers (Executive Summary)." International Rivers, March 2014 (https://www.internationalrivers.org/china%E2%80%99s-last-rivers-report).

Li Jing, "Nuclear Fuel Plant on Hold in Eastern China After Thousands Protest." *South China Morning Post*, August 10, 2016.

Li Xin, Hubacek, Klaus, Siu Ling, et al. "Wind Power in China—Dream or Reality?" *Energy*, Vol. 37, No. 1 (January 2012): 51–60.

Li Ying, "Blowing in the Wind." ChinaDialogue.net, May 31, 2016.

Ma, Damien. "Rebalancing China's Energy Strategy." Paulson Papers on Energy and Environment, January 2015.

Marcuse, Gary (director). "Waking the Green Dragon" (documentary). Vancouver, BC: Face to Face Media, 2011.

Mathews, John A. "China's Continuing Renewable Energy Revolution—Latest Trends in Electric Power Generation."

Asia-Pacific Journal: Japan Focus, Vol. 14, Issue 17, No. 6 (September 1, 2016). (Available at http://apjjf.org/2016/17/Mathews.html.)

Mathews, John A. and Tan, Hao. "Manufacture Renewables to Build Energy Security." *Nature*, Vol. 513, Issue 7517 (September 11, 2014): 166–168.

Mi Sen, "Why Nuclear Matters for China." ChinaDialogue.net, October 13, 2011.

"Nuclear Power in China." World Nuclear Association, updated June 2016.

Ng, Shinwei, Mabey, Nick, and Gaventa, Jonathan. "Pulling Ahead on Clean Technology: China's 13th Five-Year Plan Challenges Europe's Low Carbon Competitiveness." E3G Briefing Paper, March 2016 (https://www.e3g.org/docs/E3G_Report_on_Chinas_13th_5_Year_Plan.pdf).

Phillips, Tom. "China Builds World's Biggest Solar Farm in Journey to Become Green Superpower." *The Guardian*, January 19, 2017.

Plumer, Brad. "The Real War on Coal is Happening in China Right Now." *Vox*, March 6, 2016.

Pomeranz, Kenneth. "The Great Himalayan Watershed: Agrarian Crisis, Mega-Dams and the Environment." *New Left Review*, 58 (July–August 2009): 5-39.

Qi Ye, Stern, Nicholas, Wu Tong, et al. "China's Post-Coal Growth." *Nature Geoscience*, Vol. 9 (July 25, 2016): 564–566.

Renewable Energy and Energy Efficiency in China: Current Status and Prospects for 2020. WorldWatch Institute, Worldwatch Report #182 (October 2012).

Renewable Energy Prospects: China (Remap 2030 Analysis). International Renewable Energy Agency (IRENA), November 2014.

Samaranayake, Nilanthi, Limaye, Satu, and Wuthnow, Joel. *Water Resource Competition in the Brahmaputra River Basin*. Arlington, VA: CNA Analysis & Solutions, 2016.

Schneider, Keith. "New Wind and Solar Sectors Won't Solve China's Water Scarcity." Circle of Blue, February 22, 2011 (http://www.circleofblue.org/2011/world/new-wind-and-solar-sectors-wont-solve-chinas-water-scarcity/).

Spegele, Brian. "China Inc.'s Nuclear-Power Push." *Wall Street Journal*, February 23, 2016.

Stover, Dawn. "Floating Nuclear Power Plants: China is Far from First." *Bulletin of the Atomic Scientists*, June 1, 2016 (https://thebulletin.org/floating-nuclear-power-plants-china-far-first9522).

"Supporting Report 3: Seizing the Opportunity of Green Development in China." World Bank, March 2013.
Tan, Debra. "Avoiding Hydro Wars." China Water Risk, August 13, 2014.
Tan, Debra, Hu Feng, Thierot, Hubert, and McGregor, Dawn. *Towards a Water & Energy Secure China: Tough Choices Ahead in Power Expansion with Limited Water Resources.* China Water Risk, 2015.
Thierlot, Hubert. "Wind & Sun: Relief for China's Dry North." China Water Risk, July 20, 2016.
Tullos, Desiree D., Foster-Moore, Eric, Magee, Darrin, et al. "Biophysical, Socioeconomic, and Geopolitical Vulnerabilities to Hydropower Development on the Nu River, China." *Ecology and Society*, Vol. 18, No. 3 (2013), Art. 16.
Walker, Beth. "China Plans More Dams and Mega Infrastructure in Tibet." The Third Pole, March 21, 2016 (https://www.thethirdpole.net/2016/03/21/china-plans-more-hydro-projects-and-mega-infrastructure-in-tibet/).
Walker, Beth, and Liu, Qin. "China's Shift from Coal to Hydro Comes at a Heavy Price." ChinaDialogue.net, July 27, 2015.
Wang Yinan. "Drought and Earthquakes Pose 'Enormous Risk' to China's Nuclear Plans." ChinaDialogue.net, February 2, 2013.
Wen Bo. "Inland Provinces: Nuclear at Crossroads." China Water Risk, August 13, 2014.
Wen, William Hua, Luo Tianyi, and Tien Shiao. "China's Response to Air Pollution Poses Threat to Water." World Resources Institute, October 23, 2013.
Zeng Ming, Chen Li-min, Xue Song, et al. "Post-Fukushima Nuclear Power Development in China." *Power Magazine*, November 1, 2012.

INDEX

Figures, notes, and tables are indicated by "f," "n," and "t" following page numbers. Illustrations are indicated by page numbers in italics.